Basilian Fathers

St. Basil's hymnal

Containing music for vespers of all the Sundays and festivals of the year

Basilian Fathers

St. Basil's hymnal
Containing music for vespers of all the Sundays and festivals of the year

ISBN/EAN: 9783741192265

Manufactured in Europe, USA, Canada, Australia, Japa

Cover: Foto ©Thomas Meinert / pixelio.de

Manufactured and distributed by brebook publishing software (www.brebook.com)

Basilian Fathers

St. Basil's hymnal

St. Basil's Hymnal.

FIFTEENTH EDITION

CONTAINING

MUSIC

FOR

VESPERS OF ALL THE SUNDAYS AND FESTIVALS OF THE YEAR

Three Masses

AND

OVER TWO HUNDRED HYMNS

TOGETHER WITH

LITANIES, DAILY PRAYERS, PRAYERS AT MASS, PREPARATION AND PRAYERS FOR CONFESSION AND COMMUNION,

AND

THE OFFICE AND RULES

FOR

Sodalities of the Blessed Virgin Mary.

COMPILED FROM APPROVED SOURCES.

Permissu  Superiorum.

LYON & HEALY,
CHICAGO.

Permissu Superiorum

Imprimatur
+ Fergus Patritius McEvay
Archiep. Toront.
Canada.

Letter from His Eminence CARDINAL GIBBONS :
CARDINAL'S RESIDENCE,
BALTIMORE, Nov. 14th, 1896.

REV'D DEAR FATHER,—

I take great pleasure in adding my name to that of your Most Rev'd Archbishop, in commending to Catholic institutions your useful work. ST. BASIL'S HYMNAL is calculated to promote devotional singing, which is a powerful element in the cause of religion.

Faithfully yours in Xto,

Rev. L. Brennan.   J. CARL GIBBONS.

Entered according to Act of Parliament of Canada, in the year one thousand eight hundred and eighty-nine, by the Publishers, in the Office of the Minister of Agriculture.

Entered according to Act of Congress, in the year one thousand eight hundred and eighty-nine, by the Publishers, in the Office of the Librarian of Congress at Washington, U.S.A.

Preface to the Tenth Edition.

✝

IN placing the tenth edition of ST. BASIL'S HYMNAL before the public we take the opportunity of expressing our thanks to our many patrons for their generous encouragement and valuable suggestions. For the latter we are especially indebted to the devoted educational Communities throughout Canada and the United States. It is through these Religious that the Hymnal is made to serve the great end for which it was first prepared. From several quarters we have received offerings of original composition whose merit we readily appreciate, but which we are reluctantly obliged sometimes to decline on account of the limit in size and price within which our volume must be restrained.

The year 1904 was for this Book a severe trial. In the spring of that year all the plates and manuscripts, and a partially finished edition were destroyed in the disastrous fire which ruined so much of the business portion of the city. Shortly afterwards, on June 30th, 1904, he who had been the father and originator of ST. BASIL'S HYMNAL, the Rev. Father Lawrence Brennan, C. S. B., was taken from us by death and called to his reward. To his zeal, energy and ability the work and its success had been largely due. In his memory and in respect to his wishes the Basilian Fathers continue the Hymnal, and now present to their patrons the Tenth Edition with the hope that in the future as in the past it will meet with the same encouragement.

We beg to renew our acknowledgments to the many authors from whose works we have made selections, and to express our special indebtedness to the Sisters of St. Joseph, Toronto, for aid in the work of compilation.

ST. MICHAEL'S COLLEGE,
    TORONTO, CANADA.
          Feast of the Conversion of St. Paul. 1906

Letters of Approbation.

FROM THE ARCHBISHOP OF TORONTO.

My Dear Father Brennan,—St. Basil's Hymnal is an excellent and valuable compilation, and is well fitted to supply a want long felt in our parochial schools and other educational institutions, and I earnestly recommend its use for the Separate Schools and other educational institutions.

† John Walsh,
Archbishop of Toronto.

FROM THE ARCHBISHOP OF HALIFAX.

My Dear Father Brennan,—Accept my thanks for the "St. Basil's Hymn Book" so kindly sent me. I wish it the most abundant success.

Yours, etc.,

† C. O'Brien,
Archbishop of Halifax.

FROM THE ARCHBISHOP OF KINGSTON.

Dear Father Brennan,—I thank you for the copy of "St. Basil's Hymnal." The compilation is excellent, and will, I am confident, prove most useful to all Catholic people. I recommend "St. Basil's Hymnal" to the Rev. Clergy of the Archdiocese of Kingston, and to the Religious Communities and all of those who are in charge of Separate Schools.

† James Vincent Cleary,
Archbishop of Kingston.

FROM THE BISHOP OF HAMILTON.

Dear Father Brennan,—"St. Basil's Hymnal" is an excellent manual containing a rich variety of popular hymns, prayers and masses, suitable for schools, sodalities and congregational singing such as you are very zealously anxious to promote.

I will take great pleasure in recommending the book to the patronage of the Priests, Schools and Sodalities of this diocese.

† T. J. Dowling,
Bishop of Hamilton.

FROM THE BISHOP OF PETERBOROUGH.

My Dear Father Brennan,—"St. Basil's Hymnal," which you so thoughtfully sent me, was duly received, and I beg to express my sincere thanks to you for the same. It will be suitable for Schools, Choirs, etc. Please send me two dozen copies as I intend to introduce it here.

I remain yours sincerely in Christ,

† R. A. O'Connor,
Bishop of Peterborough.

Contents

	PAGE
ANTHEMS	10
ASPERGES	331
BENEDICTION	20, 33
DAILY PRAYERS	vii
HYMNS	66
God	66
Our Blessed Lord	74
Holy Name	77
Sacred Heart	81
Precious Blood	111
Blessed Sacrament	113
Holy Family	130
Blessed Virgin	131
St. Joseph	216
St. Rose of Lima	227
St. Anne	228
St. Patrick	230
St. Dominic	233
St. Stanislaus Kostka	234
St. Theresa	235
St. Agatha	237
St. Cecilia	239
All Souls	240
Advent	243
Christmas	246
Epiphany	256
Lent	258
Easter	269
Ascension	280
Pentecost	282
Trinity	289
Corpus Christi	290
Evening	293
Occasional	294
Guardian Angel	304
St. Michael	306
Angels	308

CONTENTS—Continued

	PAGE
HYMNI	6
INDULGENCED PRAYERS	x
LITANIES	312
LITANY OF THE SACRED HEART	318
LITANY OF THE SAINTS	320
LITANY OF THE BLESSED VIRGIN MARY	ix
LITANY OF THE MOST HOLY NAME OF JESUS	viii
LITTLE OFFICE OF THE IMMACULATE CONCEPTION	890
MANNER OF ASSISTING AT MASS AND VESPERS	xx
MASS	353
" DE ANGELIS	334
" PRO DEFUNCTIS	370
PRAYERS AT MASS	xi
PRAYERS FOR COMMUNION	398
PRAYERS FOR CONFESSION	396
SODALITY OF THE BLESSED VIRGIN MARY	384
SPIRITUAL CANTICLES	xxii
TE DEUM LAUDAMUS	325
VESPERS	1
MASS HYMNS	302
RESPONSES AT HIGH MASS	367
VIDI AQUAM	329
INDEX	400

J. M. J.

†

Daily Prayers.

Make the sign of the Cross, and say:
> My God, I offer Thee this day
> All I may do or think or say;
> Uniting all with what was done
> On earth by Jesus Christ, Thy Son.

AN ACT OF ADORATION.

O MY God, I adore Thee here present; I acknowledge Thee to be my Creator and Sovereign Lord; and I submit myself entirely to Thee.

Our Father, etc. Hail Mary, etc. Creed, etc.

I confess, etc. (*Here examine your conscience.*)

AN ACT OF CONTRITION.

O MY God, I am heartily sorry for having offended Thee, and I detest my sins most sincerely, not only because by them I have lost all right to heaven, and have deserved the everlasting torments of hell, but especially because they displease Thee, my God, who art so deserving of all my love, on account of Thy infinite goodness and most amiable perfections; and I firmly resolve, by Thy holy grace, never more to offend Thee, and to amend my life. Amen.

AN ACT OF FAITH.

O MY God, I most firmly believe in Thee, and all thou hast revealed to Thy Holy Catholic Church; because Thou art Truth itself, who canst neither deceive nor be deceived.

AN ACT OF HOPE.

O MY God, relying on Thy promises, and upon the merits of Jesus Christ, my Saviour, I most firmly hope in Thee, and trust that Thou wilt grant me grace to observe Thy commandments in this world, and reward me in the next.

AN ACT OF CHARITY.

O MY God, who art worthy of all my love, and infinite in every perfection, I love Thee with my whole heart; and I love my neighbour as myself for the love of Thee.

PRAYER TO OUR GUARDIAN ANGEL.

O GOOD Angel of God, to whose holy care I have been committed by the Divine bounty, deign during this night (*or day*) to enlighten, guard, guide and protect me.

The Angelus.

To be said morning, noon and night, to put us in mind that God the Son became man for our salvation.

The Angel of the Lord declared unto Mary,
And she conceived of the Holy Ghost.
        Hail Mary, etc.
Behold the handmaid of the Lord :
Be it done unto me according to Thy word
        Hail Mary, etc.
And the Word was made Flesh :
And dwelt among us.
        Hail Mary, etc.
V Pray for us, O holy Mother of God.
R That we may be made worthy of the promises of Christ.

Let us pray.

POUR fourth, we beseech Thee, O Lord, Thy grace into our hearts, that we, to whom the Incarnation of Christ, Thy Son, was made known by the message of an Angel, may by His Passion and Cross, be brought to the glory of His Resurrection, through the same Christ our Lord. Amen.

MAY the Divine assistance remain always with us : and may the souls of the faithful departed, through the mercy of God, rest in peace. Amen.

Should time permit, add, in the morning, the

Litany of the Most Holy Name of Jesus.

Lord, have mercy on us.
Christ, have mercy on us.
Lord, have mercy on us.
Jesus, hear us.
Jesus, graciously hear us.
God the Father, of heaven.
Have mercy on us.
God the Son, Redeemer of the world.
Have mercy on us.
God the Holy Ghost.
Have mercy on us.
Holy Trinity; one God.
Have mercy on us.

Jesus, Son of the living God,
Jesus, splendour of the Father,
Jesus, brightness of eternal light,
Jesus, King of glory,
Jesus, Sun of justice,
Jesus, Son of the Virgin Mary,
Jesus, most amiable,
Jesus, most admirable,
Jesus, mighty God,
Jesus, Father of the world to come.
Jesus, Angel of the great council,
Jesus, most powerful,
Jesus, most patient,
Jesus, most obedient,
Jesus, meek and humble of heart,

} *Have mercy on us.*

Jesus, Lover of chastity,
Jesus, Lover of us,
Jesus, God of Peace,
Jesus, Author of life,
Jesus, Example of virtues,
Jesus, zealous lover of souls.
Jesus, our God,
Jesus, our refuge,
Jesus, Father of the poor,
Jesus, Treasure of the faithful,
Jesus, Good Shepherd,
Jesus, true light,
Jesus, Eternal wisdom,
Jesus, infinite goodness,
Jesus, our way and our life,
Jesus, Joy of Angels,
Jesus, King of Patriarchs,
Jesus, Master of Apostles,
Jesus, Teacher of Evangelists,
Jesus, strength of Martyrs,
Jesus, Light of Confessors,
Jesus, Purity of Virgins,
Jesus, Crown of all Saints, } *Have mercy on us.*
Be merciful unto us,
Spare us, O Jesus.
Be merciful unto us,
Graciously hear us, O Jesus.
From all evil,
From all sin,
From Thy wrath, } *Jesus deliver us.*
From the snares of the devil,
From the spirit of uncleanness,
From everlasting death,
From the neglect of Thy inspirations,
Through the mystery of Thy holy Incarnation,
Through Thy nativity,
Through Thine infancy,
Through Thy most divine life,
Through Thy labours,
Through Thine agony and passion,
Through Thy Cross and dereliction,
Through Thy faintness and weariness,
Through Thy death and burial
Through Thy resurrection,
Through Thine ascension,
Through Thy Joys,
Through Thy glory, } *Jesus deliver us.*
Lamb of God, Who takest away the sins of the world.
Spare us, O Jesus.
Lamb of God, Who takest away the sins of the world.
Graciously hear us, O Jesus.
Lamb of God, Who takest away the sins of the world.
Have mercy on us, O Jesus.
Jesus, hear us.
Jesus, graciously hear us.

O LORD Jesus Christ, who hast said: "Ask, and ye shall receive; seek, and ye shall find; knock, and it shall be opened unto you;" give, we beseech Thee, to us who ask, the Grace of Thy most divine love, that with all our heart, words, and works, we may love Thee, and never cease to praise Thee. Amen.

Let us pray.

GRANT that we may have a perpetual fear and love of Thy holy Name; for Thou never failest to direct and govern those whom Thou instructest in Thy true and solid love. Through our Lord Jesus, Thy Son, who livest and reignest with Thee in the unity of the Holy Ghost God world without end. Amen.

In the evening.

Litany of the Blessed Virgin Mary.

Lord, have mercy on us.
Lord, have mercy on us.
Christ, hear us.
Christ, graciously hear us.

God the Father, of heaven,
God the Son, Redeemer of the world, } *Have mercy on us.*

Holy Mary,
Holy Mother of God,
Holy Virgin of virgins,
Mother of Christ,
Mother of divine grace,
Mother most pure,
Mother most chaste,
Mother inviolate, } *Pray for us.*

INDULGENCED PRAYERS.

Mother most amiable,
Mother most admirable,
Mother of good counsel,
Mother of our Creator
Mother of our Redeemer,
Virgin most prudent
Virgin most venerable,
Virgin most renowned,
Virgin most powerful,
Virgin most merciful,
Virgin most faithful,
Mirror of justice,
Seat of wisdom,
Cause of our joy,
Spiritual vessel,
Vessel of honour,
Vessel of singular devotion,
Mystical Rose,
Tower of David,
Tower of ivory,
House of gold,
Ark of the covenant,
Gate of heaven,
Morning Star,
Health of the sick,
Refuge of sinners,
Comforter of the afflicted,

} *Pray for us.*

Help of Christians,
Queen of Angels,
Queen of Patriarches,
Queen of Prophets,
Queen of Apostles,
Queen of Martyrs,
Queen of Confessors,
Queen of Virgins,
Queen of all Saints,
Queen conceived without original sin.
Queen of the most holy Rosary,

} *Pray for us.*

Lamb of God, Who takest away the sins of the world.
Spare us, O Lord.
Lamb of God, Who takest away the sins of the world.
Graciously hear us, O Lord.
Lamb of God, Who takest away the sins of the world.
Have mercy on us.

V Pray for us, O holy Mother of God.

R That we may be made worthy of the promises of Christ.

Let us Pray.

GRANT, we beseech Thee, O Lord God, that we, Thy servants, may be blessed with continual health of soul and body; and that by the glorious intercession of the Blessed Mary, ever Virgin, we may be delivered from present sorrow, and obtain eternal happiness, through Christ our Lord. Amen.

May the divine assistance remain always with us.
Amen.

Indulgenced Prayers.

1. Glory be to the Father, and to the Son, and to the Holy Ghost. *Three times.* (*100 days.*)
2. Eternal Father, I offer to Thee the Most Precious Blood of Jesus Christ, in satisfaction for my sins and for the needs of the Holy Church. (*100 days.*)
3. My Jesus, mercy. (*100 days.*)
4. My sweet Jesus, be not to me a Judge but a Saviour. (*50 days.*)
5. Jesus, my God, I love Thee above all things. (*50 days.*)
6. O Sacrament most holy, O Sacrament divine, all praise and all thanksgiving be every moment thine. (*100 days.*)
7. O sweetest Heart of Jesus, I implore that I may ever love Thee more

11. Jesus, Mary, Joseph, assist me in my last agony. (*100 days.*)
12. Jesus, Mary, Joseph, may I breathe forth my soul in peace in your blessed company. (*100 days.*)
13. Blessed be the Holy and Immaculate Conception of the Blessed Virgin Mary. (*300 days.*)

ACT OF CONSECRATION TO THE SACRED HEART OF JESUS.

MY loving Jesus, I give Thee my heart and I consecrate myself wholly to Thee on account of the love I bear Thee, and as a reparation for all my unfaithfulness to grace; and I purpose, with Thine aid, never to sin again.

Plen. Indul. once a month. 100 days Ind. once a day.

To be said before a Crucifix.

O GOOD and most sweet Jesus, behold, I fall on my knees before Thee, and with all the ardour of my soul, pray and beseech Thee that Thou wouldst vouchsafe to impress upon my heart lively sentiments of faith, hope and charity, with a true repentance for my sins, and a most firm resolution of amendment; whilst with deep feelings of grief I consider within myself and contemplate in spirit Thy five wounds, having before my eyes what the royal prophet expressed by these words, "They have pierced my hands and feet, they have numbered all my bones."

Say one "Our Father," and "Hail Mary," *or some other prayer for the intentions of the Church.*

Plen. Indul. on Communion Days.

MEMORARE.

REMEMBER, O most holy Virgin Mary, that from of old it has never been heard that any one fleeing to thy protection, imploring thy help, or asking thy intercession has been left unaided. Encouraged by this confidence I hasten to thee; to thee I come, and before thee, I, a weeping sinner, stand. Despise not, O Mother of the Incarnate Word, my humble petitions, but graciously hear and grant them. Amen.

(*300 days each time.*)

Prayers at Mass.

PRAYER BEFORE MASS.

O MY Saviour, I come before Thy holy Altar to assist at Thy Divine Sacrifice. Do Thou prepare my soul to receive Thy grace; fix my mind on Thee; wash away in Thy Precious Blood all the sins of which Thou seest me guilty; I hate them for the love of Thee, and most humbly beg pardon for them. Grant, O sweet Jesus, that uniting my intentions to Thine, I may spend my whole life for Thy glory, as Thou didst give Thy life for the saving of my soul. Amen.

I wish to share in the Communion of Saints by gaining all the indulgences I can to-day; I place them in the hands of our Blessed Lady for the relief of the souls in purgatory. My Jesus, mercy! Mary, help!

PRAYERS AT MASS.

PRAYER AT THE BEGINNING OF THE MASS.

While the Priest says the Judica me, Deus, *etc.*

O ALMIGHTY Lord of heaven and earth, behold I, a wretched sinner, presume to appear before Thee this day, to offer to Thee by the hands of our High Priest, Jesus Christ, Thy Son, the sacrifice of His Body and Blood, in union with that sacrifice which He offered to Thee upon the Cross; first, for Thine own honour, praise, adoration and glory; secondly, in remberance of His Death and passion, thirdly, in thanksgiving for all Thy blessings bestowed on Him and on His whole Church, whether triumphant in heaven, or militant on earth, and especially for those bestowed on me, the most unworthy of all; fourthly, to obtain pardon and remission of all my sins, and of those of all others, whether living or dead, for whom I ought to pray; and lastly, to obtain all graces and blessing both for myself and for Thy whole Church. O be thou pleased to assist me in such a manner by Thy grace, that I may behave myself this day as I ought to do in Thy Divine Presence, and that I may so commemorate the Death and Passion of Thy Son as to partake most plentifully of the fruits thereof; through the same Jesus Christ our Lord. Amen.

CONFITEOR.

I CONFESS to Almighty God, to blessed Mary ever Virgin, to blessed Michael the Archangel, to blessed John the Baptist, to the holy Apostles Peter and Paul, to all the saints and to *you, father,* that I have sinned exceedingly in thought, word, and deed, *through my fault, through my fault, through my most grievous fault,* Therefore I beseech the blessed Mary ever Virgin, blessed Michael the Archangel, blessed John the Baptist, the holy Apostles Peter and Paul, and all the saints, and *you, father,* to pray to the Lord our God for me.

The Priest goes up to the Altar, and as he advances, full of holy fear, says in a low tone of voice:

PRAYERS.

TAKE away from us our sins, we beseech Thee, O Lord, that we may be worthy to enter with pure minds into the Holy of Holies; through Jesus Christ our Lord. Amen.

WE beseech Thee, O Lord, by the merits of Thy Saints whose relics are here, and of all the Saints, that thou wouldst mercifully forgive me all my sins, Amen.

THE INTROIT

The Introit is the first prayer the Priest reads at the right or Epistle side of the Altar. This prayer reminds us how much those who lived holy lives, under the Old Law, wished for the coming of our Blessed Redeemer. *Glory be to the Father,* is added in honour of the Blessed Trinity.

PRAYER DURING THE READING OF THE INTROIT.

LET the Name of the Lord be blessed both now and for ever. From the rising to the setting of the sun let all praise be given to the Name of the Lord. Glory be to the Father, and to the Son, and to the Holy Ghost. As it was in the beginning, is now, and ever shall be, world without end. Amen.

THE KYRIE ELEISON.

Lord, have mercy on us. (*thrice.*)
Christ, have mercy on us. (*thrice*)
Lord, have mercy on us. (*thrice*)

PRAYERS AT MASS.

THE GLORIA.

GLORY be to God on high, and on earth peace to men of good will. We praise Thee, we bless Thee; we adore Thee; we glorify Thee. We give Thee thanks for Thy great glory, O Lord God, heavenly King, God the Father Almighty. O Lord Jesus Christ, the only begotten Son; O Lord God, Lamb of God, Son of the Father, Who takest away the sins of the world, have mercy upon us; Who takest away the sins of the world, receive our prayers: Thou Who sittest at the right hand of the Father, have mercy on us. For Thou only art holy: Thou only art the Lord: Thou only, O Jesus Christ, with the Holy Ghost, art most high in the glory of God the Father. Amen.

At the end of the Gloria, the Priest kisses the Altar and turns to the people saying:

The Lord be with you.

The Clerk answers:

And with Thy Spirit:

AT THE COLLECTS.

O ALMIGHTY and eternal God, we humbly beseech Thee mercifully to give ear to the prayers here offered Thee by Thy servant in the name of Thy whole Church, and in behalf of us Thy people. Accept them to the honour of Thy Name, and the good of our souls; and grant to us all mercy, grace, and salvation; through our Lord Jesus Christ. Amen.

AT THE EPISTLE.

THOU hast vouchsafed, O Lord, to teach us Thy sacred truths by Thy prophets and apostles; O grant that we may so improve by their doctrine and examples in the love of Thy holy Law, that we may show forth by our lives whose disciples we are; that we may no longer follow the corrupt inclinations of flesh and blood, but master all our passions; that we may be ever directed by Thy light, and strengthened by Thy grace, to walk in the way of Thy commandments, and to serve Thee with clean hearts; through our Lord Jesus Christ. Amen.

BEFORE THE GOSPEL.

CREATE a clean heart in me, O God, and grant that I may listen to Thy holy Gospel with respect, and bless Thy Name for ever.

AT THE GOSPEL

MAYEST Thou be ever adored and praised, O Lord, who, not content to instruct and inform us by Thy prophets and apostles, hast even vouchsafed to speak to us by Thy only Son our Lord and Saviour Jesus Christ, commanding us by a voice from Heaven to hear Him; O grant that we may so improve by His doctrine and example in the love of Thy holy Name, and of Thy holy Law, that we may shew forth by our lives whose disciples we are, that we may no longer follow the corrupt inclinations of flesh and blood, but master all our passions, that we may be ever directed by Thy light, and strengthened by Thy grace, to walk in the way of Thy commandments and to serve Thee with clean hearts; through our Lord Jesus Christ. Amen.

THE NICENE CREED

I BELIEVE in one God, the Father Almighty, Creator of heaven and earth and of all things visible and invisible. And in one Lord Jesus Christ, the only begotten Son of God, born of the Father before all ages. God of God; Light of Light; true God of true God; begotten not made; consubstantial with the

Father, by whom all things were made. Who for us men, and for our salvation, came down from heaven, and was incarnate by the Holy Ghost of the Virgin Mary, AND WAS MADE MAN, [*Kneel in reverence for Christ's Incarnation.*] He suffered under Pontius Pilate, was crucified, dead, and buried. The third day, according to the scriptures, He rose again; and ascended into heaven, and sitteth at the right hand of the Father, and He shall come again with glory to judge both the living and the dead; of whose kingdom there shall be no end. And I believe in the Holy Ghost, the Lord and giver of life, who proceedeth from the Father and the Son: Who together with the Father and the Son is adored and glorified: Who spoke by the prophets. And One Holy Catholic and Apostolic Church. I confess one baptism for the remission of sins. And I look for the resurrection of the dead, and life of the world to come. Amen.

The Lord be with you.
And with thy spirit.

AT THE OFFERTORY.

ACCEPT O holy Father, almighty and eternal God, this unspotted Host, which I, Thy unworthy servant, offer unto Thee for my many sins, my faults, and my carelessness. I offer it also for all here present in this Church, as well as for all faithful Christians, both living and dead, that it may help both them and me to gain eternal life.

AT THE OFFERING OF THE CHALICE.

WE offer Thee, O Lord the chalice of salvation, humbly begging Thy mercy, that it may ascend to Thee for our salvation, and that of the whole world. Amen.

OFFERING OF THE FAITHFUL.

The Priest makes the following prayer for himself and for the people:

PRAYER.

ACCEPT us, O Lord, who come to Thee with contrite and humble hearts: and grant that the sacrifice we offer this day in Thy sight may be pleasing to Thee, O Lord God.

BLESSING OF THE BREAD AND WINE.

PRAYER.

COME, O almighty and eternal God, and bless this sacrifice prepared for the glory of Thy holy Name.

WASHING OF THE FINGERS.

PRAYER.

O JESUS, most pure of heart: O spotless Lamb of God; help me that I may keep my heart pure; that all through my life I may never displease Thee by any wicked thing. Give me the blessing of the clean of heart.

PRAYER TO THE BLESSED TRINITY.

The Priest returns to the middle of the Altar, and, bowing down, offers the Sacrifice to the Most Holy Trinity.

PRAYER.

O BLESSED Trinity ; Father, Son, and Holy Ghost, accept this Holy Mass which we offer Thee in memory of the Passion, Resurrection, and Ascension of our Lord Jesus Christ, and in honour of the Blessed Mary, ever Virgin, of Blessed John the Baptist, the holy Apostles Peter and Paul, St. Joseph, my Angel Guardian and patron Saints. And may all the Saints and Angels whom we now honour upon earth, intercede for us in Heaven. Amen.

THE ORATE FRATRES OR "BRETHREN PRAY."

The Priest turns to the congregation, and, with his hands stretched out, invites them to pray with him.

PRAYER.

BRETHREN, pray that my sacrifice and yours may be acceptable to God, the Father Almighty.

The Clerk answers :

MAY the Lord receive this sacrifice from thy hands, to the praise and glory of His Name, for our benefit, and that of all His holy Church.

THE SECRET PRAYERS.

The Priest now prays in a low tone of voice.

During this time, do you in charity think of the thousands who are to pass to-day from this world to the next. Say most earnestly for them this

PRAYER.

HEART of Jesus, once in agony, have pity on the dying.

THE PREFACE.

The *Preface* leads to the *Canon*, and the Altar bell is rung to tell us that the Priest is entering upon the most solemn part of the Mass.

> World without end,
> Amen.
> The Lord be with you.
> And with Thy Spirit.
> Lift up your hearts.
> We have lifted them up to the Lord.
> Let us give thanks to the Lord our God,
> It is meet and just.

IT is truly meet and just, that we should always, and in all places, give thanks to Thee, O holy Lord, Father Almighty, Eternal God, through Christ our Lord. Through Whom the Angels praise Thy majesty, adore Thee, reverence Thee, and sing Thy everlasting praise. Together with them we beseech Thee that Thou wouldst allow our voices also to be admitted, whilst we humbly say :—

THE SANCTUS.

(The bell rings.)

HOLY, holy, holy, Lord God of Hosts. Heaven and earth are full of Thy glory. Hosanna in the highest. Blessed is He that cometh in the Name of the Lord. Hosanna in the highest.

PRAYERS AT MASS.

THE CANON OF THE MASS.

MOST merciful Father, Who hast given us Thy only Son to be our daily Sacrifice, incline Thine ear to our prayers, and favour our desires; protect, unite, and govern Thy whole Church throughout the world; pour forth Thy blessings on his present Holiness, on our Bishop, and all true professors of the Catholic faith.

I OFFER Thee, O Eternal Father, with this Thy minister at the altar, this oblation of the Body and Blood of Thy only Son, to Thy honour and glory; in remembrance of my Saviour's passion, in thanksgiving for all thy benefits, in satisfaction for all my sins, and for the obtaining of Thy grace, whereby I may be enabled to live virtuously and die happily. I desire Thee likewise to accept it, O God, for my parents [*if alive*], relatives, friends and benefactors; grant them all blessings, spiritual and temporal. I offer it up also [*name the particular intention*]. Likewise for all that are in misery; for those that I have in any way injured either by word or deed; for all my enemies, for all those for whom my prayers are desired, especially *N.;* for the conversion of all sinners, and enlightening all that sit in darkness. Pour forth Thy blessings on all, according to their different necessities. Through the merits of Thy only Son our Lord.

GIVE ear, we beseech Thee, to the prayers of Thy servant, who is here appointed to make this oblation in our behalf; and grant it may be effectual for the obtaining of all those blessings which he asks for us.

BEHOLD, O Lord, we all here present to Thee in this bread and wine the symbols of our perfect union. Grant, O Lord, that they may be made for us the true Body and Blood of Thy dear Son; that, being consecrated to Thee by this holy Victim, we may live in Thy service, and depart this life in Thy grace.

AT THE ELEVATION OF THE HOST.

I BELIEVE, O Jesus, that Thou art truly present here, as God and Man, under the form of bread. I adore Thee with the deepest reverence, as my Lord and my God. O Jesus, may I live for Thee only, may I die for Thee gladly: O Jesus, living or dying, let me be Thine!

ELEVATION OF THE CHALICE.

O MY Saviour, I believe that Thou art here. I believe that Thy most Precious Blood, which was poured out once upon the Cross for a sacrifice to atone for our sins, is substantially present in this chalice, under the appearance of wine. Ah! holy Blood of my Redeemer, I beseech Thee, wash and purify me from all my sins.

AFTER THE ELEVATION.

O JESUS, Who after Thy death upon the Cross was laid in the grave and didst raise Thyself to life on the third day, help me to keep my soul in the life of grace. Help me so to live that on the last day I may rise in glory and be happy with Thee in Heaven.

PRAYER FOR THE DEAD.

O MOST merciful Lord Jesus, give unto them eternal rest. Be mindful, O Lord, of Thy servants, who are gone before us with the sign of faith, and sleep in the sleep of peace. [*Name.*] To these, O Lord, and to all that rest in Christ, grant, we beseech Thee, a place of refreshment, light and peace; through the same Christ our Lord. Amen.

PRAYERS AT MASS.

Let us pray.

INSTRUCTED by Thy saving precepts, and following Thy divine institution, we presume to say :—

OUR Father, Who art in heaven, hallowed be Thy name, Thy kingdom come Thy will be done on earth as it is in heaven. Give us this day our daily bread; and forgive us our trespasses, as we forgive them that trespass against us. And lead us not into temptation, but deliver us from evil. Amen.

DELIVER us, we beseech Thee, O Lord, from all evils, past, present, and to come; and by the prayers of the Blessed Virgin Mary, and all the Saints, mercifully grant peace in our days, that, with Thy help we may be always free from sin and safe from harm. Through the same Jesus Christ Thy Son our Lord, Who with Thee, in the unity of the Holy Ghost, liveth and reigneth, God, world without end. Amen.

AT THE BREAKING OF THE HOST.

THY Body was broken and Thy Blood was shed for us; grant, O sweet Jesus, that we, who receive Thee in this Holy Sacrament, may ever believe in Thee, and hope in Thee, and love Thee, more and more. Amen.

THE AGNUS DEI.

LAMB of God, Who takest away the sins of the world, have mercy on us.
Lamb of God, Who takest away the sins of the world have mercy on us.
Lamb of God, Who takest away the sins of the world, grant us peace.

PREPARATION FOR HOLY COMMUNION.

LORD Jesus Christ, who saidst to Thy Apostles, Peace I leave with you, my peace I give unto you; look not upon my sins but upon the faith of Thy Church, and give her that peace which Thou dost love to see among her children; who livest and reignest God for ever and ever. Amen.

LORD Jesus Christ, Son of the living God, Who, by the will of Thy Father and by the power of the Holy Ghost, hast by Thy death given life to the world; deliver me by this, Thy most Sacred Body and Blood, from all my sins and from all evils; and make me always follow Thy commandments, and never let me be separated from Thee; Who, with the same God and Father and the Holy Ghost, livest and reignest, God, for ever and ever. Amen.

AT THE COMMUNION.

MAY this Holy Communion, which I am about to receive, O Lord, keep my soul and body from all evil. Who with God the Father, in the unity of the Holy Ghost, livest and reignest, God, for ever and ever. Amen.

I WILL take the Bread of Heaven, and call upon the Name of the Lord.

The Priest strikes his breast three times saying:

LORD, I am not worthy that Thou shouldst enter under my roof; say but the word and my soul shall be healed.

ACT OF SPIRITUAL COMMUNION.

O MY Jesus, I believe that thou art truly present in this Holy Sacrament, I love Thee above all things, and I desire Thee with my whole soul, but since I cannot now receive Thee sacramentally, come at least spiritually into my heart. I embrace Thee as if Thou wert already come, I unite myself wholly to Thee. Never suffer me to separate from Thee.

PRAYERS AT MASS.

WHAT shall I give to the Lord for all that He hath given to me? I will take the chalice of salvation, and call upon the Name of the Lord. Praising I will call upon the Lord, and I shall be saved from my enemies.

PRAYER.

DEAR Jesus, wash my soul in Thy Precious Blood. May the Blood of our Lord Jesus Christ preserve my soul to everlasting life. Eternal Father, I offer Thee the Precious Blood of Jesus Christ in satisfaction for my sins, and for the needs of Holy Church. Amen.

AT THE ABLUTIONS.

GRANT, O Lord, that what we have taken with our mouth we may receive with a pure mind; and may it do us good both for time and eternity. Amen.

MAY Thy Body, O Lord, which I have received, and Thy Blood which I have drunk remain with me; and grant that no stain of sin may be left on my soul, which has been fed with such pure and holy Sacraments. Who livest and reignest one God, world without end. Amen.

THE POST COMMUNION.

MY God, I thank Thee for all Thou hast done for me. In return for all Thy mercies I wish never more to displease Thee. Make me wholly thine, and let me always love Thee more and more.

The Lord be with you.
And with thy spirit.

Let us pray.

JESUS, meek and humble of heart, make my heart like to Thine. O Sacred Heart of Jesus, I implore, that I may ever love Thee more and more. O Mary, conceived without sin, pray for us who have recourse to thee. Saint Joseph, friend of the Sacred Heart, pray for us.

Let us bless the Lord.
Thanks be to God.

(In Masses for the dead.)

May they rest in peace. Amen.

The Priest bowing down before the Altar says:

PRAYER.

O HOLY Trinity, let what I have done be pleasing to Thee; and grant that the sacrifice which I, though unworthy, have offered up in the sight of Thy majesty, may be accepted by Thee; and through Thy mercy may I, and all for whom it has been offered, receive forgiveness of our sins. Through Christ our Lord. Amen.

The Lord be with you.
And with thy spirit.

PRAYERS AT MASS.

THE LAST GOSPEL.

The beginning of the holy Gospel according to St. John.

IN the beginning was the Word, and the Word was with God, and the Word was God; the same was in the beginning with God. All things were made by Him, and without Him was made nothing that was made: In Him was life, and the life was the light of men: and the light shineth in darkness, and the darkness did not comprehend it. There was a man sent from God, whose name was John. This man came for a witness, to give testimony of the light, that all men might believe through him. He was not the light, but came to give testimony of the light. He was the true light which enlightened every man that cometh into this world. He was in the world, and the world was made by Him, and the world knew Him not. He came unto His own, and His own received Him not. But as many as received Him, to them He gave power to become the sons of God: to those that believe in His name, who are born not of blood, nor of the will of the flesh, nor of the will of man, but of God. AND THE WORD WAS MADE FLESH [*Here the people kneel down*], and dwelt among us; and we saw His glory, as it were the glory of the Only-Begotten of the Father, full of grace and truth.

Thanks be to God.

> Great God, we thank Thee for the grace
> Of hearing Holy Mass this day;
> On Sundays may we always come
> To hear the Holy Mass and pray.
> And may the grace of Holy Mass
> Be with us still in all our need.
> And keep us from the stain of sin,
> In every thought and word and deed.

THE DIVINE PRAISES.*

The Divine Praises are generally said by the Priest at the end of Mass and Vespers.

Blessed be God.
Blessed be His holy Name.
Blessed be Jesus Christ, true God and true man.
Blessed be the Name of Jesus.
Blessed be His Most Sacred Heart.
Blessed be Jesus in the most holy Sacrament of the Altar.
Blessed be the great mother of God, Mary most holy.
Blessed be her holy and Immaculate Conception.
Blessed be the name of Mary, Virgin and Mother.
Blessed be God in His Angels and in His Saints.

*Indulgence: One year for every time it is said.

✝

The Manner of Assisting at Mass and Vespers.

LOW MASS.

According to the Rubrics of the Missal, all assisting at Low Mass should kneel during the whole service, except at the Gospel. Custom, however, has modified the law as follows:

1. When the celebrant enters the sanctuary, all shall rise. They remain standing until the Priest descends from the Altar to begin Mass, when all shall kneel.
2. They remain kneeling until the Gospel. As the Altar boy ascends to place the Missal on the left side of the Altar, all shall rise and remain standing during the Gospel (and during the *Credo*, should it be said), until the celebrant says "*Dominus Vobiscum.*"
3. While the Priest is making the announcements, or preaching, the people should be seated. If the Gospel is read to the congregation, they should stand.
4. Should the *Credo* be said, the congregation genuflects with the Priest at the words "*et incarnatus est* * * * ET HOMO FACTUS EST.*"
5. After "*Dominus Vobiscum*" all sit down and continue so till the *Sanctus*, when they shall reverently kneel. Thus they remain during the Priest's Communion and also during the Communion of the faithful, should there be any to receive.
6. When the Priest receives the first ablution, all may sit down.
7. They kneel again, however, as soon as he goes to the book.
8. After the blessing, all rise and stand during the last Gospel, genuflecting at "ET VERBUM, CARO FACTUM EST."
9. When the Priest descends from the Altar, they kneel and recite with him the prayers after Mass.
10. *Not until the Priest has retired from the Sanctuary should any person leave the church or his place therein.*

HIGH MASS.

11. On entrance of the celebrant all rise.
12. The congregation kneel when the Priest intones the *Asperges me*, and stand when he sprinkles them with holy water, and remain standing until the prayer is sung. They may sit down while the Priest is vesting.
13. As the Priest descends from the Altar to begin Mass they kneel.
14. At the intonation of the "*Gloria*" all stand, and as the celebrant takes his seat, all sit down.
15. When he reascends the Altar, all rise and stand during the singing of the prayers. (*It is customary to kneel during the singing of the prayer for the departed, in Masses of* REQUIEM.)

16. When he begins to *read* the Epistle, all sit down, and arise as the Altar boy ascends with the Missal to the Gospel side.

17. Should there be a sermon, they kneel during the "*Veni Creator*," and stand while the preacher reads the Gospel.

18. When the celebrant leaves his seat to intone the "*Credo*," all rise and remain standing while he recites it, genuflecting at "*et incarnatus est*," and sitting down when the celebrant is seated.

19. During the singing of "*et incarnatus est* * * * ET HOMO FACTUS EST" all kneel, and at its close re-seat themselves. A different custom exists in many well regulated churches.

20. As the Priest again ascends the Altar, all rise, and sit down again after he has sung "*Oremus.*"

21. When he sings "*Per omnia sæcula sæculorum*," at the Preface, all rise and stand until the *Sanctus*, when they kneel and remain kneeling till after the Communions of both Priest and people, and then sit down during the purification and covering of the chalice.

22. When the celebrant goes to the Book, all stand. They stand during prayers, kneel for blessing, and stand during the last Gospel, at the end of which they kneel and *remain so till the celebrant has left the Sanctuary*.

SOLEMN HIGH MASS.

The rules are the same as for High Mass. Note, however:

23. That the people do not stand while the celebrant *reads* the Gospel, but only when the Deacon commences with "*Dominus Vobiscum*" to sing it.

24. When the altar boy incenses the congregation at the Offertory, all should stand.

VESPERS.

25. All should stand when the celebrant enters the Sanctuary, and remain standing until he has arrived at the Altar.

26. All should kneel while the celebrant is saying the first prayer at the foot of the Altar; they rise when he rises to go to his seat, and remain standing until the celebrant sits down after intoning the *Deus in adjutorum*.

27. At the *Gloria Patri* at the end of each Psalm, all should bow the head, but not stand up.

28. During the singing of the *Chapter* at the end of the psalms all should stand up and remain standing until the celebrant is seated. If the celebrant should kneel during the singing of the hymn, the people should kneel also.

29. During the singing of the *Magnificat* and Prayer, the people should stand, making the sign of the cross at the beginning of the *Magnificat*.

30. When the celebrant kneels at the Altar, before the exposition of the Blessed Sacrament, all should kneel, and remain so until the Blessed Sacrament is put into the tabernacle at the end of the Benediction.

CONCERNING THE CHOIR.

31. All members are governed by the foregoing rules in so far as they do not interfere with the singing.

32. They should try to give the responses in the tone assumed by the celebrant or given them by the organist. A Sanctuary Choir should never fail here. The organist can do much to help both celebrant and choir by a timely touch of the proper note at critical moments.

33. The celebrant should *never* be kept waiting for the choir to finish. The interlude at the Offertory should end at the "*Orate fratres*;" the *Sanctus* should close at the single stroke of the bell; and the *Benedictus* should close at the "*Nobis quoque peccatoribus.*" Should the celebrant not be ready, then the organist will do well to softly run over the notes of the "*Per omnia sæcula sæculorum.*"

Spiritual Canticles.

THE Sovereign Pontiff, Pius VII., in order to encourage the faithful to sing spiritual canticles, and to check, as far as possible, the singing of dangerous profane songs, by a rescript from the Office of the Secretary of Memorials, Jan. 16, 1817, granted:

An indulgence of one year, every time, to all who shall promote the singing of spiritual canticles.

An indulgence of one hundred days to all who, with at least contrite heart, shall practise this pious exercise.

A plenary indulgence, once a month, to all who, having promoted or practised this pious exercise during the month, shall, on any day, being truly penitent, after confession and communion, pray for the intention of the Sovereign Pontiff.

✝

"Sing ye to the Lord a *New Canticle:* sing well unto Him with a loud voice, and bless His name." (Ps. xxxii., 3, xcv., 2.)

"I will sing to the Lord, who gaveth me good things; yea, I will sing to the name of the Lord the most high." (Ps. xli., 6.)

Vespers for Sundays.

FIRST VESPERS.

Pater Noster, Ave Maria (In secret.)

Priest. Deus in adjutorium .... meum in - ten - de.
Domine, ad adjuvandum .... me fes - ti - na.
Gloria Patri et Filio et .... Spiritu - i Sanc - to:
Sicut erat in principio et .... nunc et semp - er,
Et in sæcula .... sæcu - lorum. A - men.

From Septuagesima Sunday instead of Alleluia, sing:

Al - le - lu - ia. Laus ti-bi Do-mine Rex æ - ter - næ glo - ri - æ.

DIXIT DOMINUS. Psalm cix.

FIRST CHANT.

1 Dixit Dominus Domino me - o.* sede a dex - tris me - is.

2 Donec ponam ini - mi - cos tu - os * scabellum pe - dum tu - o - rum.
3 Virgam virtutis tuæ, emittet Dominus ex Si - on :* dominare in medio inimico - rum tu - o - rum.
4 Tecum principium in die virtutis tuæ, in splendoribus sanc - to - rum: * ex utero ante luci - ferum ge - nui te.
5 Juravit Dominus, et non pœnitebit e - um :* Tu es Sacerdos in æternum, secundum ordi - nem Mel - chi - sedech.
6 Dominus a dextris tu - is, * confregit in die iræ su - æ re - ges.
7 Judicabit in nationibus, implebit ru - i - nas ; * conquassabit capita in terra mul - to - rum
8 De torrente in via bi - bet ; * propterea exal-ta-bit ca-put. *Gloria Patri, etc.*

SECOND CHANT.

1 Dixit Dominus Domino me - o:* sede a dex - tris me - is.

VESPERS

CONFITEBOR. Psalm cx.

FIRST CHANT.

1 Confitebor tibi, Do-mine, in toto cor - de me - o;* in consilio justo rum, et congre-ga-ti - o - ne.

2 Magna o - pera Do - mini,* exquisita in omnes volun - tates e - jus.
3 Confessio et magnificentia o - pus e - jus, * et justitia ejus manet in sæ - culum sæ - culi.
4 Memoriam fecit mirabilium suorum misericors et mise - ra - tor Do - minus:* escam dedit ti men - ti - bus se.
5 Memor erit in sæculum testa - men - ti su - i;* virtutem operum suorum an - nuntiabit po - pulo su - o:
6 Ut det illis hæredi - ta - tem gen - tium ;* opera manuum ejus veritas et ju - di - cium.

7 Fidelia omnia mandata ejus con - firmata in sæ - culum sæ - culi, * facta in veritate et æ - qui - tate.
8 Redemptionem misit po - pulo su - o;* mandavit in æternum testa - men - tum su - um.
9 Sanctum et terrible no - men e - jus:* initium sapientiæ ti - mor Do - mini.
10 Intellectus bonus omnibus faci - en - tibus e - um ; * laudatio ejus manet in sæ - culum sæ - culi.

Gloria Patri, etc.

SECOND CHANT.

1 Con-fite-bor tibi, Domine in toto cor-de me-o* in consilio justo-rum, et con-gre-ga - ti - o - ne.

BEATUS VIR. Psalm cxi.

FIRST CHANT.

1. Beatus vir, qui ti-met Dominum ;*in mandatis ejus vo-let ni - - mis.

VESPERS.

2 Potens in terra erit se-men e-jus; *
generatio rectorum be-ne-di-ce-tur.

3 Gloria et divitiæ in do-mo e-jus; *
et justitia ejus manet in sœ-culum sœ-culi.

4 Exortum est in tenebris lu-men
rec-tis: * misericors, et mise-ra-tor,
et justus.

5 Jucundus homo, qui miseretur et
commodat; disponet sermones suos in
ju-di-cio;* quia in æternum non-com-mo-ve-bitur.

6 In memoria æterna e-rit jus-tus: *
ab auditione mala non ti-me-bit.

7 Paratum cor ejus sperare in Dom-ino; confirmatum-est-cor e-jus: * non
commovebitur, donec despiciat ini-mi-cos-su-os.

8 Dispersit, dedit pauperibus; jus-titia ejus manet in sœ-culum sœ-culi; *
cornu ejus exalta-bi-tur in gloria.

9 Peccator videbit, et irasce-tur,
dentibus suis fremet, et ta-bes-cet; *
desidcrium pecca-to-rum pe-ri-bit.

Gloria Patri, etc,

SECOND CHANT.

1 Beatus vir, qui timet Do-minum: * in manda-tis ejus vo--let ni-mis.

LAUDATE PUERI. Psalm cxii.

FIRST CHANT.

1 Lauda-te, pueri, Do-minum: * Laudate no-men Do-mi-ni.

2 Sit nomen Domini be-ne-dic-tum, *
ex hoc nunc, et us-que in sœ-culum.

3 A solis ortu usque ad-oc-ca-sum,*
laudabile no-men Do-mini.

4 Excelsus super omnes gen-tes Do-minus, * et super cœlos glo-ria e-jus.

5 Quis sicut Dominus Deus noster,
qui in al-tis ha-bitat, * et humilia
respicit in cœ-lo et in terra?

6 Suscitans a ter-ra in-opem,* et de
stercore eri-gens pau-perem.

7 Ut collocet eum cum prin-ci-pibus, * cum principibus po-puli su-i.

8 Qui habitare facit steril-em-in-do-mo, * matrem filiorum-læ-tantem
Gloria Patri, etc.

SECOND CHANT.

Lauda-te, pu-e-ri Do-minum: * Laudate no-men Do-mini.

VESPERS.

In Exitu Israel. Psalm cxiii.

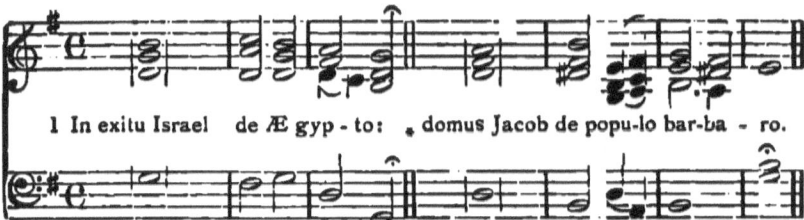

1 In exitu Israel de Æ gyp - to: * domus Jacob de popu-lo bar-ba - ro.

2 Facta est Judæa sancitifi - ca - tio e - jus, * Israel po - tes - tas e jus.
3 Mare vi - dit, et fu - git : * Jordanis conver - sus est retror - sum.
4 Montes exultaverunt ut a-ri- etes,* et colles si-cut a-gni o-vium.
5 Quid est tibi, mare - quod fu - gis - ti? * et tu, Jordanis, quia conver-sus es re - tror sum?
6 Montes, exultastis si-cut a-ri-etes?* et colles, si-cut a-gni o-vium?
7 A facie Domini mo - ta est ter - ra,* a facie De - i Jacob.
8 Qui convertit petram in sta-gna a * qua-rum, * et rupem in fon-tes a - qua - rium.
9 Non nobis, Dom - ne, ncn no - bis, * sed nomini tu-o da glo-ri-am.
10 Super misericordia tua et veri-ta - te tu - a ; *nequando dicant gentes: Ubi est De-us e-o-rnm?
11 Deus autem nos - ter in cœ - lo. : * omn'a quæcumque vo-lu-it, fe-cit.
12 Simulacra gentium argen - tum et au-rum,* opera ma-nu-um ho-minum.
13 Os habent, et non - lo - quen - tur :* oculos habent, et non-vi-de-bunt.
14 Aures habent, et - non au - dient ; * nares habent, et non o-do-ra-bunt.
15 Manus habent, et non palpa bunt ; pedes habent, et non am - bu - la - bunt ;* non clamabunt in gut-tu-re-su-o.

16 Similes illis fiant qui fa - ciunt e-a* et omnes qui con-fi-dunt in e-is.
17 Domus Israel spera-vit in Do-mi-no? * adjutor eorum et protec - tor e - o- rum est.
18 Domus Aaron spera - vit in Do - mino; * adjutor eorum et protec-tor e - o - rum est.
19 Qui timent Dominum, spera ve - runt in Do - mino ; * adjutor eorum et protec-tor e-o-rum est.
20 Dominus memor fu - it nos - tri, * et bene - dixit nobis.
21 Benedixit do-mui Is-ra-el, * bene - dixit do - mui A - a - ron.
22 Benedixit ommibus qui ti - ment Do - mi - num, * pusillis cum - ma - jo - ri - bus.
23 Ajiciat Domi - nus su - per vos, * super vos, et super fi - li - os ves - tros.
24 Benedicti - vos a Do-mino, * qui fecit cœ - lum et ter - ram.
25 Cœlum - cœli Do - mino: * terram autem dedit fili - is ho - minum.
26 Non mortui lauda - bunt te, Do - mine, * neque omnes qui descendunt in in - fer - num.
27 Sed nos qui vivimus, bene - dicimus Do - mino, * ex hoc nunc, et us - que in sæ - cu - lum.

Gloria Patri, etc.

Laudate Dominum. Psalm cxvi.

(This Psalm is often sung in place of "In exitu Israel.")

VESPERS.

Hymnus.

LUCIS CREATOR.

(From Pentecost to Advent, and from Second Sunday after Epiphany to First Sunday in Lent.)

FIRST CHANT

1 Lu - cis cre - a - tor op - ti - me, Lu - cem di -

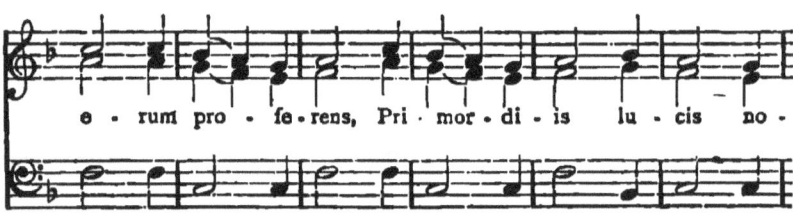

e - rum pro - fe - rens, Pri - mor - di - is lu - cis no -

væ, Mun - di pa - rans o - ri - gi - nem. A - men.

2 Qui mane junctum vesperi
Diem vocari præcipis:
Illabitur tetrum chaos,
Audi preces cum fletibus.

3 Ne mens gravata crimine,
Vitæ sit exul munere,
Dum nil perenne cogitat,
Seseque culpis illigat.

4 Cœleste pulset ostium,
Vitale tollat præmium:
Vitemus omne noxium,
Purgemus omne pessimum.

5 Præsta, Pater piissime,
Patrique compar Unice,
Cum Spiritu Paraclito,
Regnans per omne sæculum.
   Amen.

℣ Dirigatur, Domine, oratio mea.

℟ Sicut incensum in conspectu tuo.

VESPERS.

LUCIS CREATOR

SECOND CHANT.

1 Lu-cis cre-a-tor op-ti-me, Lu-cem di-
e-rum pro-fe-rens, Pri-mor-di-is lu-cis novæ, Mun-di pa-rans o-ri-gi-nem. A-men.

CREATOR ALME.

CHANT, PAGES 6 AND 7.] (*For Advent.*)

1 CREATOR alme siderum,
Æterna lux credentium ;
Jesu, Redemptor omnium,
Intende votis supplicum.

2 Qui dæmonis ne fraudibus
Periret orbis, impetu
Amoris actus, languidi
Mundi medela factus es.

3 Commune qui mundi nefas
Ut expiares, ad Crucem
E Virginis Sacrario
Intacta prodis victima.

℣ Rorate cœli desuper, et nubes pluant justum.

4 Cujus potestas gloriæ,
Nomenque cum primum sonat,
Et cœlites et inferi
Tremente curvantur genu.

5 Te deprecamur, ultimæ
Magnum diei Judicem :
Armis supernæ gratiæ
Defende nos ab hostibus.

6 Virtus, honor, laus, gloria
Deo Patri cum Filio,
Sancto simul Paraclito,
In sæculorum sæcula. Amen.

℟ Aperiatur terra, et germinet Salvatorem.

VESPERS.

AUDI, BENIGNE CONDITOR.

[CHANT PAGES 6 AND 7.]   (*For Lent*).

1. AUDI, benigne Conditor,
   Nostras preces cum fletibus,
   In hoc sacro jejunio
   Fusas quadragenario.

2. Scrutator alme cordium,
   Infirma tu scis virium :
   Ad te reversis exhibe
   Remissionis gratiam.

3. Multum quidem peccavimus,
   Sed parce confitentibus :

℣ Angelis suis Deus mandavit de te.

Ad nominis laudem tui
Confer medelam languidis.

4. Concede nostrum conteri
   Corpus per abstinentiam :
   Culpæ ut relinquant pabulum
   Jejuna corda criminum.

5. Præsta, beata Trinitas,
   Concede, simplex Unitas,
   Ut fructuosa sint tuis.
   Jejuniorum munera. Amen.

℞ Ut custodiant te in omnibus viis tuis

VEXILLA REGIS.
(*For Passion time.*)

GREGORIAN CHANT

1 Vex-il-la re-gis pro-de-unt:......
Ful-get cru-cis mys-te-ri-um,....
Qua vi-ta mor-tem per-tu-lit,......

VESPERS.

VEXILLA REGIS—Continued.

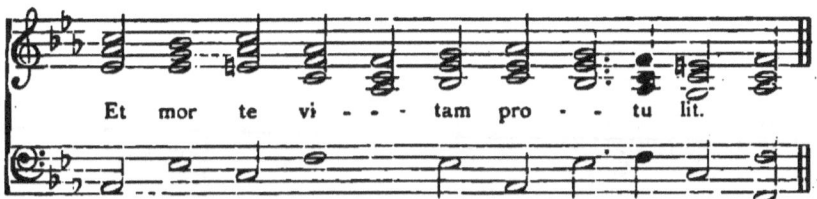

Et mor te vi - - - tam pro - - tu lit.

2 Quæ vulnerata lanceæ
Mucrone diro, criminum
Ut nos lavaret sordibus, .
Manavit unda et sanguine.

3 Impleta sunt quæ concinit
David fideli carmine.
Dicendo nationibus:
Regnavit a lingo Deus.

4 Arbor decora et fulgida,
Ornata Regis purpura,
Electa digno stipite
Tam sancta membra tangere.

5 Beata cujus brachiis
Pretium pependit sæculi,
Statera facta corporis,
Tulitque prædam tartari.

6 O Crux, ave, spes unica,'
Hoc Passionis tempore
Piis adauge gratiam,
Reisque dele crimina.

7 Te, fons salutis Trinitas,
Collaudet omnis spiritus:
Quibus Crucis victoriam
Largiris, adde præmium.

℣ E ipe me, Domine, ab homine malo.   ℞ A viro iniquo e ipe me.

Ad Regias Agni.

CHANT PAGES 6 AND 7.]   (*For Paschal time.*)

1 Ad regias Agni dapes,
Stolis amicti candidis,
Post transitum Maris Rubri,
Christo canamus Principi.

2 Divina cujus charitas
Sacrum propinat saguinem,
Almique membra corporis
Amor Sacerdos immolat,

3 Sparsum cruorem postibus
Vastator horret Angelus:
Fugitque divisum mare,
Merguntur hostes fluctibus.

4 Jam Pascha nostrum Christus est,
Paschalis idem Victima.
Et pura puris mentibus
Sinceritatis azyma.

5 O vera cœli Victima,
Subjecta cui sunt tartara,
Soluta mortis vincula,
Recepta vitæ præmia.

6 Victor, subactis inferis.
Trophæa Christus explicat,
Cœloque aperto, subditum,
Regem tenebrarum trahit.

7 Ut sis perenne mentibus
Paschale, Jesu, gaudium,
A morte dira criminum
Vitæ renatos libera.

8 Deo Patri sit gloria,
Et Filio, qui a mortuis
Surrexit, ac Paraclito,
In sempiterna sæcula.   Amen.

℣ Mane nobiscum, Domine. Alleluia.   ℞ Quoniam advesperascit.   Alleluia.

Magnificat.

1 Mag · ni · · · · · fi - cat.* anima me - a Do-mi-num

2 Et exultavit spiritus me - us: * in
Deo salu - ta - ri me - o.
3 Quia respexit humilitatem ancillæ
su-æ: * ecce enim ex hoc beatam me
dicent, omnes gen-ra-ti-o-nes.
4 Quia fecit mihi magna qui po - tens
est: * et sanctum no - men e - jus.
5 Et misericordia ejus a progenie in
pro-ge nies : * timen-ti-bus e-um.
6 Fecit potentiam in brachio su - o: *

dispersit superbos mente cor - dis su -i.
7 Deposuit potentes de se - de: * et
exal - ta - vit hu - miles.
8 Esurientes implevit bo - nis · * et di-
vites dimit - sit - in - an es.
9 Suscepit Israel puerum su - um: *
recordatus misericor diæ su - æ.
10 Sicut locutus est ad patres nostros ;*
Abraham et semini e - jus in - sæ - cula.
Gloria Patri, etc.

No 1.—Alma Redemptoris Mater,

(From Advent to Purification.)

No. 2—Alma Redemptoris.

VESPERS.

AVE REGINA—Continued

13

CHORUS. *Pastorale.*

℣ Dignare me laudare te, Virgo sacrata.
℟ Da mihi virtutem contra hostes tuos.

VESPERS.

REGINA CŒLI—No. 1.
(Easter to Pentecost.)

VESPERS.

REGINA CŒLI—Continued.

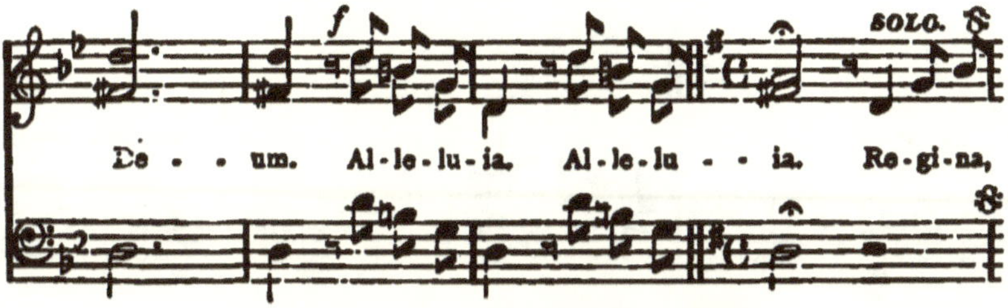

Gaude et lætare, Virgo Maria. Alleluia.
Quia surrexit, Dominus vere. Alleluia.

REGINA CŒLI.—No. 2.

WEBBE.

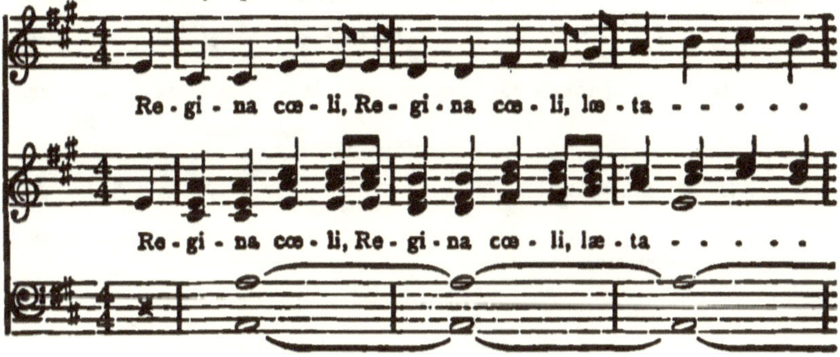

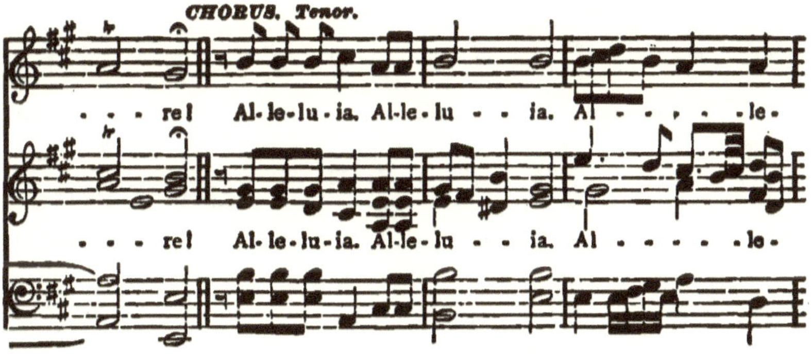

VESPERS.

REGINA CŒLI—Continued.

Benediction.

O SALUTARIS.—No. 1.

BENEDICTION.

21

BENEDICTION.

BENEDICTION.

O SALUTARIS—Continued.

O SALUTARIS.—No. 4.

BENEDICTION.

O SALUTARIS—Continued.

No. 1.—Tantum Ergo.

BENEDICTION.

TANTUM ERGO—Continued.

Præ-stet fi-des sup-ple-men-tum Sen-su-um de-fec-tu-i
Pro-ce-den-ti ab u-tro-que Com-par sit lau-da-ti-o.   A-men.

No. 2—TANTUM ERGO.

Maestoso.   LAMBILOTTE.

Tan-tum er-go   Sa-cra-men-tum Ve-ne-re-mur cer-nu-
Gen-i-tor-i,   Gen-i-to-que   Laus et ju-bi-la-ti-

Et anti-qu-um   do-cu-men-tum No-vo ce-dat ri-tu-
Sal-us, hon-or, vir-tus quo-que Sit et be-ne* dic-ti-

Præ-stet fi-des sup-ple-men-tum sen-su-um   sen-su-um de-
Pro-ce-den-ti   ab-u-tro-que   com-par sit com-par sit lau-

TANTUM ERGO—Continued.

No. 3.—Tantum Ergo.

TANTUM ERGO—Continued.

No. 4.—Tantum Ergo.

BENEDICTION.

TANTUM ERGO—Continued.

BENEDICTION. 31

No. 5.—Tantum Ergo.

TANTUM ERGO.—Continued.

V. Panem de coelo praestitisti eis. (Alleluia).
R. Omne delectamentum in se habentem. (Alleluia).

Adoro Te Devote

Andante religioso.   OLD HYMNAL.

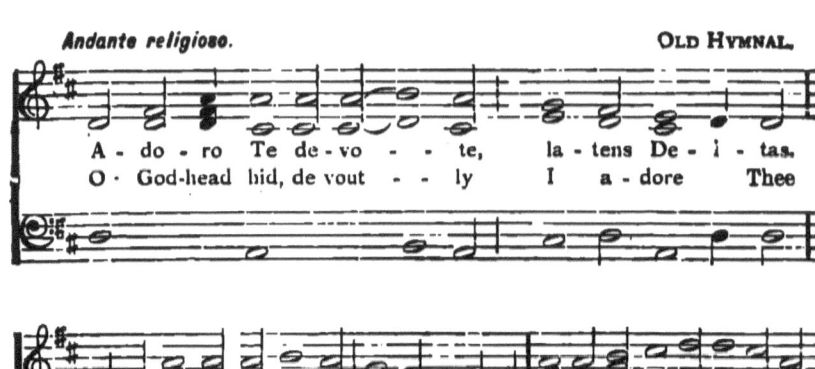

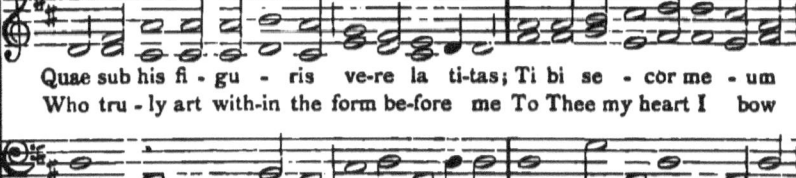

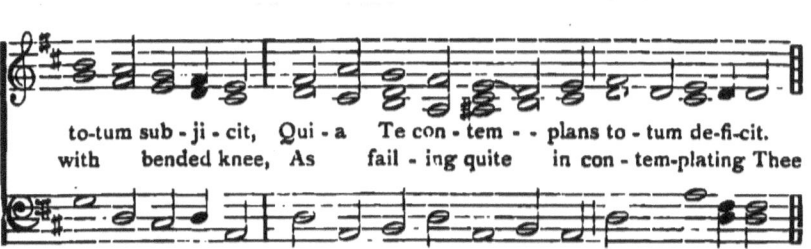

Visus, gustus, tactus, in Te fállitur,
Sed auditu solo tuto créditur,
Credo quidquid dixit Dei Filius
Nil hoc varitàtis verbo vèrius.

In cruce latèbat sola Dèitas,
At hic latet simul et Humànitas:
Ambo tamen credens atque cònfitens,
Peto quod petivit latro pœnitens.

Plagas. sicut Thomas, non intueor,
Deum tamen meum Te confiteor.
Fac me Tibi semper magis credere,
In Te spem habere. Te diligere.

O memoriale mortis Dòmini:
Panis vivus, vitam præstans homini!
Præsta meæ menti de Te vivere,
Et Te illi semper dulce sàpere.

Pie Pelicane, Jesu Dòmine,
Me immundum munda Tuo sanguine,
Cujus una stilla salvum facere,
Totum quit ab omni mundum scelere.

Jesu, quem velatum nunc aspicio
Oro, fiat illud, quod tam sitio,
Ut, Te revelata cernens facie,
Visu sim beatus Tuæ gloriæ.

Jesu Corona Virginum.

(Feast of Virgins.)

BLANCHI.

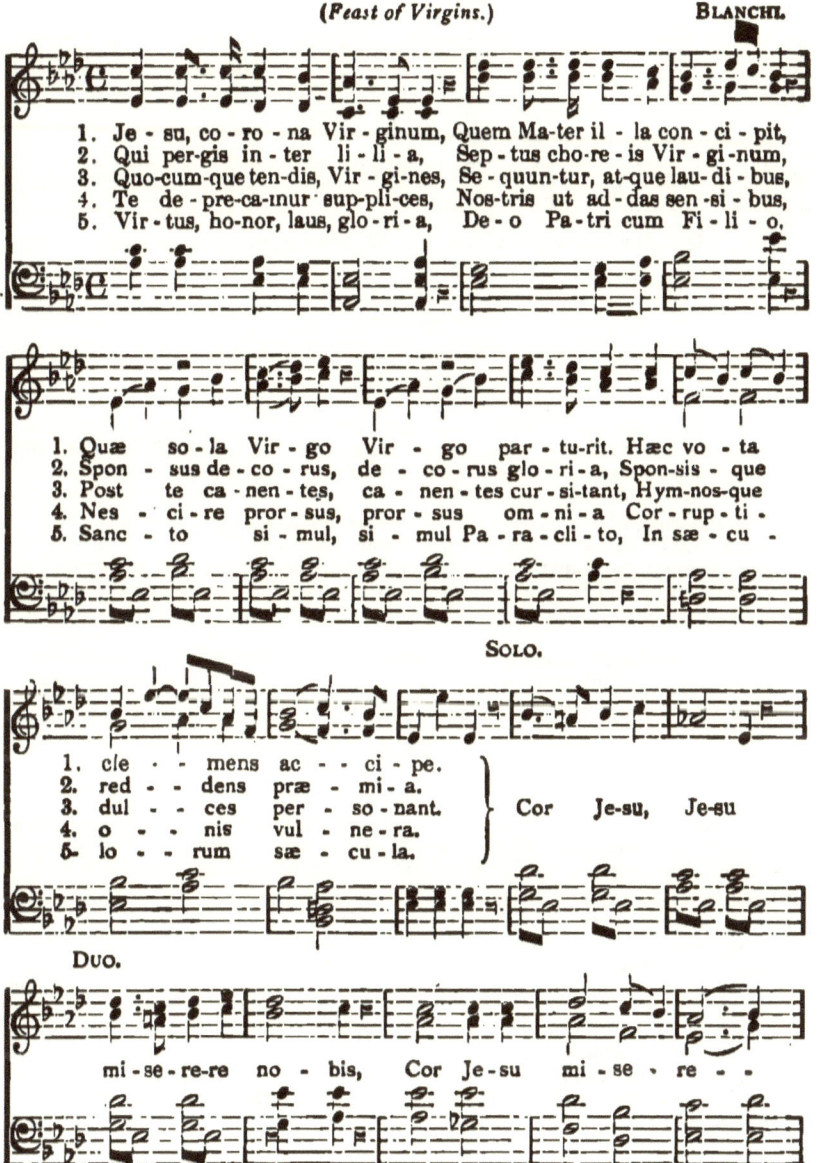

VESPERS.

JESU CORONA VIRGINUM—Continued.

re . Cor Je-su mi-se-re-re no - - bis.

℣ Specie tua et pulchritudine tua. ℟ Intende, prospere procede, et regna

SECOND VESPERS.
(FOR AN APOSTLE.)
Psalms—*Same as First Vespers, page 1.*

Exultet Orbis.

Exultet orbis gaudiis:
Coelum resultet laudibus
Apostolorum gloriam
Tellus et astra concinunt.

Vos sæculorum judices
Et vera mundi lumina,
Votis precamur cordium;
Audite voces supplicum.

Qui templa cœli clauditis,
Serasque verbo solvitis,
Nos a reatu noxios
Solvi jubete, quæsumus.

Præceptor quorum protinus
Languor, salusque sentiunt,
Sanate mentes languidas
Augete nos virtutibus:

Ut, cum redibit Arbiter
In fine Christus sæculi,
Nos sempiterni gaudii
Concedat esse compotes.

Patri, simulque Filio,
Tibique, sancte Spiritus,
Sicut fuit, sit iugiter
Sæclum per omne gloria.
Amen.

V. In omnem terram exivit sonus eorum.
R. Et in fines orbis terræ verba eorum.

V. Annuntiaverunt opera Dei.
R. Et facta ejus intellexerunt.

Tristes Erant.
(*For Paschal time.*)

Tristes erant Apostoli
De Christi acerbo funere,
Quem morte crudelissima
Servi necarant impii.

Sermone verax Angelus
Mulieribus prædixerat:
Mox ore Christus gaudium
Gregi feret fidelium.

Ad anxios Apostolos
Currunt statim dum nuntiæ,
Illæ micantis obvia
Christi tenent vestigia.

Galiææ ad alta montium
Se conferunt Apostoli,
Jesuque, voti compotes
Almo beantur lumine.

Ut sis perenne mentibus
Paschale, Jesu, gaudium,
A morte dira criminum
Vitæ renatos libera

Deo patri sit gloria,
Et Filio qui a mortuis
Surrexit, ac Paraclito,
In sempiterna sæcula.
Amen.

(*From Ascension to Pentecost*)

Jesu, tibi sit gloria,
Qui victor in cœlum redis,
V. Sancti et justi in Domino gaudete,
Alleluia.

Cum Patre et almo Spiritu,
In sempiterna sæcula. Amen.
R. Vos elegit Deus in hereditatem
sibi, Alleluia.

VESPERS.

THIRD VESPERS.

(FOR AN APOSTLE.) PSALMS—*Dixit Dominus*, page 1 ; *Laudate Pueri*, page 3.

CREDIDI. Psalms cxv.

CHANT AS FOR *Confitebor*, PAGE 2.

CREDIDI, propter-quod lo - cutus-sum ; * ego autem humilia - tua sum nim - is.

2 Ego dixi in ex cessu me-o : * Omnis ho - mo men - dax.

3 Quid re - tribuam Do - mino, * pro omnibus quæ re - tribu - it mi - hi ?

4 Calicem salu - taris ac - ci-piam, *et nomen Domini invocabo.

5 Vota mea Domino reddam coram omni - populo e -jus : * pretiosa in conspectu Domini mora sanc-to rum e -jus.

6 O Domine quia ego-servus tu us :* ego servus tuus et filius an-cil læ tu-æ.

7 Diripuisti vincula me - a : * tibi sacrificabo hostiam laudis, et nomen Domini in - vo -ca - bo.

8 Vota mea: Domino reddam in conspectu omnis-populi e - jus : * in atriis domus Domini, in medio tui, Je - ru salem.

Gloria Patri, etc.

IN CONVERTENDO. Psalm cxxv.

CHANT AS FOR *Beautus Vir*, PAGES 2 AND 3.

IN convertendo Dominus captivi - ta - tem Si - on, *facti sumus sicut con - so - la - ti.

2 Tunc repletum est gau - dio os nostrum, * et lingua nostra exul - ta - tione.

3 Tunc dicent inter gen - tes : *Magnificavit Dominus fa - ce - re cum eis.

4 Magnificavit Dominus fa - ce - re no-biscum ;* facti - sumus læ - tan tes.

5 Converte, Domine, captivi - ta tem nos - tram * sicut tor - rens in Aus-tro.

6 Qui seminant - in la - cry - mis, * in exultati - o ne me - tent.

7 Euntes-ibant et fle-bant, * mittentes se - mi-na - su - a.

8 Venientes autem venient cum ex - ul - ta - tione, *portantes mani - pu - los su-os. Gloria Patri, etc.

DOMINE PROBASTI. Psalm cxxxviii.

DOMINE, probasti me, et cognovisti me ; * tu cognovisti sessionem meam et resurrectionem meam.

2 Intellexisti cogitationes meas de longe ; *semitam meam et funiculum meum investigasti.

3 Et omnes vias meas prævidisti ; *quia non est sermo in lingua mea.

4 Ecce, Domine, tu cognovisti omnia novissima et antiqua ; *tu formasti me, et posuisti super me manum tuam.

5 Mirabilis facta est scientia tua ex me ; * confortata est, et non potero ad eam.

6 Quo ibo a spiritu tuo ? * et quo a facie tua fugiam.

7 Si ascendero in cœlum, tu illic es ; *si descendero in infernum, ades.

8 Si sumpsero pennas meas diluculo; et habitavero in extremis maris.

9 Etenim illuc manus tua deducet me : *et tenebit me dextera tua.

10 Et dixi ; Forsitan tenebræ conculcabunt me, * et nox illuminatio mea in deliciis meis.

11 Quia tenebræ non obscurabuntur a te, et nox sicut dies illuminabitur : * sicut tenebræ ejus, ita et lumen ejus.

12 Quia tu possedisti renes meos : *suscepisti me de utero matris meæ.

13 Confitebor tibi, quia terribiliter magnificatus es : *mirabilia opera tua et anima mea cognoscit nimis.

14 Non est occultatum os meum a te, quod fecisti in occulto : *et substantia mea in inferioribus terræ.

15 Imperfectum meum viderunt occuli et in libro tuo omnes scribentur : * dies formabuntur, et nemo in eis.

DOMINE PROBASTI—Continued.

16 Mihi autem nimis honorificati sunt-amici tui, Deus : * nimis confortatus est principatus eorum.

17 Dinumerabo eos, et super arenam multiplicabuntur : * exsurrexi, et adhuc sum tecum.

18 Si occideris, Deus, peccatores : * viri sanguinum declinate a me :

19 Quia dicitis in cogitatione : *Accipient in vanitate civitates tuas.

20 Nonne qui oderunt te, Domine, oderam ? * et super inimicos tuos tabescebam ?

21 Perfecto odio oderam illos : * et inimici facti sunt mihi.

22 Proba me, Deus, et scito cor meum : *interroga me, et cognosce semitas meas.

23 Et vide si via iniquitatis in me est : * et deduc me in via æterna.

FOURTH VESPERS.

(*Vespers of B. V. M. and of Virgins.*)
Dixit Dominus, page 1.   Laudate pueri, page 3.

LÆTATUS SUM.   Psalm cxxi.

LÆTATUS sum in his quæ dicta sunt mihi ; * in domum Domini ibimus.

2 Stantes erant pedes nostri : * in atriis tuis, Jerusalem.

3 Jerusalem, quæ ædificatur ut civitas : cujus participatio ejus in idipsum.

4 Illuc enim ascenderunt tribus, tribus Domini, * testimonium Israel ad confitendum nomini Domini.

5 Quia illic sederunt sedes in judicio * sedes super domum David.

6 Rogate quæ ad pacem sunt Jerusalem, *et abundantia diligentibus te.

7 Fiat pax in virtute tua, *et abundantia in turribus tuis.

8 Propter fratres meos et proximos meos : *loquebar pacem de te.

9 Propter domum Domini Dei nostri, * quæsivi bona tibi.

Gloria Patri, etc.

NISI DOMINUS.   Psalm cxxvi.

CHANT AS FOR *Beatus Vir*, PAGES 2 AND 3.

NISI Dominus ædifi-ca-verit do-mum, * in vanum laboraverunt qui ædi-fi-cant e-am.

2 Nisi Dominus custodierit ci - vi - ta - tem, * frustra vigilat qui custo - dit e - am.

3 Vanum est vobis ante lu - cem sur - gere : * surgite postquam sederitis, qui manducatis pà - nem do - lo - ris.

4 Cum dederit dilectis suis - som - num : * ecce hæreditas Domini, filii - merces, fruc - tus ven - tris.

5 Sicut sagittæ in ma-nu po - ten - tis,* ita filii ex - cus - so-rum.

6 Beatus vir qui implevit desiderium su-um ex ip - sis : * non confundetur cum loquetur inimicis su - is in por - ta.

Gloria Patri, etc.

LAUDA JERUSALEM.   Psalm cxlvii.

CHANT AS FOR *Laudate Dominum*, PAGE 5.

LAUDA Jeru - salem, Domi - num : * lauda Deum tu - um, Si - on.

2 Quoniam confortavit seras porta-rum tu - ar - um, * benedixit filiis tu - is in te.

3 Qui posuit fines tu - os pa - cem, * et adipe frumenti sa - tiat te.

4 Qui emittit eloquium suum ter-ræ * volociter currit ser - mo e - jus.

5 Qui dat nivem si-cut la - nam * nebulam sicut - cinerem spar - git.

6 Mittit crystallum suam si - cut buc - cel - las : * ante faciem frigoris ejus quis sus - ti - ne - bit ?

7 Emittet verbum suum, et liquefa-ciet e - a : * flabit spiritus ejus, - et fiu - ent a - quæ.

8 Qui annuntiat verbum su - um Ja - cob : * justitias et judicia su - a I - srael.

9 Non fecit taliter omni na - ti - o - ni,* et judicia sua non manifesta - vit - e is.

Gloria Patri, etc

VESPERS.
AVE, MARIS STELLA.—No. 1.

Moderato.

A - ve, ma - ris stel . . . . . . la, De - i

Ma - ter al . . . . . ma, At - que sem - per

Vir . . . . go, Fe - lix cœ - - li por . . . . . ta,

Sumens illud Ave	Monstra te esse matrem;	Vitam præsta puram,
Gabrielis ore,	Sumat per te preces,	Iter para tutum,
Funda nos in pace	Qui pro nobis natus,	Ut videntes Jesum,
Mutans Evæ nomen.	Tulit esse tuus.	Semper collætemur.
Solve vincla reis,	Virgo singularis,	Sit laus Deo Patri.
Profer lumen cæcis;	Inter omnes mitis,	Summo Christo decus,
Mala nostra pelle,	Nos culpis solutos,	Spiritui Sancto,
Bona cuncta posce.	Mites fac et castos.	Tribus honor unus.
		Amen.

No. 2—AVE MARIS STELLA

1. A - ve Ma - ris. stel - la. De - i Ma - ter al - ma,

At-que sem - per Vir - go, Fe - lix cœ - li por - ta,

VESPERS

AVE, MARIS STELLA—Continued.

At-que sem-per Vir - go, Fe-lix cœ-li por-ta.

O Gloriosa Virginum
(AIR JESU DULCIS MEMORIA.)

Andante.

O Glo-ri-o - - sa Vir-gi-num Sub-

li'-mis in-ter si-de-ra.... Qui te cre - a - vit.

par-vu-lun.. Lac-ten - te nu - tris u-be - re.

Quod Heva tristis abstulit
Tu reddis almo germine ;
Intrent ut astra flebiles.
Cœli recludis cardines.

Tu Regis alti janua,
Et aula lucis fulgida;
Vitam datam per Virginem,
Gentes redemptæ, plaudite.

Jesu, tibi sit gloria
Qui natus es de Virgine,
Cum Patre, et almo Spiritu,
In sempiterna sæcula. Amen.

THE MOST BLESSED VIRGIN.

AVE MARIA.—Concluded.

pec - ca - to - ri - bus, nunc et in ho - ra, in ho - ra mortis nos-træ. O - ra pro no - bis, pro no-bis pec - ca - to - ri - bus, nunc et in ho - ra, in ho - ra mor-tis nos-træ, A - - - men. Nunc et in ho - ra, in ho-ra mor-tis nos-træ, A - - - - - men, A - men, A - - men

VESPERS.
THE ANGELUS.

VESPERS.
The Angelus—Continued.

VESPERS.

The Angelus.—Continued.

VESPERS.
The Angelus.—Continued.

O Maria, Sine Labe Concepta.

VESPERS.

O MARIA, SINE LABE CONCEPTA.

Fortem Virili Pectore.

(Neither Virgins nor Martyrs)

CHANTS PAGES 6 AND 7.

FORTEM virili pectore
Laudemus omnes feminam,
Quæ sanctitatis gloria
Ubique fulget inclyta.

Hæc sancto amore saucia,
Dum mundi amorem noxium
Horrescit, ad cœlestia
Iter peregit arduum.

Carnem domans jejuniis,
Dulcique mentem pabulo

℟. Diffusa est gratia in labiis tuis,

Orationis nutriens,
Cœli potitur gaudiis.

Rex Christe virtus fortium,
Qui magna solus efficis,
Hujus precatu quæsumus,
Audi benignus supplices.

Deo Patri sit gloria,
Ejusque soli Filio,
Cum Spiritu Paraclito,
Nunc et per omne sæculum. Amen.

℟ Propterea henedixit te Deus in æternum.

FOR THE FOLLOWING FEASTS OF THE B V. M., ETC., ARE TAKEN FROM FOURTH VESPERS PAGE 38.

(The Espousals, January 23rd.)

℣ Desponsatio est hodie sanctæ Mariæ Virginis
℟ Cujus vita inclyta cunctas illustrat Ecclesias

VESPERS.

(Purification, Feb. 2nd).

V. Responsum accepit Simeon a Spiritu Sancto.
R. Non visurum se mortem, nisi videret Christum Domini.

(Annunciation, March 25th).

V. Ave, Maria, gratia plena.   R. Dominus tecum.

(The Most Pure Heart, 3rd Sunday after Pentecost).

V. Viam mandatorum tuorum cucurri.   R. Cum dilatasti cor meum.

(Assumption, August 15th).

V. Exaltata est sancta Dei Genitrix.
R. Super choros Angelorum ad cœlestia regna.

(Nativity, Sept. 8th).

V. Nativitas est hodie sanctæ Mariæ virginis.
R. Cujus vita inclyta cunctas illustrat Ecclesias.

(Seven Dolors, 3rd Sunday of Sept).

O QUOT UNDIS.

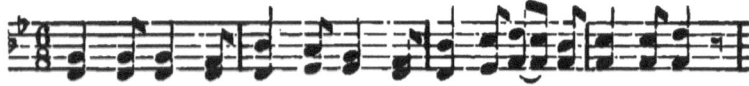

1 O Quot un-dis lac-ry-ma-rum, Quo do-lo-re vol-vi-tur,
2 Os su-a-ve, mi-te pec-tus Et la-tus dul-cis-si-mum,
3 Cen-ti-es-que mil-li-es-que Strin-git arc-tis nex-i-bus.
4 Ei-a, Mat-er, ob-se-cra-mus Per tu-as bas lac-ry-mas,
5 Es-to Pat-ri, Fi-li-o-que, Et co-æ-vo Fla-mi-ni,

Luc-tu-o-sa de cru-en-to Dum re vul-sum sti-pi-te
Dex-ter-am-que vul-ner-a-tam, Et sin-is-tram sau-ci-am,
Pec-tus il-lud, et la-cer-tos, Il-la fi-git vul-ne-ra;
Fi-li-i-que tris-te fun-us, Vul-ne-rum-que pur-pur-am,
Es-to Sum-mæ Tri-ni-ta-ti Semp-i-ter-na glo-ri-a

VESPERS.

O QUOT UNDIS—Continued.

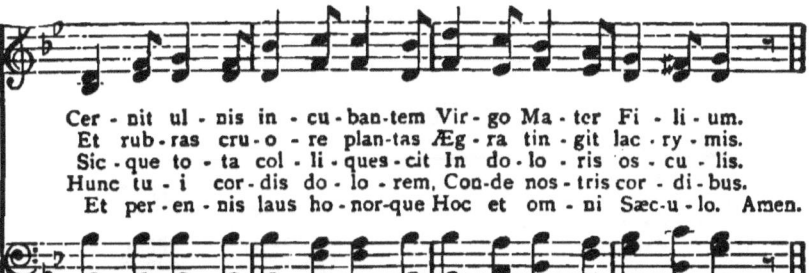

Cer - nit ul - nis in - cu - ban - tem Vir - go Ma - ter Fi - li - um.
Et rub - ras cru - o - re plan - tas Æg - ra tin - git lac - ry - mis.
Sic - que to - ta col - li - ques - cit In do - lo - ris os - cu - lis.
Hunc tu - i cor - dis do - lo - rem, Con - de nos - tris cor - di - bus.
Et per - en - nis laus ho - nor - que Hoc et om - ni Sæc - u - lo. Amen.

℣. Regina martyrum, ora pro nobis.   ℟. Quæ juxta crucem Jesu constitisti.

(*The Most Holy Rosary, 1st Sunday of October*).

(*The Maternity, 2nd Sunday of October*.)

℣. Bendicta tu in mulieribus.   ℟ Et benedictus fructus ventris tui.

(*The Purity, 3rd Sunday of October*).

℣. Cum jucunditate Virginitatem beatæ Mariæ semper virginis celebremus.   ℟ Ut ipsa pro nobis intercedat ad Dominum Jesum Christum.

PRÆCLARA CUSTOS VIRGINUM.

Chants Pages 6 and 7.

PRÆCLARA custos Virginum,
Intacta Mater Numinis,
Cœlestis aulæ janua,
Spes nostra, cœli gaudium.

Inter rubeta lilium,
Columba formosissima,
Virga e radice germinans
Nostro medelam vulneri.

Turris draconi impervia,
Amica stella naufragis,

Tuere nos a fraudibus,
Tuaque luce dirige.

Erroris umbras discute,
Syrtes dolosas amove,
Fluctus tot inter deviis.
Tutam reclude semitam.

Jesu, tibi sit gloria,
Qui natus es de Virgine,
Cum Patre, et almo Spiritu,
In sempiterna sæcula. Amen

(*Immaculate Conception, 8th of December.*)

Hymnus—*Præclara custos.*

℣ Immaculata conceptio est hodie Sanctæ Mariæ Virginis.   ℟ Quæ serpentis caput virgineo pede contrivit.

(*The Patronage, 2nd Sunday of November.*)

VESPERS.

FIFTH VESPERS.

(FOR MARTYRS.)

PSALMS—*Same as First Vespers.*

DEUS, TUORUM MILITUM.

CHANTS PAGES 6 AND 7.

DEUS, tuorum militum
Sors et corona, præmium,
Laudes canentes Martyris
Absolve nexu criminis.

Hic nempe mundi gaudia,
Et blanda fraudum pabula,
Imbuta felle deputans,
Pervenit ad cœlestia.

Pœnas cucurrit fortiter,
Et sustulit viriliter,

℣ Gloria et horore coronasti eum, Domine.
℟ Et constituisti eum super opera manuum tuarum.

Fundensque pro te sanguinem,
Æterna dona possidet.

Ob hoc precatu supplici
Te poscimus, piissime :
In hoc triumpho Martyris
Dimitte noxam servulis.

Laus et perennis gloria
Patri sit, atque Filio,
Sancto simul Paraclito,
In sempiterna sæcula. Amen.

℣ Justus ut palma florebit.
℟ Sicut cedrus Libani multiplicabitur.

SANCTORUM MERITIS.

(*For several Martyrs.*)

Hi sunt quos fatue mundus abhorruit
Hunc fructu vacuum, floribus aridum
Contempsere tui nominis asseclæ,
Jesu, Rex bone Cœlitum

Hi pro te furias atque minas truces
Calcarunt hominum, sævaque verbera
His cessit lacerans fortiter ungula,
Nec carpsit penetralia.

Cæduntur gladiis more bidentium
Non murmur resonat, non querimonia

V. Lætamini in Domino, et exultate, justi.
R. Et gloriamini, omnes recti corde.

Sed corde impavido mens bene conscia
Conservat patientiam.

Quæ vox, quæ poterit lingua retexere
Quæ tu Martyribus munera præparas?
Rubri nam fluido sanguine fulgidis
Cingunt tempora laureis.

Te, summa O Deitas, unaque, poscimus
Ut culpas abigas, noxia subtrahas,
Des pacem famulis, ut tibi gloriam
Annorum in seriem canant. Amen.

V. Extultabunt Sancti in gloria.
R. Lætabuntur in cubilibus suis.

SIXTH VESPERS

(FOR MARTYRS.)

PSALMS—*For first four see First Vespers, page 1; Fifth, Credidi, page 51*
HYMNUS—*Sanctorum Meritis, page 52.*

VESPERS.

SEVENTH VESPERS.

(FOR CONFESSORS, ETC.)

PSALMS—*Same as First Vespers,*

ISTE CONFESSOR.—No. 1.

Is - te Con - fes - sor Do - mi - ni, co - len - tes

Quem pi - e laud ant po - pu - li. per or - bem, Hac di - e

læ - tus me - ru it be - a - tas. Scan - de - re se - des.
Or, su - pre - mos Lau - dis ho no - res.

Qui pius, prudens, humilis, pudicus,
Sobriam duxit sine labe vitam,
Donec humanos animavit auræ
Spiritus artus.

Cujus ob præstans meritum frequenter
Ægra quæ passim jacuere, membra,
Viribus morbi, domitis, saluti
Restituuntur.

℣. Amavit eum Dominus et ornavit eum.

Noster hinc illi chorus obsequentem
Concinit laudem, celebresque palmas;
Ut piis ejus precibus juvemur
Omne per ævum.

Sit Salus illi, decus, atque virtus,
Qui, super cœli solio coruscans,
Totius mundi seriem gubernat
Trinus et unus. Amen.

℟. Stolam gloriæ induit eum.

VESPERS.

ISTE CONFESSOR.—No. 2.

Is - te Con - fes - sor Do - mi - ni, co - len - tes
Quem pi - e lau - dant po - pu - li per or - bem, Hac di - e
læ - tus me - ru - it be - a - tas Scan - de - re se - des.
Or, su - pre - mos Lau - dis ho - no - res.

EIGHTH VESPERS.

For Confessors, etc.

Psalms—*For first four, see First Vespers, page 1.*

MEMENTO DOMINE. Last Psalm, cxxxi.

Chant as for *Laudate Dominum* Page

MEMENTO, Do - mine, Da - vid, *
et omnis mansue tu - dinis e - jus,
2 Sicut jura - vit Do - mino, * votum
vovit De - o Ja - cob
3 Si introiero in tabernaculum, do - mus
me - æ : * si ascendero in lectum stra - ti
me - i :
4 Si dedero somnum o - culis me - is,
* et palpebris meis dormi - ta - ti - o - nem.
5 Et requiem temporibus meis, donec
inveniam lo - cum - Do - mino, * tabernaculum De - o Ja - cob

6 Ecce audivimus eam in - Eph - ra - ta:
* invenimus eam in camp - is sil - væ.
7 Introibimus in taberna-culum e - jus:*
adorabimus in loco, ubi steterunt pe - des
e - jus.
8 Surge, Domine, in re - quiem tu - am, *
tu et arca sanctifica - tio - nis tu - æ.
9 Sacerdotes tui induantur jus - ti -
tiam, * et sancti tui - ex - ul - tent.
10 Propter David ser - vum tu - um, *
non avertas faciem Chris - ti tu - i.
11 Juravit Dominus David veritatem,

et non frustra-bitur e-am: * De fructu ventris tui-ponam super se-dem tu am.

12 Si custodierint filii tui testamentum me-um, * et testimonia mea hæc quæ doce-bo e-os:

13 Et filii eorum usque-in sæ-cu-lum,* sedebunt super se-dem tu-am.

14 Quoniam elegit Do-minus Si-on, ⁓ elegit eam in habitatio-nem si-bi.

15 Hæc requies mea in sæ-culum sæculi: * hic habitabo, quoniam ele-gi e-am.

℣ Justum deduxit Dominus per vias rectas.

16 Viduam ejus benedicens be-ne-di-cam: * pauperes ejus satura-bo pa-ni-bus.

17 Sacerdotes ejus induam sa-lu-ta ri, * et sancti ejus exultatione e-xul-ta-bunt.

18 Illuc producam cor-nu Dav-id: * paravi lucernam Chris-to me-o.

19 Inimicos ejus induam confu-si-o-ne: * super ipsum autem efflorebit sanctifica-ti-o me-a.

Gloria Patri, etc.

℟ Et Ostendit illi regnum Dei.

HYMNUS—*Iste Confessor, page 54*

SPECIAL VESPERS.

Christmas.

PSALMS—*Dixit Dominus, page 1; Confitebor tibi, page 2; Beatus vir, page 2.*

DE PROFUNDIS. Psalm cxxix.

CHANT AS FOR *Laudate Pueri*, PAGE 3.

DE profundis clamavi ad te, Do-mine: * Domine, exaudi vo-cem me-am.

2 Fiant aures tuæ intenden-tes * in vocem deprecatio-nis me-æ.

3 Si iniquitates observaveris, Do-mine, * Domine, quis sus-ti-ne-bit?

4 Quia apud te propitiatio est,* Et propter legem tuam susti nu-i te, Do-mine.

5 Sustinuit anima mea in verbo e-jus: * Speravit anima me-a in Do-mino.

6 A custodia matutina usque ad noc-tem, * speret Isra-el in Do-mino.

7 Quia apud Dominum misericordia, * et copiosa apud e-um re-demp-tio.

8 Et ipse redimet Is-rael * ex omnibus iniquita-ti-bus e-jus.

Gloria Patri, etc.

Memento Domine David, page 5.

JESU REDEMPTOR OMNIUM.

CHANTS PAGES 6 AND 7.

JESU, Redemptor omnium, Quem lucis ante originem Parem paternæ gloriæ Pater supremus edidit.

Tu lumen et splendor Patris, Tu spes perennis omnium, Intende quas fundunt preces Tui per orbem servuli.

Memento, rerum Conditor, Nostri quod olim corporis, Sacrata ab alvo Virginis Nascendo, formam sumpseris.

Testatur hoc præsens dies Currens per anni circulum, Quod solus e sinu Patris Mundi salus adveneris.

VESPERS.

Hunc astra, tellus, æquora,
Hunc omne quod cœlo subest,
Salutis Auctorem novæ
Novo salutat cantico.

Et nos beata quos sacri
Rigavit unda Sanguinis,
℣ Crastina die delebitur iniquitas terræ.
℟ Et regnabit super nos salvator mundi.

Natalis ob diem tui,
Hymni tributum solvimus.

Jesu, tibi sit gloria,
Qui natus es de virgino
Cum Patre et almo Spiritu
—In sempiterna sæcula. Amen.
℣ Notum fecit Dominus. Alleluia
℟ Sulutare suum. Alleluia.

Epiphany.

PSALMS—*Same as First Vespers, page 1*

CRUDELIS HERODES, DEUM.

CHANTS PAGES 6 AND 7.

CRUDELIS Herodes, Deum
Regem venire quid times?
Non eripit mortalia
Qui regna dat cœlestia,

Ibant Magi, quam viderant
Stellam sequentes præviam:
Lumen requirunt lumine:
Deum fatentur munere.

Lavacra puri gurgitis,
Cœlestis Agnus attigit,

℣ Reges Tharsis et insulæ munera
offerent

Peccata, quæ non detulit,
Nos abluendo sustulit.

Novum genus potentiæ!
Aquæ rubescunt hydriæ,
Vinumque jussa fundere,
Mutavit unda originem.

Jesu, tibi sit gloria,
Qui apparuisti gentibus,
Cum Patre et almo Spiritu,
In sempiterna sæcula. Amen.

℟ Reges Arabum et Saba dona addu
cent.

Feast of the Most Holy Name.

(*Second Sunday after Epiphany.*)

PSALMS—*For first four, see First Vespers, page 1; last Psalm, Credidi, page 37*

JESU DULCIS MEMORIA.

CHANTS PAGES 6 AND 7.

JESU dulcis memoria,
Dans vera cordis gaudia:
Sed super mel et omnia
Ejus dulcis præsentia.

Nil canitur suavius,
Nil auditur jucundius,
Nil cogitatur dulcius,
Quam Jesus Dei Filius.

Jesu, spes pœnitentibus,
Quam pius es petentibus!

℣ Sit Nomen Domini benedictum.
Alleluia

Quam bonus te quærentibus!
Sed quid invenientibus?

Nec lingua valet dicere,
Nec littera exprimere:
Expertus potest credere
Quid sit Jesum diligere.

Sis, Jesu, nostrum gaudium,
Qui es futurus præmium
Sit nostra in te gloria,
Per cuncta semper sæcula, Amen

℟ Ex hoc nunc et usque in sæculum
Alleluia.

Feast of the Holy Family.

(*Third Sunday after Epiphany.*)

PSALMS—*Same as Fourth Vespers.*

O LUX BEATA.

O Lux beata Cœlitum,
Et summa spes mortalium,
Jesu, O cui domestica
Arrisit orto caritas.

Maria, dives gratia,
O sola quæ casto potes
Fovere Jesum pectore,
Cum lacte donans oscula.

Tuque ex vetustis patribus
Delecte custos Virginis,
Dulci patris quem nomine
Divina proles invocat.

De stirpe Jesse Nobili
Nati in salutem gentium,

V. Verbum caro factum est. Alleluia.
R. Et habitavit in nobis. Allelulia.

Audite nos qui supplices
Vestras ad aras sistimus.

Dum sol redux ad vesperum
Rebus nitorem detrahit,
Nos hic manentes intimo
Ex corde vota fundimus.

Qua vestra sedes floruit
Virtutis omnis gratia,
Hanc detur in domesticis
Referre posse moribus.

Jesu, tibi sit gloria,
Qui natus es de Virgine,
Cum Patre, et almo Spiritu,
In sempiterna sæcula. Amen.

V. Ponam universos filios tuos doctos
  a Domino.
R. Et multitudinem pacis filiis tuis.

Easter Sunday.

PSALMS—*Same as First Vespers.*

Ascension Thursday and Sunday after.

PSALMS—*Same as First Vespers.*

SALUTIS HUMANÆ.

SALUTIS humanæ Sator,
Jesu, voluptas cordium,
Orbis redempti Conditor
Et casta lux amantium :

Qua victus es clementia,
Ut nostra ferres crimina,
Mortem subires innocens,
A morte nos ut tolleres !

Perrumpis infernum chaos.
Vinctis catenas detrahis ;

V. Ascendit Deus in jubilatione. Alleluia.
R. Et Dominus in voce tubæ. Alleluia.

Victor triumpho nobili
Ad dexteram Patris sedes.

Te cogat indulgentia,
Ut damna nostra sarcias,
Tuique vultus compotes
Dites beato lumine.

Tu dux ad astra, et semita,
Sis meta nostris cordibus.
Sis lacrymarum gaudium,
Sis dulce vitæ præmium. Amen.

V. Dominus in cœlo. Alleluia.
R. Paravit sedem suam. Alleluia.

VESPERS. 59

Patronage of St. Joseph.

(Third Sunday after Easter.)

PSALMS—*Same as First Vespers, page 1.*
HYMNUS—*Te Joseph, page 62.*

℣ Sub umbra illius quem desideraver-
am sedi. Alleluia.

℞ Et Fructus ejus dulcis gutturi meo
Alleluia.

Pentecost.

PSALMS—*Same as First Vespers, page 1.*

VENI, CREATOR.

GREGORIAN.

Ve - ni, Cre - a - - tor Spi - - - - ri - tus,

Men - tes tu - o - rum vi - - si - ta,

Im - ple. su - - per - na - - gra - - ti - a.

VESPERS.

VENI, CREATOR—Continued.

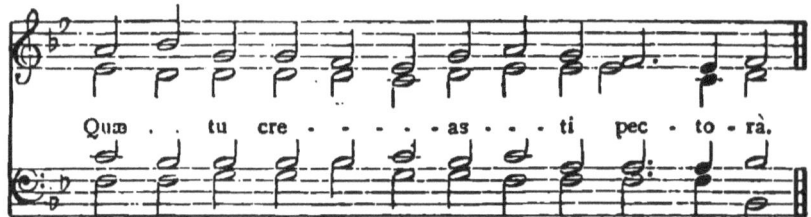

Quæ .. tu cre - - - as - - ti pec - to - ra.

Qui diceris Paraclitus,
Altissimi donum Dei,
Fons vivus, ignis, charitas,
Et spiritalis unctio.

Tu septiformis munere,
Digitus paternæ dexteræ,
Tu rite promissum Patris,
Sermone ditans guttura.

Accende lumen sensibus,
Infunde amorem cordibus,
Infirma nostri corporis
Virtute firmans perpeti.

Hostem repellas longius,
Pacemque dones protinus:
Ductore sic te prævio,
Vitemus omne noxium

Per te sciamus da Patrem,
Noscamus atque Filium,
Teque utriusque Spiritum
Credamus omni tempore.

Deo Patri sit gloria,
Et Filio, qui a mortuis
Surrexit, ac Paraclito,
In sæculorum sæcula. Amen.

V. Repleti sunt omnes Spiritu Sancto Alleluia.

R. Et cœperunt loqui, Alleluia.

V. Loquebantur variis linguis Apostoli. Alleluia.

R. Magnalia Dei. Alleluia.

OREMUS
For other occasions, see page 384.

Trinity Sunday.

PSALMS—*Same as First Vespers, page 1.*

JAM SOL RECEDIT IGNEUS.

CHANTS PAGES 6 AND 7.

Jam sol recedit igneus:
Tu, lux perennis, Unitas,
Nostris, beata Trinitas.
Infunde amorem cordibus.

Te mane laudum carmine
Te deprecamur vespere;

V. Benedicamus Patrem et Filium cum Sancto Spiritu.

R. Laudemus et superexaltemus eum in sæcula.

Digneris, ut te supplices
Laudemus inter Cœlites.

Patri, simulque Filio,
Tibique Sancte Spiritus,
Sicut fuit, sit jugiter,
Sæculum per omne gloria. Amen.

V. Benedictus es Domine in firmamento cœli.

R. Et laudabilis et gloriosus in sæcula.

VESPERS   61

Corpus Christi.

PSALMS—*Dixit Dominus, page 1; Confitebor, page 2; Credidi,*
Beati Omnes, Psalm cxxvii.

CHANT AS FOR *Laudate Pueri,* PAGE 23.

BEATI omnes, qui timent Do - minum,
* qui ambulant in vi - is e - jus.
2 Labores manuum tuarum quia mandu - ca - bis: * beatus es, et be - ne ti - bi e - rit.
3 Uxor tua sicut vitis a - bun - dans, * in lateribus do - mus tu - æ.
4 Filii tui sicut novellæ oli - va - rum, * in circuitu mens - æ tu - æ.

5 Ecce sic benèdicetur ho - mo, * qu ti - met Do - minum.
6 Benedicat tibi Dominus ex Si - on : * et videas bona Jerusalem omnibus die - bus vi - tæ tu - æ.
7 Et Videas filios filiorum tu - o - rum, * pacem sup - er Is - ra - el.
Gloria Patri, etc.

Lauda Jerusalem,
Pange Lingua.

Pan - ge, lin - gua......... glo - ri - o - - - si

cor - - po - ris mys - - - - te - ri - - - um,

San - gui - nis - que pre - ti - o - si, quem in mun - di

VESPERS

PANGE LINGUA—Continued.

Nobis datus, nobis natus
 Ex intacta Virgine,
Et in mundo conversatus,
 Sparso verbi semine,
Sui moras incolatus
 Miro clausit ordine.

In supremæ nocte cœnæ
 Recumbens cum fratribus,
Observata lege plene
 Cibis in legalibus,
Cibum turbæ duodenæ
 Se dat suis manibus.

Verbum caro, panem verum,
 Verbo carnem efficit,
Fitque sanguis Christi merum,

Et si sensus deficit,
 Ad firmandum cor sincerum
 Sola fides sufficit.

Tantum ergo Sacramentum
 Veneremur cernui,
Et antiquum documentum
 Novo cedat ritui:
Præstet fides supplementum
 Sensuum defectui.

Genitori Genitoque
 Laus et jubilatio,
Salus, honor, virtus quoque
 Sit et benedictio,
Procedenti ab utroque
 Compar sit laudatio. Amen.

V. Panem de cœlo præstitisti eis, alleluia.

R. Omne delectamentum in se habentem, alleluia.

St. Joseph.

(*19th March.*)

PSALMS—*Same as First Vespers, page 1.*

Te Joseph, Celebrent.

CHANT PAGE 53

TE, Joseph, celebrent agmina Cœlitum,
Te cuncti resonent christiadum chori,
Qui clarus meritis, junctus es inclytæ
Casto fœdere Virgini.

Almo cum tumidam germine conjugem
Admirans, dubio tangeris anxius,
Afflatu superi Flaminis Angelus
Conceptum puerum docet.

VESPERS.

Tu natum Dominum stringis ad exteras
Ægypti profugum tu sequeris plagas;
Amissum Solymis quæris, et invenis,
Miscens gaudia fletibus.

Post mortem reliquos mors pia consecrat.
Palmamque emeritos gloria suscipit :

V. Constituit eum dominum domus suæ.
R. Et principem omnis possessionis suæ.

Tu vivens, Superis par, frueris Deo,
Mira sorte beatior.

Nobis, summa Trias, parce precantibus,
Da, Joseph meritis, sidera scandere
Ut tandem liceat nos tibi perpetim
Gratum promere canticum. Amen.

V. Gloria et divitiæ in domo ejus.
R. Et justitia ejus manet in Sæculum
Sæculi.

St. John the Baptist.

(24th June.)

PSALMS— *Same as First Vespers.*

UT QUEANT LAXIS.

CHANTS PAGES 54 AND 55.

Ut queant laxis resonare fibris
Mira gestorum famuli tuorum,
Solve polluti labii reatum,
Sancte Joannes.

Nuntius celso veniens Olympo,
Te patri magnum fore nasciturum,
Nomen, et vitæ seriem gerendæ
Ordine promit.

Ille promissi dubius superni,
Perdidit promptæ modulos louquelæ

V. Fuit homo missus a Deo.
R. Cui nomen erat Joannes.

Sed reformasti genitus peremptæ
Organa vocis.

Ventris obstruso recubans cubili,
Senseras Regem thalamo manentem :
Hinc parens, nati meritis, uterque
Abdita pandit.

Sit decus Patri, genitæque Proli,
Et tibi compar utriusque virtus,
Spiritus semper, Deus unus, omni
Temporis ævo. Amen.

V. Iste Puer magnus coram Domino.
R. Nam et manus ejus cum ipso est.

Precious Blood.

(First Sunday of July.)

PSALMS—*For first four, see First Vespers, last, Lauda Jerusalem.*

FESTIVIS RESONENT.

CHANT PAGE 52.

Festivis resonent compita vocibus,
Cives lætitiam frontibus explicent,
Tædis flammiferis ordine prodeant
Instructi pueri et senes.

Quem dura moriens Christus in arbore
Fudit multiplici vulnere Sanguinem
Nos facti memores dum colimus, decet
Saltem fundere lacrymas.

Humano generi pernicies gravis
Adami veteris crimine contigit :
Adami integritas et pietas novi
Vitam reddidit omnibus.

Clamorem validum summus ab æthere
Languentis Geniti si Pater audiit,
Placari potius sanguine debuit,
Et nobis veniam dare.

Hoc quicumque stolam sanguine proluit,
Abstergit maculas, er roseum decus,
Quo fiat similis protinus Angelis,
Et Regi placeat, capit.

A recto instabilis tramite postmodum
Se nullus retrahat, meta sed ultima

℣. Redemisti nos, Domine, in sanguine tuo.
℟. Et fecisti nos Deo nostro regnum

Tangatur : tribuet nobile præmium,
Qui cursum Deus adjuvat.

Nobis propitius sis, Genitor potens,
Ut quos unigenæ Sanguine Filii
Emisti, et placido Flamine recreas,
Cœli ad culmina transferas. Amen.

℣. Te ergo quæsumus, tuis famulis subveni.
℟. Quos pretioso sanguine redemisti

St. Michael.

(29th September.)

PSALMS—*For first four, see First Vespers, page 1.*

CONFITEBOR TIBI. Psalm cxxxvii.

CHANTS AS FOR *Laudate Dominum*, PAGE 5.

CONFITEBOR tibi Domine in toto
cor - de me - o : * quoniam audisti
verba or - is me - i.
2 In conspectu Angelorum psal - lam
ti - bi : * adorabo ad templum sanctum
tuum, et confitebor no - mini tu - o.
3 Super misericordia tua, et verita
te tu - a : . * quoniam magnificasti super
omne, nomen sanc - tum tu - um.
4 In quacumque die invocavero te,
ex - au - di me : * multiplicabis in anima
me - a vir - tu - tem.
5 Confiteantur. tibi Domine omnes
re - ges ter - ræ : * quia audierunt omnia
verba or - is tu - i.

6 Et cantent in vi - is Do - mini: *
quoniam magna est glo - ria Do - mi - ni.
7 Quoniam excelsus Dominus, et humi - lia re - spicit : * et alta a lon - ge
cog - nos - cit.
8 Si ambulavero in medio tribulationis, vivi - fica - bis me :* et super iram inimicorum meorum extendisti manum
tuam, et salvum me fecit dex - tera
tu - a.
9 Dominus retri - bu - et pro me: *
Domine misericordia tua in sæculum:
opera manuum tuarum ne - de - spi - cias.

Gloria Patri, etc.

TE SPLENDOR.

CHANTS PAGES 26 AND 27.

Te, splendor et virtus Patris,
Te, vita, Jesu, cordium,
Ab ore qui pendent tuo,
Laudamus inter Angelos.

Tibi mille densa millium
Ducum corona militat:
Sed explicat Victor Crucem
Michael, salutis signifer.

Draconis hic dirum caput
In ima pellit tartara,

℣ In conspectu Angelorum psallam
tibi, Deus meus.
℟ Adorabo ad templum sanctum
tuum, et confitebor nomini tuo.

Ducemque cum rebellibus
Cœlesti ab arce fulminat.

Contra ducem superbiæ
Sesquamur hunc nos Principem,
Ut detur ex Agni throno
Nobis corona gloriæ.

Patris simulque Filio,
Tibique, Sancte Spiritus,
Sicut fuit, sit jugiter
Sæclum per omne gloria. Amen.

℣ Stetit Angelus juxta aram templi.
℟ Habens thuribulum aureum in
manu sua.

SS. Peter and Paul.

PSALMS—*Same as for Third Vespers, page 37*

DECORA LUX.

Decora lux æternitatis, auream
Diem beatis irrigavit ignibus,
Apostolorum quæ coronat Principes,
Reisque in astra liberam pandit viam.

Mundi Magister, atque cœli Janitor,
Romæ parentes, arbitrique Gentium,
Per ensis ille, hic per Crucis victor necem.
Vitæ senatum laureati possident.

V. In omnen terram exivit sonus eorum.
R. Et in fines orbis terræ verba eorum.

O Roma felix, quæ duorum Principum
Es consecrata glorioso sanguine:
Horum cruore purpurata cæteras
Excellis orbis una pulchritudines.

Sit Trinitati sempiterna gloria,
Honor, potestas, atque jubilatio,
In unitate, quæ gubernat omnia,
Per universa sæculorum sæcula. Amen.

V. Annuntiaverunt opera Dei,
R. Et facta ejus intellexerunt

Dedication of Churches.

PSALMS—*First four, same as for First Vespers, page 1 ; last, Lauda Jerusalem, page 38.*

CŒLESTIS URBS JERUSALEM.

Cœlestis Urbs Jerusalem,
Beata pacis visio,
Quæ celsa de viventibus
Saxis ad astra tolleris,
Sponsæque ritu cingeris
Mille Angelorum millibus.

O sorte nupta prospera,
Dotata Patris gloria,
Respersa Sponsi gratia,
Regina formosissima,
Christo jugata Principi,
Cœli corusca Civitas,

Hic margaritis emicant,
Patentque cunctis ostia :
Virtute namque prævia

Mortalis illuc ducitur,
Amore Christi percitus
Tormenta quisquis sustinet.

Scalpri salubris ictibus,
Et tunsione plurima,
Fabri polita malleo
Hanc saxa molem construunt,
Aptisque juncta nexibus
Locantur in fastigio.

Decus Parenti debitum
Sit usquequaque Altissimo,
Natoque Patris unico,
Et inclyto Paraclito,
Cui laus, potestas, gloria
Æterna sit per sæcula. Amen.

V. Hæc est domus Domini firmiter ædificata.
R. Bene fundata est supra firmam petram.

V. Domum tuam Domine decet sanctitudo.
R. In longitudinem dierum.

J. * M. * J.

†

Hymns of Adoration and Praise.

GOD.

1—God of My Heart.

God of my heart! Its earliest love, its last repose,........ Nor peace, nor...... joy it ev--er knows From Thee apart.

2   God of my soul!
      For Thee its fevered nature thirsts,
      To live with Thee it pants, it trusts,
         While ages roll.

3   God of my mind!
      To Thee its thoughts in rapture rise;
      It spurns the earth, it cleaves the skies,
         Its God to find.

4   God of my life!
      When cruel foes around me stand,

      Direct my aim and nerve my hand
         Amid the strife.

5   God of my death!
      That hour is only known to Thee:
      Receive, when life's last moments flee,
         My latest breath.

6   God of the blest!
      Throw open, Lord, Thy gates on high,
      And let me enter there, that I
         With Thee may rest.

GOD.

2—Nearer, My God, to Thee.

2. Deep in Thy Sacred Heart
   Let me abide,
  Thou that has bled for me,
   Sorrowed, and died;
  Sweet shall my weeping be,
   Grief surely leading me,
  Nearer, my God, to Thee,
   Nearer to Thee.

3. Friends may depart from me,
   Night may come down,
  Clouds of adversity
   Darken and frown;

  Still through my tears I'll see
   Hope gently leading me
  Nearer, my God, to Thee,
   Nearer to Thee.

4. And when the goal is won,
   How like a dream,
  In the dim retrospect,
   Sorrow will seem.
  'Sweet will my transports be
   Jesus, thy face to see,
  When I have come, at last
   Nearer to Thee.

3—Holy God, We Praise Thy Name.

1. Holy God, we praise Thy Name! Lord of all, we bow before Thee! All on earth Thy scep-tre claim, All in heav'n a-bove a-dore Thee: In-fi-nite Thy vast do-main, Ev-er-last-ing is Thy Name.

2. Hark! the loud celestial hymn,
    Angel choirs above are singing!
 Cherubim and Seraphim,
    In unceasing chorus praising;
 ‖: Fill the Heavens with sweet accord;
    Holy! Holy! Holy Lord. :‖

3. Lo! the apostolic train,
    Join Thy sacred Name to hallow!
 Prophets swell the loud refrain,
    And with white-robed martyrs follow;
 ‖: And from morn till set of sun,
    Through the Church the song goes on. :‖

4. Holy Father, Holy Son,
    Holy Spirit, Three we name Thee,
 While in essence only One,
    Undivided God we claim Thee:
 ‖: And adoring bend the knee,
    While we own the mystery. :‖

5. Thou art King of glory Christ!
    Son of God, yet born of Mary,
 For us sinners sacrificed,
    And to death a tributary:
 ‖: First to break the bars of death,
    Thou hast open'd Heav'n to Faith.

GOD.

4—I Love Thee, O Thou Lord Most High.

1. I love Thee, O Thou Lord most high! Because Thou first hast loved me; I seek no other liberty, But that of being bound to Thee.

CHORUS.

My God I here protest to Thee, No other will I have than Thine; What ever Thou hast given me, I here again to Thee resign.

2. All mine is Thine, say but the word,
   Whate'er Thou willest shall be done;
   I know Thy love, all-gracious Lord,
   I know it seeks my good alone.

3. Apart from Thee, all things are nought;
   Then grant, O my supremest bliss

Grant me to love Thee as I ought,—
Thou givest all in giving this!

4. My memory no tho't suggest,
   But shall to Thy pure glory tend;
   My understanding find no rest,
   Except in Thee its only end.

GOD.

STRIKE, STRIKE THE HARP—Continued.

forth her prais - es, Glo - ry to the God a - bove.

D.C.

2. Honor Him, ye hosts of heav'n!
Worship Him, ye realms above!
Not with outward form alone,
But with hearts that purely love.

3. He who rules the earth, the ocean
Keepeth silent watch o'er thee,
He can tell with what devotion,
Bows the heart or bends the knee.

6—O Come, Loud Anthems Let Us Sing.

SOLO. *Andante.*

1. O come, loud an - thems let us sing, Loud
2. In - to His pre - sence let us haste, To
3. The depths of earth are in His hand, Her
4. O let us to His courts re - pair, And

thanks to our Al - might - y King; For we our
thank Him for His fa - vours past; To Him ad -
se - cret wealth at His com - mand; The strength of
bow with ad - o - ra - tion there; Down on our

voi - ces high should raise, When our sal - va - tion's
dress, in joy - ful songs, The praise that to His
hills that reach the skies, Sub - ject - ed to His
knees, de - vout - ly all, Be - fore the Lord, our

GOD.

O COME, LOUD ANTHEMS—Continued.

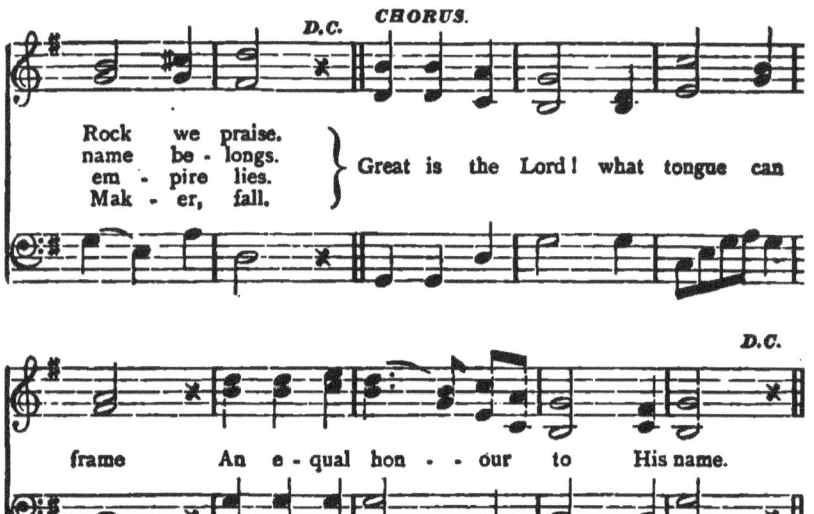

Rock we praise.
name be - longs.
em - pire lies.
Mak - er, fall.
} Great is the Lord! what tongue can frame An e - qual hon - - our to His name.

7—Praise Ye the Lord.

OLD HYMNAL.

1 Praise ye the Lord; on ev-'ry height Songs to His glo-ry raise; Ye an-gel hosts, ye stars of night, Send forth your voice of

GOD. 73

PRAISE YE THE LORD—Continued.

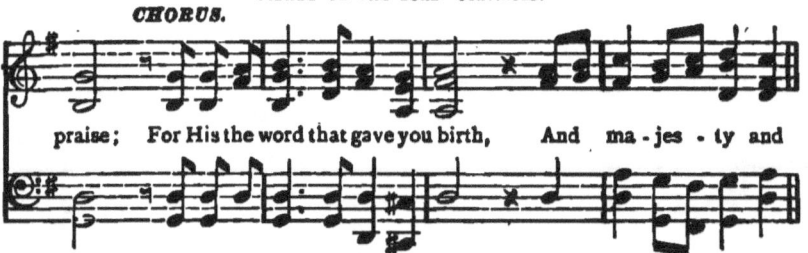

2 O fire and vapour, hail and snow,
  Ye servants of His will;
  O stormy winds, that only blow
  His mandates to fulfil;
  Ye mountains, rocks, to heav'n that rise;
  Fair cedars of the wood;
  All things of life that wing the skies,
  Or track the plains for food.

3 Ye judges, rulers, kings, whose hand
  The sceptre waves on high;
  O youths and virgins of the land;
  O age and infancy;
  Praise ye His Name, to whom alone
  All homage should be given,
  Whose glory from th' eternal throne
  Spreads wide o'er earth and heav'n.

OUR BLESSED LORD.
8—Jesus, Sweet Jesus.

2 Jesus, my Jesus, so priceless in worth,
Joy of the angels and hope of the earth;
Strong are the links and the bonds which confine
My heart and my soul to Thee, Jesus, all mine.

OUR BLESSED LORD. 75

9—Jesus is God.

Allegro Moderato.

1. Jesus is God; the solid earth, The ocean broad and bright, The countless stars, like golden dust That strew the skies at night, The wheeling storm, the dreadful fire, The pleasant wholesome air, The summer's sun, the winter's frost, His own creations were.

2. Jesus is God, the glorious bands
   Of golden angels sing
   Songs of adoring praise to Him,
   Their Maker and their King.
   He was true God in Bethlehem's crib,
   On Calvary's Cross true God,
   He who in heaven eternal reigned,
   In time on earth abode.

3. Jesus is God; alas, they say
   On earth the numbers grow
   Who His Divinity blaspheme
   To their unfailing woe·

And yet, what is the single end
Of this life's mortal span,
Except to glorify the God
Who for our sakes was Man!

4. Jesus is God; let sorrow come
   And pain and every ill;
   All are worth while—for all are means
   His glory to fulfil;
   Worth while a thousand years of life
   To speak one little word,
   If by our *Credo* we might own
   The Godhead of our Lord.

HOLY NAME. 77

JESU! SAVOUR OF MY SOUL—Continued

f A - ve, A - ve, Je - sus mild, Deign to hear Thy low - ly child.

2 Other refuge have I none, All my trust in Thee is stayed,
  Hangs my helpless soul on Thee, All my help from Thee I bring;
  Leave, oh leave me not alone, Cover my defenceless head,
  Still support and strengthen me. With the cover of Thy wing.

11—O Jesus, Jesus, Dearest Lord.

Moderato.

1 O Je-sus, Jesus dear-est Lord, For-give me if I say, For
2 O won-der-ful! that Thou shouldst let So vile a heart as mine, Love
3 O Light in dark-ness, Joy in grief, O Heav'n be-gun on earth! Je-

ve - ry love, Thy sacred Name, A thousand times a day. I
Thee with such a love as this, And make so free with Thine. The
sus! my Love! my treasure! who Can tell what Thou art worth? O

love Thee so, I know not how My transports to con - trol; Thy
craft of this wide world of ours, Poor wis-dom seems to me; Ah!
Je - sus, Je-sus, sweetest Lord, What art Thou not to me? Each

HOLY NAME.

O JESUS, JESUS, DEAREST LORD—Continued.

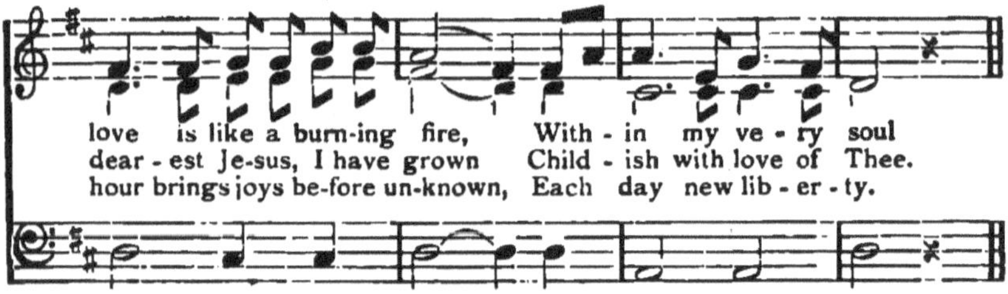

love is like a burn-ing fire, With-in my ve-ry soul
dear-est Je-sus, I have grown Child-ish with love of Thee.
hour brings joys be-fore un-known, Each day new lib-er-ty.

12—O Jesus, Thou the Beauty Art.

Andante.

O Je-sus, Thou the beauty art, Of an-gel worlds a-bove,.. Thy name is mu-sic to the heart, En-chanting it with love, Ce- -les-tial sweetness un-al loyed. Who eat Thee hunger.. still, Who drink of Thee still feel a void Which naught but Thou cans't fill

HOLY NAME.   79

O JESUS, THOU THE BEAUTY ART—Continued.

2 O Jesu, love unchangeable,
　For Whom my soul doth pine !
O fruit of life celestial !
O sweetness all divine !
When once Thou visitest the heart,
　Then truth begins to shine ;
Then earthly vanities depart ;
　Then wakens love divine.

3 O fairest of the sons of day !
　More fragrant than the rose !
O brighter than the dazzling ray
　That in the sunbeams glows ;
May every heart confess Thy name,
　And ever Thee adore ;
And, seeking Thee, itself inflame,
　To seek Thee more and more.

13—Sweet Name Which Makes the Dying Live.

Music by SISTER OF MERCY, St. Xavier's, Chicago, Ill.

Sweet name which cooled the martyr's fire
And o'er each torment new
A charm of heavenly comfort shed,
A fresh celestial dew !

Sweet name, which bids temptation fly,
And baffles satan's power;
What name like thine can bear me up
In death's appalling hour !

SACRED HEART.

JESUS, THE VERY THOUGHT OF THEE—*Continued.*

2 O hope of every contrite heart,
   O joy of all the meek,
To those who fall how kind Thou art,
   How good to those who seek.
But what of those who find ? Ah! this
   Nor tongue nor pen can show ;
The love of Jesus what it is
   ‖:None but His loved ones know. :‖

3 Jesus, our only joy be Thou,
   As Thou our hope will be ;
Jesus, be Thou our glory now,
   And through eternity.
O King of Love, thy blessed fire
   Does such sweet flames excite
That first it raises the desire,
   ‖:Then fills it with delight. :‖

15—Give Me, O Jesus Dear, a Place to Dwell.

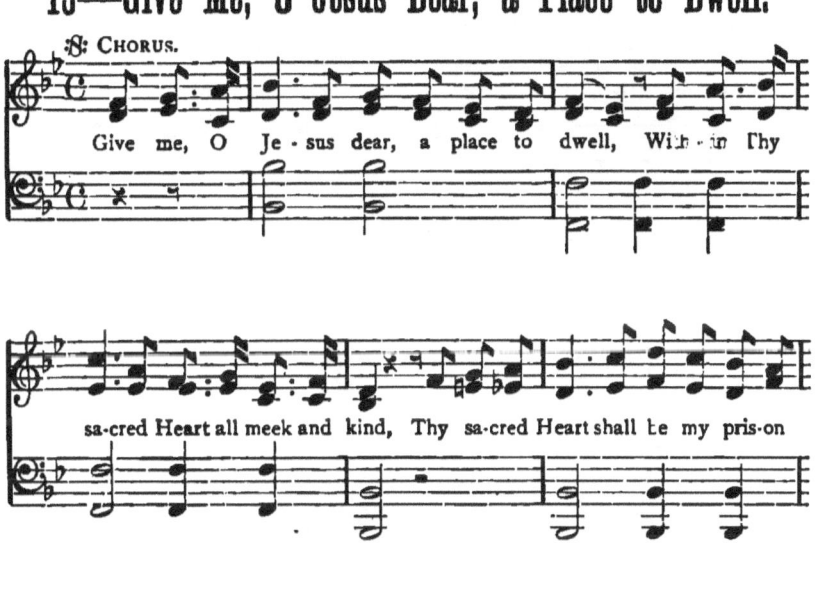

SACRED HEART.

GIVE ME, O JESUS DEAR, A PLACE TO DWELL—*Continued.*

1 For see my foes are con-stant-ly a - round, To tempt my soul, to catch it in their snares, True safe-ty in Thy sacred Heart is found, There shall I fly with all my man-y cares.
2 What is this world but constant care and woe, A world of care, a world of cold de - ceit; Thy Heart a-lone can peace and joy be-stow, Can give my soul its hap - pi - ness com - plete.
3 Where could I find a no-bler, love - lier heart, A heart more wor-thy ob-ject of my love? Such love-li - ness that but to see a part, Can rav - ish with de - light the saints a - bove.
4 Oh, what a joy! if in Thy Heart di - vine, To end this life my hap-py lot should be! Oh, what a peaceful death should then be mine! It would be life in-deed, not death to me.

16—Behold the Heart! Whose Love for Man.

Allegro Moderato. S. H. MESSENGER.

2.
The Kingdom of the Prince of peace,
　Whose reign of love shall never cease;
Meek and humble sovereign!
　All our passions govern
And our League of love increase!
　　　　　Chorus.

3.
Oh! reign of gentle lowliness,
　Of pure, devoted holiness,
Of the gracious merit
　Of a selfless spirit,
Heal our wounds, our sorrows bless!
　　　　　Chorus.

4.
By all the love and rapture sweet
　That swayed the Blessed Marguerite,
Let Thy cross be ours,
　And Thy thorns, our flowers,
Thy blest flames, our sure retreat,
　　　　　Chorus.

SACRED HEART.

17—Sweet Heart of Jesus be My Love.

2 Oh! happy union fruit of love,
   All other bonds are vain;
   It sweetens here each bitter grief,
   And lightens every pain.
   I bless, O Lord, Thy kingly heart,
   My sweetest treasure here:
   It fills my soul with heavenly joy,
   And dries each falling tear.

3 Thro' Mary's heart, dear Lord I come
   To seek a rest divine :
   And through the wounds in Thy blest side,
   I place my heart in Thine.
   O take it Lord, and in return
   I ask one gift of Thee.
   That Thou wilt fill it with Thy love
   For all eternity.

SACRED HEART. 85

18—O Sacred Heart that on the Cross.

Moderato.

1. O Sacred Heart that on the Cross Gave up Thy latest breath for me; This hour of song and sacrifice, With willing mind I give to Thee.

CHORUS.

O Sacred Heart, sweet Sacred Heart, Shrine of our faith, temple of love,

O Sacred Heart, sweet Sacred Heart, Bring us to Thee in heav'n above.

2 From Bethlehem to Calvary's hour,
　Thy beatings were for me alone;
　Yet have I scorned its gentle power,
　For all Thy many favours shown.

3 With deep resolve I turn to Thee,
　And pardon ask for every sin,
　My heart henceforth shall beat with Thine,
　Nor let the slightest evil in.

4 O give me grace to do Thy will,
　And keep my soul from every stain;
　That when my last sad hour has come,
　I may not look to Thee in vain.

SACRED HEART.

19—I Dwell a Captive in this Heart.

L. BERGÉ.

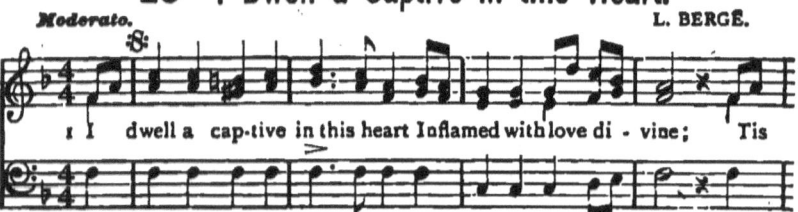

1 I dwell a captive in this heart Inflamed with love divine; Tis

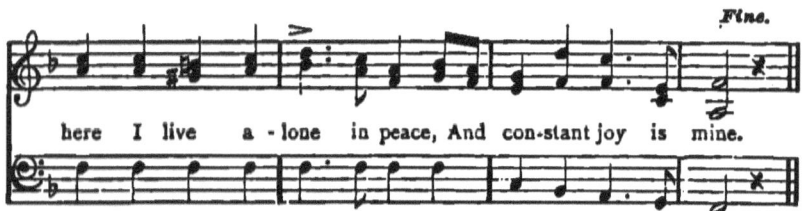

here I live alone in peace, And constant joy is mine.

DUET.

It is the Heart of God's own Son, In His humanity, Who

all enamoured of my soul, Here burns with love of me. I dwell, &c.

2 Here like the dove within the Ark,
   Securely I repose ;
  Since now the Lord is my defence,
   I fear no earthly foes.
  What though I suffer, still in love
   I ever true will be ;
  My love of God shall deeper grow,
   When crosses fall on me.

3 From every bond of earth, O Lord,
   Thy grace hath set me free ;
  My soul delivered from the snare
   Enjoys true liberty.
  Nought more can I desire than this,
   To see Thy face in Heav'n ;
  And this I hope since He on earth
   His heart in pledge hath giv'n.

SACRED HEART.

20—Hear the Heart of Jesus Pleading.

1 Hear the Heart of Jesus pleading, "Come, and sweetly rest in Me, With a peace and joy exceeding, Meek and humble ever be; In My Heart serene and holy, All your selfish cares resign." Dearest Jesus meek and lowly, Make, oh, make our hearts like Thine.

2 "Purer than the lily's whiteness,
   Fairer than the fairest snows,
In the beauty and the brightness,
   Of your souls I seek repose,
Calmly keep your hearts before Me,
   From the stain of passion free."
Heart of Jesus! we implore Thee,
   Make, oh, make us pure like Thee!

5 Heart of love! in Thee confiding,
   We shall learn to do Thy will;
In Thy sacred wounds abiding,
   Burning love our breasts shall fill.
We shall bless Thee, and obey Thee,
   Ever serve Thee faithfully;
Sweetest Heart! we humbly pray Thee,
   Let us live and die in Thee!

21—Sacred Heart! In Accents Burning.

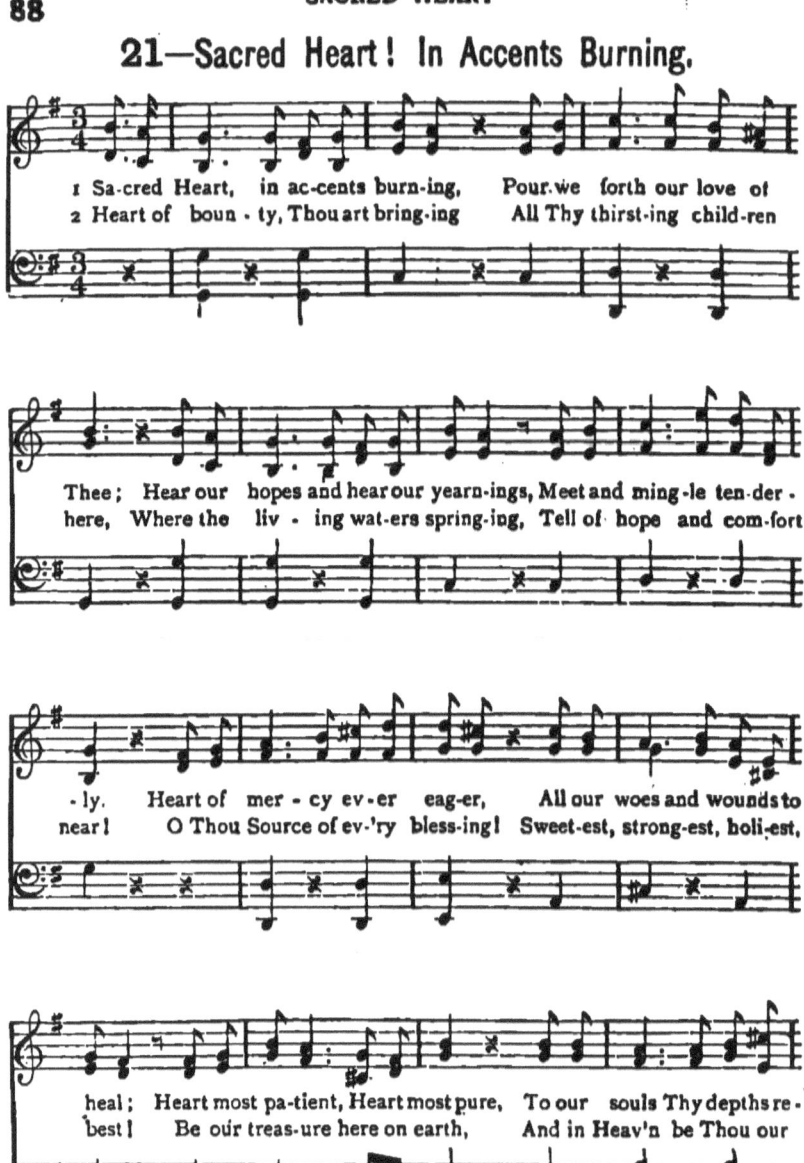

1. Sacred Heart, in accents burning, Pour we forth our love of Thee; Hear our hopes and hear our yearnings, Meet and mingle tenderly. Heart of mercy ever eager, All our woes and wounds to heal; Heart most patient, Heart most pure, To our souls Thy depths re-

2. Heart of bounty, Thou art bringing All Thy thirsting children here, Where the living waters springing, Tell of hope and comfort near! O Thou Source of ev'ry blessing! Sweetest, strongest, holiest, best! Be our treasure here on earth, And in Heav'n be Thou our

SACRED HEART.   89

SACRED HEART ! IN ACCENTS BURNING—Continued.

CHORUS.

veal. } Sa-cred Heart   of our Redeemer ! Pierced with love on Calva-
rest !

-ry;   Heart of Je - sus ev-er lov-ing, Make us burn with love of

Thee. Praise to Thee !   Sacred Heart.

22—Like a Strong and Raging Fire.

1 Like a strong and rag-ing fire   In a nar   row fur-nace
2 'Twas to cast   a-broad Love's fire, That our God from Heav-en
3 Bless - ed Lord ! Thy Heart is clov-en, With the cross of bit - ter

SACRED HEART.

LIKE A STRONG AND RAGING FIRE—Continued.

pent, Glows the Sac - red Heart's de-si - re   In the Ho - ly Sacra-
came; May those sparks our love in - spire,   May we burn with that blest
woe, There are thorns a-round It wov-en,   And the blood-drops from It

ment Round that sac-red fur-nace throng-ing, Shall these hearts re-fuse to
flame! All our sins, our slights, our coldness, All our in- - sults we de-
flow; Let us take Thy cross, and bear it, Let Thy thorn - y crown be

burn? Heart of love and ten-der long-ing Shall we make Thee no re
plore, Par-don, Lord, our dar-ing boldness, We will never wound Thee
ours, 'Twill be sweet - er far to wear it, Than a crown of fair-est

CHORUS.

turn?
more! } Bend-ing low in a-dor - a-tion, While our souls are borne a-
flow'rs.

SACRED HEART.

O SACRED HEART—Continued.

2 O Sacred Heart! O Sacred Heart!
  So spotless and so pure:
  Our weakness and our misery,
  May rest in Thee secure.

3 O Sacred Heart! O Sacred Heart!
  Consumed with purest fires,
  The cross, the thorns, the open wound,
  Reveal Thy fond desires.

24—Upon the Altar, Night and Day.

Moderato.

1 Up-on the Al-tar, night and day, The Heart of Je-sus lies, And night and day throughout the world, Do men Its claims despise; For by their cold ungrateful lives, They pierce It through and through, And if pure and true must be the soul, That fain would hide in Thee, Oh!

2 Be-neath a crown of cru-el thorns, Thy Heart is all on fire; And brightly shines from out Its flames, The cross of Thy desire. And joyous victims we shall be, Consumed before Thy throne, If

3 We of-fer Thee our hum-ble gifts, For poor they are and small, Our hearts, our souls, our little lives, Dear Heart! we give Thee all;

CHORUS—Oh draw us close to Thee, sweet Lord! And burning zeal impart, To

CHORUS—Then draw us closer still to Thee, O Sacred Heart divine! In

SACRED HEART.

UPON THE ALTAR, NIGHT AND DAY—Continued.

by the scourg-es of their crimes, Its ag - o - nies re - new.
now re-pair, by praise and pray'r, The wrongs of Thy dear Heart!
let Thy roy - al love sup-ply, For all our mis - er - y!
dead to sin, if dead to self, We live to Thee a - lone!
joy and grief, in life and death, Our hearts are ev - er Thine.

25—Peace, be Still! Our God is Dwelling.

Maestoso.

1 Peace be still! our God is dwell-ing Si-lent on His al - tar
CHORUS.—Heart of Jesus! strength su - per-nal! Send us pow - er from a-

throne; Let us kneel, our bosoms swell-ing, With a joy but sel-dom
bove; Heart of Jes - us! light e - ter - nal! Fill our souls with light and

known. Heart of Je-sus! come we hith - er, With our bur-dens meekly
love!

PEACE, BE STILL! OUR GOD IS DWELLING—Continued.

2 Thou hast called.the heavy-laden,
  Called the poor, the frail to Thee,
  See us then, O Son of Maiden!
  None could poorer frailer be,
  Thou dost know the woes and weakness
  Of a nature prone to ill,
  Heart of mercy! Heart of meekness!
  Be our shield, our succour still!

26—To Thy Pure and Burning Heart.

SACRED HEART.

27—O Sacred Heart! O Love Divine.

1 O Sacred Heart! O Love Divine! Do keep us near to Thee; And make our love so like to Thine, That we may holy be.

CHORUS.

Heart of Jesus hear! O Heart of Love Divine! Listen to our prayer;.... Make us always Thine.

2 O Temple pure! O House of gold!
Our heaven here below!
What sweet delights, what wealth untold
From Thee do ever flow

3 O wounded Heart, O Font of tears!
O Throne of grief and pain!
Whereon for the eternal years,
Thy love for man does reign.

4 Ungrateful hearts, forgetful hearts,
The hearts of men have been,
To wound Thy side with cruel darts
Which they have made by sin.

SACRED HEART.

28—A Message from the Sacred Heart.

1 A message from the Sacred Heart! What may this message be? "My child, my child! give Me thy heart; My heart has bled for Thee," This is the message Jesus sends to my poor heart to-day, And from His Throne in Heaven He bends to hear what I shall say.

2 A message to the Sacred Heart!
Oh! bear it back with speed:
"Come, Jesus, reign within my heart,
Thy Heart is all I need."
This prayer I'll pray while here I pine,
From Heaven and Thee apart,
Nor cease, dear Lord, till I am Thine
Forever, Heart to Heart.

SACRED HEART

FROM BANKS, OH! ALL YE LEAGUERS—Continued

love Thee more and more with every day. day.

30—As the Radiant Dawn is Stealing.

Allegretto   S. H. MESSENGER

As the ra-diant dawn is stealing Far up the glowing east, To Thy faithful ones re-veal-ing, A-gain the happy Feast, Sacred Heart in spirit low-ly I...... con-se-crate to-day.. Heart and soul, that I may wholly be Thine

SACRED HEART

AS THE RADIANT DAWN IS STEALING—Continued.

2 Thou art here in loving meekness,
  Through ever changing years;
 Thou hast strength for human weak-
  And balm for human tears. [ness
 On the cross Thy heart was bleed ng
  My sins to wash away;
 Now Thy heart for mine in pleading
  With fondest love to-day.

3 Thou whose angel choirs are telling
  Of majesty divine,
 How cans't Thou desire the dwelling
  Of such a heart as mine?
 Love divine, grant that I never
  From Thee by sin depart,
 And my hope and stay forever
  Will be Thy sacred heart.

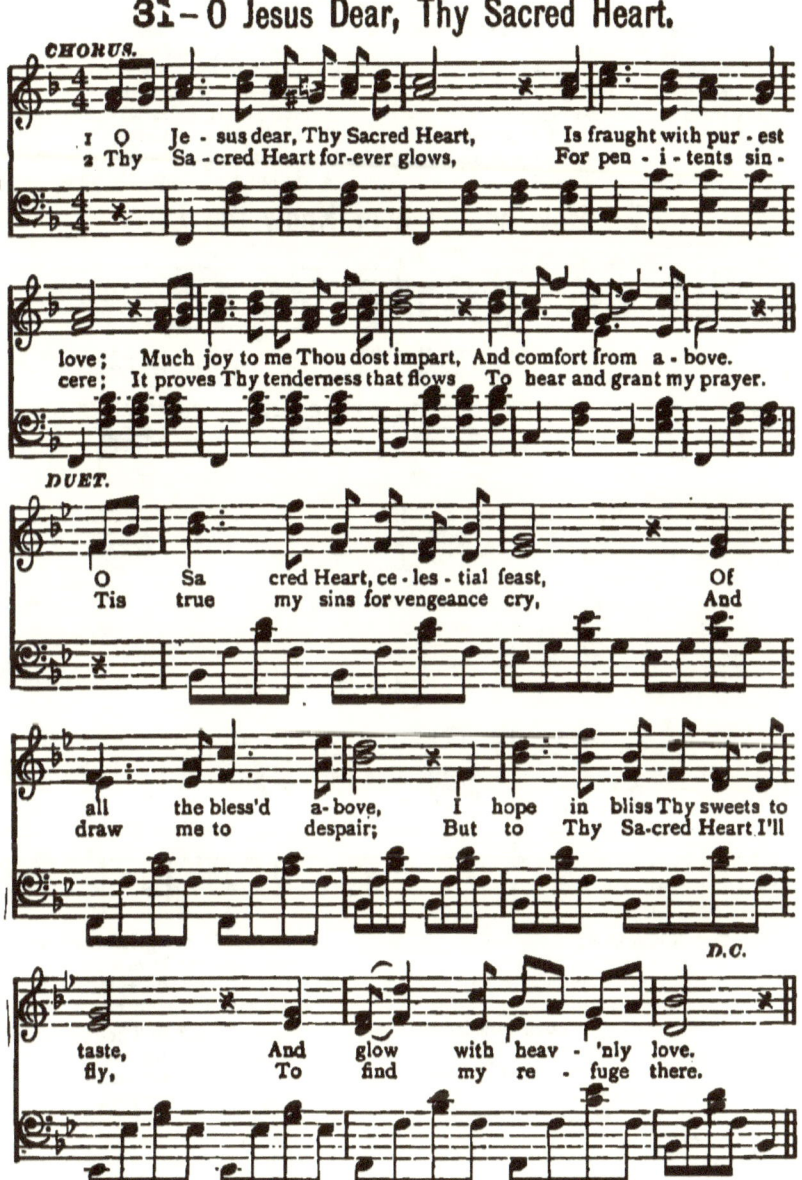

SACRED HEART.

O JESUS DEAR, THY SACRED HEART—Continued.

3 Thy Sacred Heart was pierced for me,
  And bled at every pore!
  From past offences set me free,
  Oh! them I shall deplore.
  My tears shall never cease to flow
  Because from Thee I've strayed,
  Who with such weight of pain and woe
  My ransom freely paid.

4 O! let me kiss Thy sacred feet,
  Thy bleeding hands and side:
  To suffer pain for Thee is meet,
  Who freely for me died.
  O Sacred Heart, celestial feast,
  Of all the bless'd above,
  I hope in bliss Thy sweets to taste
  And glow with heavenly love.

32—How shall I ever Know the Love

1 How shall I ever know the love
  Thou hast, O God for me?
  Nor men below, nor saints above,
  That love can tell or see.

  Nor Angels know, nor heaven's Queen,
  The loving God Thou art;
  Thy love is only felt and seen
  By Jesu's Sacred Heart.

CHORUS.
  O Heart of Jesus! I implore
  That I may love Thee more and more.

2 As God, Thou loved'st me before
  The world or time began:
  And now, as if to love me more,
  Thou lovest me as man.
  It seems, dear Lord, Thou wouldst forsake
  Thy glory, to impart
  Thy life to me, when Thou didst take
  A living human Heart.

3 The earth beneath, the Heaven above,
  Thy mercy would entwine,
  To thus unite in links of love
  The human and divine.

  And so that in our griefs and joys
  Thou mightest have a part,
  And feel with us and sympathize,
  Thou hast a human Heart.

4 O Sacred Heart! in Thee enshrined
  Is all that angels prize;
  Within Thy holy depths I find
  My solace and my joys,
  For Thee and for Thy love I yearn,
  Teach me the heavenly art,
  To be like Thee—Thy lessons learn,
  O meek and humble Heart.

SACRED HEART.

33—To Jesus' Heart all Burning.

2 O Heart for me on fire,
   With love no man can speak,
   My yet untold desire,
   God gives me for Thy sake,
3 Too true I have forsaken
   Thy flock by wilful sin,

Yet now let me be taken
Back to Thy fold again.
4 As Thou art meek and lowly,
   And ever pure of Heart,
   So may my heart be wholly
   Of Thine the counterpart.

SACRED HEART

34—HEART OF JESUS! DEAREST TREASURE!

Duo.

1. Heart of Jesus! dearest treasure, Joy of angels, hope of heaven! Thou hast lov'd us without measure, All Thy riches to us given. Full of mercy, full of meekness, Naught refusing to our weakness, By the
2. Sin and Satan, 'gainst us leaguing, Rise in fury to affright us; Foul temptations souls besieging, From Thy service would invite us. Hear and help us, Heart most tender, Lest in weakness we surrender; In the

35 — Heart of Jesus, we are Grateful.

SACRED HEART. 107

HEART OF JESUS, WE ARE GRATEFUL—Continued.

treas-ures dost un-fold. Heart of Je-sus, we will thank Thee, We will love Thee more and more; Heart of Je-sus, we will praise Thee, And we'll thank Thee o'er and o'er.

2 Heart of Jesus, Thou hast taught us
How to seek and how to find,
And that lesson now has brought us
To Thy heart so sweet and kind.
What we ask, with faith believing,
Thou hast pledged Thy word to give,
And Thy word is not deceiving,

3 Heart of Jesus, whilst we waited
For the favors now obtained,
Not a moment had we doubted
That by prayer they'd be gained.
Thou hadst told us that our treasures
Would be found in Thy dear heart,
And we knew that without measure

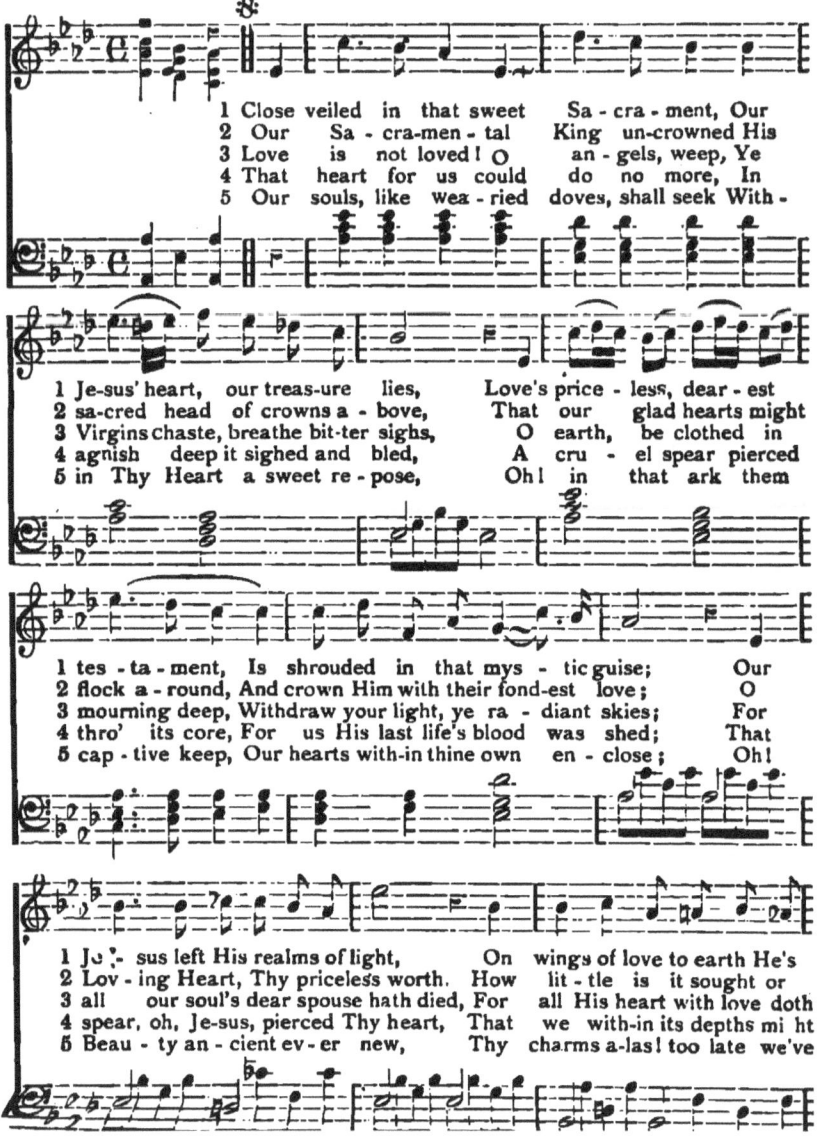

112 PRECIOUS BLOOD

HAIL, JESUS, HAIL! WHO FOR MY SAKE—Continued.

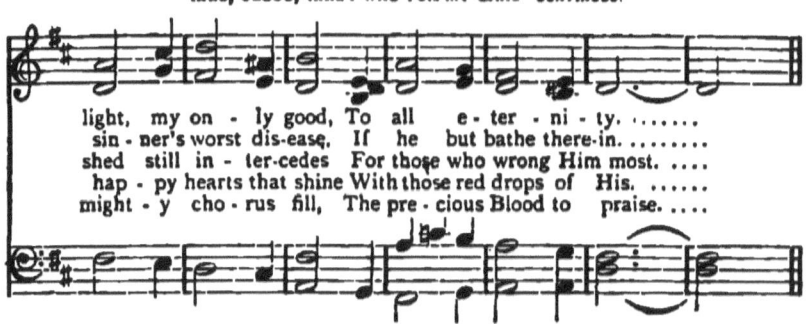

light, my on - ly good, To all e - ter - ni - ty. ....
sin - ner's worst dis-ease, If he but bathe there-in. ....
shed still in - ter-cedes For those who wrong Him most. ....
hap - py hearts that shine With those red drops of His. ......
might - y cho - rus fill, The pre - cious Blood to praise. ....

38* Soul of my Saviour, Sanctify my Breast.

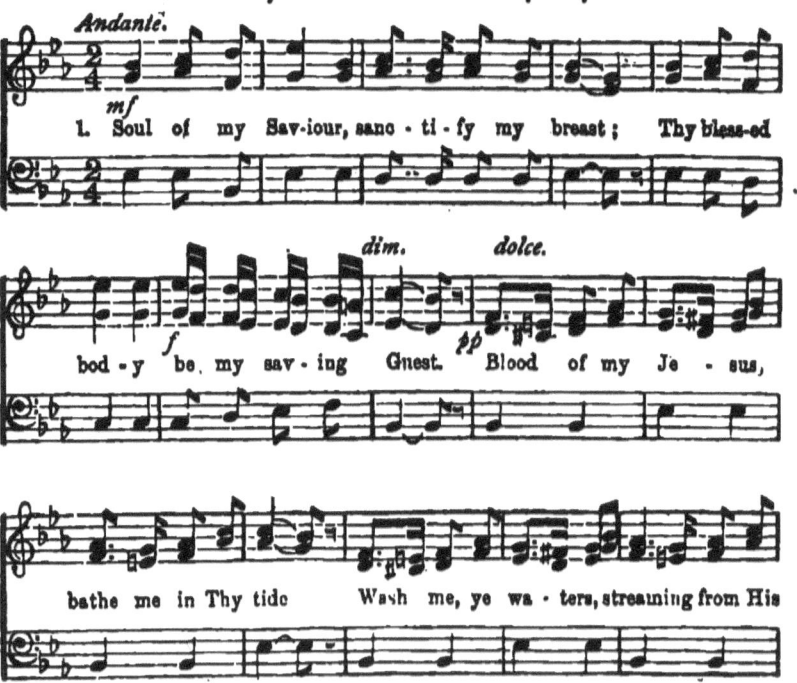

1. Soul of my Sav-iour, sanc - ti - fy my breast; Thy bless-ed bod - y be my sav - ing Guest. Blood of my Je - sus, bathe me in Thy tide Wash me, ye wa - ters, streaming from His

BLESSED SACRAMENT

2. O Cross! O Death of Jesus, soothe my fears:
Jesus, O hear my sighs, regard my tears!
O, hide me in Thy wounds, there may I stay,
And never, never more be turned away,
And never, never more be turned away

3. Save me, O save me from my deadly foe!
Call me at death from off my bed of woe!
And take me to Thy arms to hymn Thy praise,
Among Thy Saints in heaven thro' endless days,
Among Thy Saints in heaven thro' endless days.

39—What Happiness Can Equal Mine?

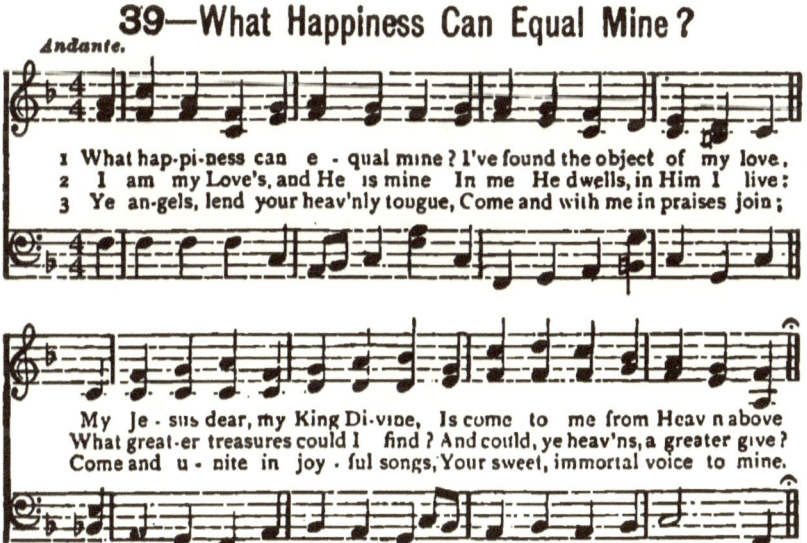

1. What hap-pi-ness can e-qual mine? I've found the object of my love,
My Jesus dear, my King Divine, Is come to me from Heav'n above

2. I am my Love's, and He is mine In me He dwells, in Him I live:
What great-er treasures could I find? And could, ye heav'ns, a greater give?

3. Ye an-gels, lend your heav'nly tongue, Come and with me in praises join;
Come and u-nite in joy-ful songs, Your sweet, immortal voice to mine.

BLESSED SACRAMENT.

WHAT HAPPINESS CAN EQUAL MINE—Continued.

He chose my heart for His abode, He there becomes my daily bread;
O sacred banquet, heav'nly feast! O o-ver-flowing source of grace,
Oh, that I had your burning hearts, To love my God, my spouse most dear!

There on me flows His heal-ing Blood; There with His Flesh my soul is fed,
Where God the food, and man the guest, Meet and u-nite in sweet embrace!
Oh, that He would with flaming darts Raise in my heart a heav'nly fire.

40—In this Sacrament Sweet Jesus.

1 In this Sa-cra-ment, sweet Je-sus, Thou dost give Thy Flesh and Blood, With Thy soul and God head al-so,

BLESSED SACRAMENT.

IN THIS SACRAMENT SWEET JESUS—CONTINUED.

As our own most precious food. .... As our own most precious food.

2 Yes, dear Jesus, I believe it,
And Thy presence I adore;
And with all my heart I love Thee,
May I love Thee more and more.

3 Come, sweet Jesus, in Thy mercy,
Give Thy Flesh and Blood to me:
Come to me, O dearest Jesus;
Come, my soul's true life to be.

4 Come, that I may live forever,
Thou in me and I in Thee,
Living thus I shall not perish,
But shall live eternally.

41—What Light is Streaming from the Skies.

Moderato.

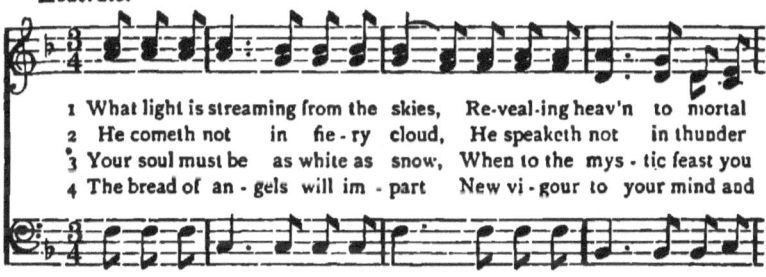

1 What light is streaming from the skies, Re-veal-ing heav'n to mortal
2 He cometh not in fie-ry cloud, He speaketh not in thunder
3 Your soul must be as white as snow, When to the mys-tic feast you
4 The bread of an-gels will im-part New vi-gour to your mind and

eyes, What voice is singing from the spheres Angelic hymns to mor-tal ears?
loud, He looseth not the storm-wind's breath, To frighten men with fear of death
go. There to receive—O heavenly bliss! Upon your lips the Saviour's kiss.
heart, You will become a child of truth, Endowed with everlasting youth.

116 BLESSED SACRAMENT.

WHAT LIGHT IS STREAMING FROM THE SKIES—CONTINUED.

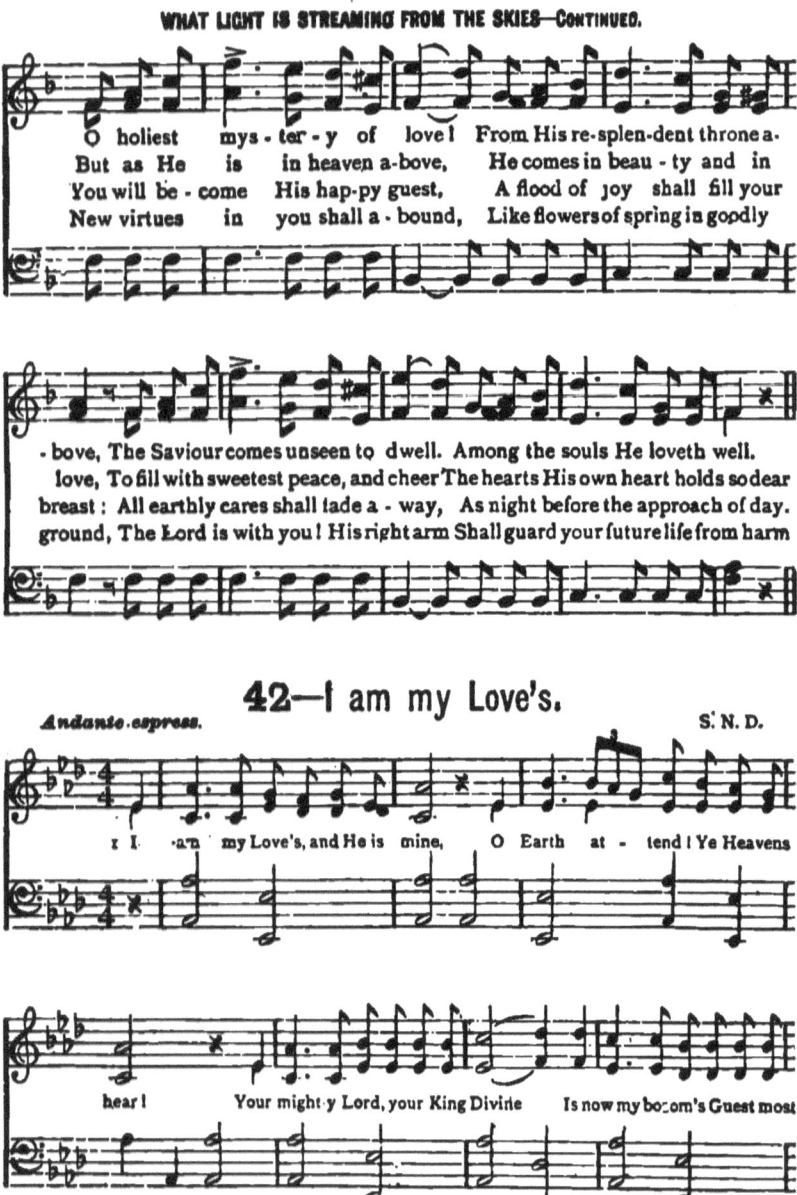

O holiest mys-ter-y of love! From His re-splen-dent throne a-
But as He is in heaven a-bove, He comes in beau-ty and in
You will be-come His hap-py guest, A flood of joy shall fill your
New virtues in you shall a-bound, Like flowers of spring in goodly

-bove, The Saviour comes unseen to dwell. Among the souls He loveth well.
love, To fill with sweetest peace, and cheer The hearts His own heart holds so dear
breast: All earthly cares shall fade a-way, As night before the approach of day.
ground, The Lord is with you! His right arm Shall guard your future life from harm

42—I am my Love's.

Andante espress. S. N. D.

1 I am my Love's, and He is mine, O Earth at-tend! Ye Heavens
hear! Your might-y Lord, your King Divine Is now my bosom's Guest most

2 Close lock'd within His fond embrace,
His Sacred Heart reclines on mine;
Its throbbings flood my soul with grace
And rapt'rous love and bliss divine.
Lo! Angels near me hover round,
From opening skies bright legions dart,
For Jesus their dear King they've found
Within the Heaven of my heart.

BLESSED SACRAMENT.

43—Jesus, my Lord, my God.

1. Jesus, my Lord my God, my all! How can I love Thee as I ought? And how revere this wondrous gift, So far surpassing hope or thought?

CHORUS.

Sweet Sacrament! we Thee adore, O make us love Thee more and more O make us love Thee more and more.

2. Had I but Mary's sinless heart
   To love Thee with, my dearest King,
   O with what bursts of fervent praise
   Thy goodness, Jesus, would I sing!

3. Thy Body, Soul, and God-head, all
   O mystery of love divine!—
   I cannot compass all I have,
   For all Thou hast and art are mine!

4. Sound, sound His praises higher still,
   And come, ye Angels, to our aid,
   'Tis God! 'tis God! the very God,
   Whose pow'r both men and angels made!

44—O Jesus Christ, Remember.

1 O Jesus Christ, remember, When Thou shalt come again, Upon the clouds of heaven With all Thy shining train; When ev'ry eye shall see Thee, In Deity revealed, Who now upon this altar In silence art concealed.

2 Remember, then, O Saviour,
　I supplicate of Thee,
That here I bowed before Thee,
　Upon my bended knee;
That here I own'd Thy presence,
　And did not Thee deny;
And glorify Thy greatness,
　Though hid from human eye.

3 Accept, divine Redeemer,
　The homage of my praise,
Be Thou the light, and honour,
　And glory of my days-
Be Thou my consolation
　When death is drawing nigh;
Be Thou my only Treasure,
　Through all eternity.

2 From Thy Father's throne descending
Thou becom'st our daily bread;
Midst celestial hosts attending
With Thy Flesh our souls are fed.
Come, Thou source of ev'ry blessing,
Warm our hearts with love divine,
Let Thy grace our souls possessing,
Make us be forever Thine,

46—When Our Saviour Wished to Prove.

2 When the dark and stormy night
   Fills the soul with wild affright;
   From the cloudlet where He hides
   Soon a ray of comfort glides.
   Where the tear of mis'ry falls,
   Where the voice of sorrow calls;
   Still He speaks with love divine,
   Give me, oh give me that heart of thine.

3 Can the Saints' ecstatic flight,
   Can the winged Seraphs' might,
   To their Lord approach more near
   Than do we poor sinners here?
   God Himself we here receive,
   Nobler gift He cannot give,
   Yet He breathes with love divine,
   Give me, oh give me that heart of thine.

BLESSED SACRAMENT.

47—My God, my Life, my Love.

2 My faith beholds Thee, Lord !
   Concealed in human food,
   My senses fail, but in Thy word
   I trust and find my God.

3 Oh, when wilt Thou be mine,
   Sweet lover of my soul?
   My Jesus dear, my King divine,
   Come o'er my heart to rule

4 Oh! come and fix Thy throne
   Within my very heart ;
   Oh! make it burn for Thee alone,
   And from me ne'er depart.

BLESSED SACRAMENT.

48 — When at Thy Altar.

1. When at Thy Altar, Lord, I kneel And think upon Thy love, Oh make my heart Thy goodness feel And cling to Thee above, O Son of God, we bow before Thee, Blessed Saviour we adore Thee, Son of God we bow before Thee, Blessed Saviour we Thee adore.

2. Oh manna! which my sovereign Lord,
   In mercy, left for me;
   Without this mystery adored,
   What would this exile be?
       Chorus.

3. A desert land of woe and care,
   A dreary land of strife,
   Who could its weight of sorrows bear
   Without this Bread of Life.
       Chorus.

4. My soul here finds a sovereign balm,
   A cure for every grief,
   'Mid pain and care a heavenly calm,
   A solace and relief.
       Chorus.

5. O Bread of Angels aid my flight,
   When from this world I soar,
   To dwell in realms of bliss and light,
   For ever—evermore.
       Chorus.

BLESSED SACRAMENT.

49—O Bond of Love.

Moderato.

1. O bond of love, that dost u-nite The ser-vant to his lov-ing Lord; Could I dare live and not re-quite Such love— then death were meet re-ward; I can-not live un-less to prove Some love for such un-meas-ured love, I can-not live un-less to

BLESSED SACRAMENT

O Bond of Love—Continued

prove Some love for such un-meas-ured love.

Chorus.

O Bread of Heaven, beneath this veil Thou dost my very God conceal, My Jesus dearest treasure hail! I love Thee and adoring kneel.

2. My dearest God! who dost so bind
   My heart with countless chains to Thee!
   O sweetest love, my soul shall find
   In Thy dear bonds true liberty.
   Thyself Thou hast bestowed on me,
   Thine, Thine forever I will be.
   CHORUS.—

3. O sweetest dart of love divine!
   If I have sinned, this vengeance take;
   Come pierce this guilty heart of mine,
   And let it die for His dear sake.
   Who once expired on Calvary,
   His heart pierced through for love of me.
   CHORUS—

4. Beloved Lord! In Heaven above
   Sweet Jesus; Thou awaitest me
   To gaze on Thee with changeless love,
   This is my hope laid up for me.
   For how canst Thou deny me heaven
   Who, here, to me Thyself hath given!
   CHORUS.—

BLESSED SACRAMENT.

50—O Lord, I am not Worthy.

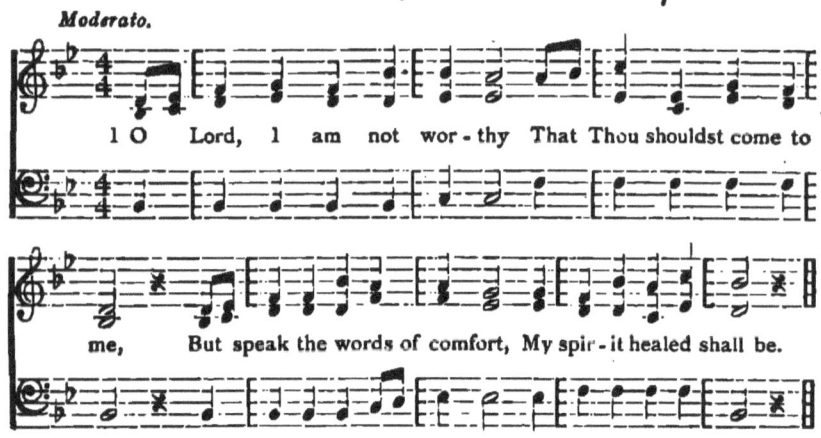

1 O Lord, I am not wor-thy That Thou shouldst come to me, But speak the words of comfort, My spir-it healed shall be.

2 And humbly I'll receive Thee.
The Bridegroom of my soul,
No more by sin to grieve Thee,
Or fly Thy sweet control.

3 Mighty, Eternal Spirit,
Unworthy tho' I be
Prepare me to receive Him
And trust the Word to me.

51—My Jesus, from His Throne above.

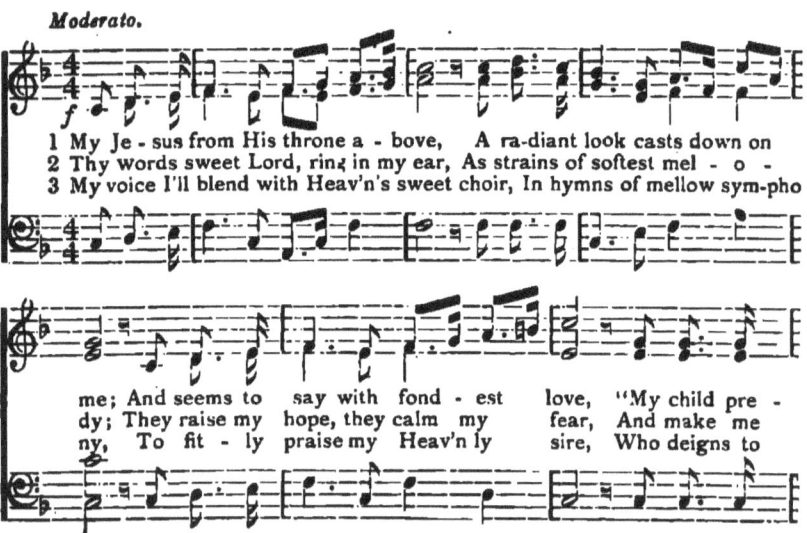

1 My Je-sus from His throne a-bove, A ra-diant look casts down on me; And seems to say with fond-est love, "My child pre-
2 Thy words sweet Lord, ring in my ear, As strains of softest mel-o-dy; They raise my hope, they calm my fear, And make me
3 My voice I'll blend with Heav'n's sweet choir, In hymns of mellow sym-pho-ny, To fit-ly praise my Heav'n ly sire, Who deigns to

BLESSED SACRAMENT.

MY JESUS FROM HIS THRONE ABOVE—Continued.

pare, I go to thee.' Then, Saviour come, do not de-
long t'approach to Thee. Be - hold me Lord, be-neath this
come and dwell with me. From this day hence my Lord di-

lay, Descend with speed from Heav'n a - bove, And on this
dome, And at this great and sol - emn hour Im-plor - ing
vine, I con - se-crate my - self to Thee; O may I

great and glorious day, Con-sume my heart with Thy pure love.
Thee to make Thy home, Within my young heart's nuptial bower.
be for - ev - er Thine, In time and in e - ter - ni - ty.

52—Jesus, Jesus, Come to me.

Lento.

1 Je - sus, Je - sus, come to me, O, how much I long for

JESUS, JESUS, COME TO ME—Continued.

2 Empty is all worldly joy,
Ever mixed with some alloy;
Give me my true Sovereign Good,
Jesus, Thy Own Flesh and Blood.

3 On the Cross three hours for me
Thou didst hang in agony;
I my heart to Thee resign;
O what rapture to be Thine!

53—O What Could My Jesus Do More

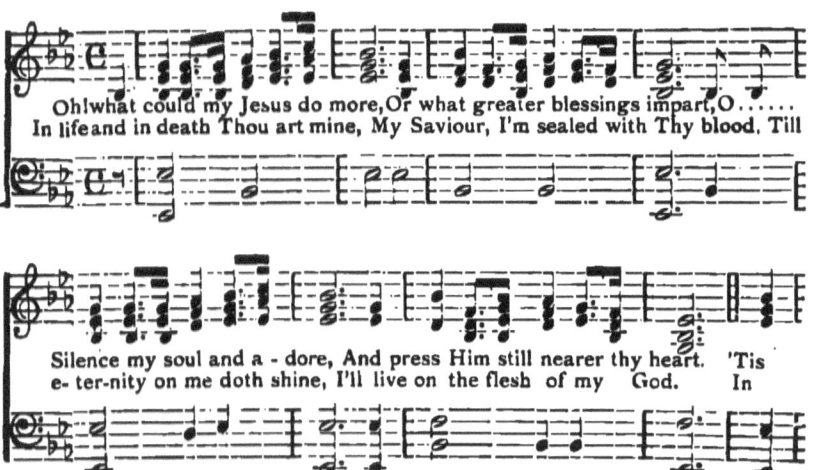

BLESSED SACRAMENT.

O WHAT COULD MY JESUS DO MORE—Continued.

here from my labour I'll rest, Since He makes my poor heart His a-bode, To Him all my cares I'll ad-dress and speak to the heart of my God.
Jesus triumphant I'll live, In Je-sus triumphant I'll die, The terrors of death calmly brave In His bosom breathe out my last sigh.

54—Ave Verum.

A - ve ve-rum Cor-pus na-tum, de Ma-ri - a Vir - gi - ne,..
Ve - re pas-sum, im-mo-la-tum in cru - ce pro ho - mi - ne,..
Cu - jus la-tus per - fo-ra - - tum, flu - xit a - qua

HOLY FAMILY

AVE VERUM. CONTINUED

et.... san - gui - ne..... Es - to no-bis præ-gus-ta - - tum,

mor-tis.... in ex - a - mi - ne... O Je - su dul - cis,
O Je - su pi - e,

O......... Je - su fi - li...... Ma - ri - æ-

55—Happy We, Who, Thus United.

1 Hap - py we, who, thus u - nit-ed, Join in cheer - ful mel - o - dy,
2 Je - sus, whose al-might - y bid-ding All cre - a-ted things ful - fil,
3 Sweet-est In-fant! make us pa-tient And o - be-dient, for Thy sake;
4 Ma - ry!thou a-lone wert chos-en To be Moth-er of thy Lord;
5 Dear - est Mo-ther!make us hum-ble, For thy Son will take His rest
6 Jos- eph!thou wert called the Father Of thy Mak er and thy Lord;
7 Suf - fer us to call thee Fa-ther, Show to us a fa-ther's love;

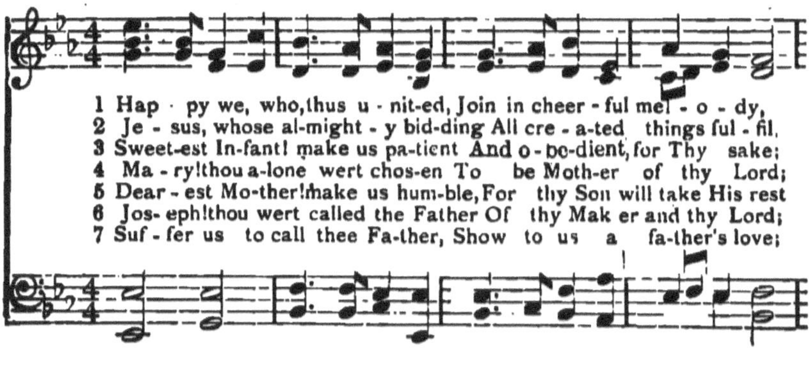

BLESSED VIRGIN MARY.

HAPPY WE, WHO, THUS UNITED—Continued.

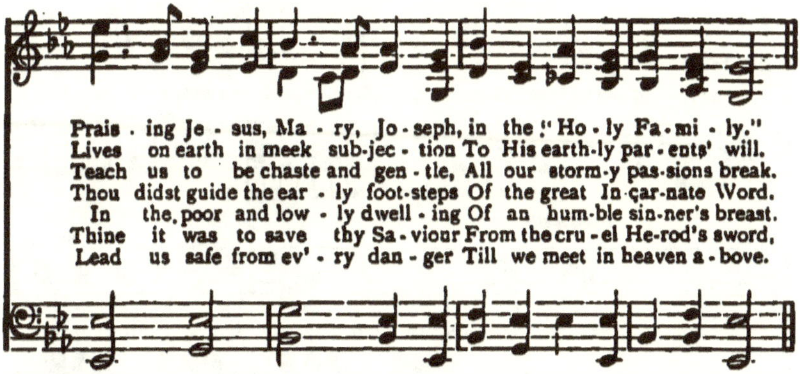

Prais - ing Je - sus, Ma - ry, Jo - seph, in the "Ho - ly Fa - mi - ly."
Lives on earth in meek sub-jec - tion To His earth-ly par - ents' will.
Teach us to be chaste and gen - tle, All our storm-y pas-sions break.
Thou didst guide the ear - ly foot-steps Of the great In - car-nate Word.
In the poor and low - ly dwell - ing Of an hum-ble sin-ner's breast.
Thine it was to save thy Sa - viour From the cru - el He-rod's sword.
Lead us safe from ev' - ry dan - ger Till we meet in heaven a - bove.

CHORUS. *Animate.*

Je - sus, Ma - ry, Jo - seph, help us, That we ev - er true may be
To the pro - mis - es that bind us To the "Ho - ly Fam - i - ly."

56—Holy Queen! We Bend Before Thee.

1 Ho - ly Queen! we bend be - fore thee, Queen of pu - ri - ty di--

BLESSED VIRGIN MARY

HOLY QUEEN! WE BEND BEFORE THEE—Continued.

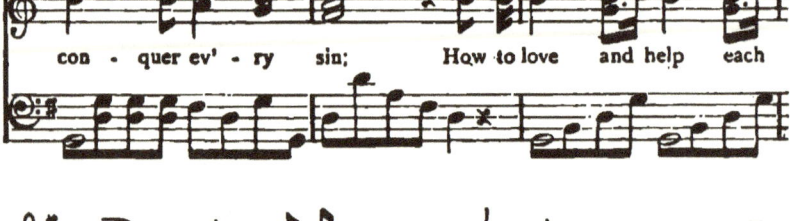

2 Thou, to whom a Child was given
   Greater than the sons of men,
   Coming down from highest heaven
   To create the world again!

3 O, by that Almighty Maker,
   Whom thyself, a Virgin bore!
   O, by the supreme Creator,
   Link'd with thee for evermore!

4 By the hope thy name inspires!
   By our doom reversed through thee,
   Help us, Queen of Angel choirs!
   To a blest eternity!

57—Hail, Heavenly Queen.

BLESSED VIRGIN MARY.

HAIL, HEAVENLY QUEEN—Continued.

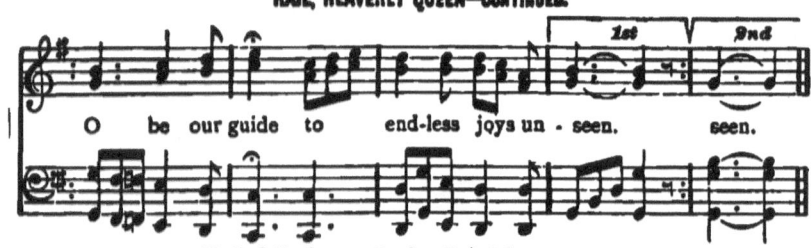

O be our guide to endless joys unseen. seen.

2 "Hail, full of grace," with Gabriel we repeat;
Thee, Queen of heav'n from him we learn to greet;
Then give us peace which heav'n alone can give,
And dead thro' Eve, thro' Mary let us live.

3 O break our chains, our captive souls release;
O give us light, and let our darkness cease;
Let ev'ry ill that preys upon our hearts,
Fly at Thy voice which every good imparts.

4 Our lives unstain'd, in purity preserve;
Nor e'er permit our ways from truth to swerve,
That when our time has rolled its rapid round,
We may, with Christ, in heav'nly bliss be crown'd.

58—O Purest of Creatures.

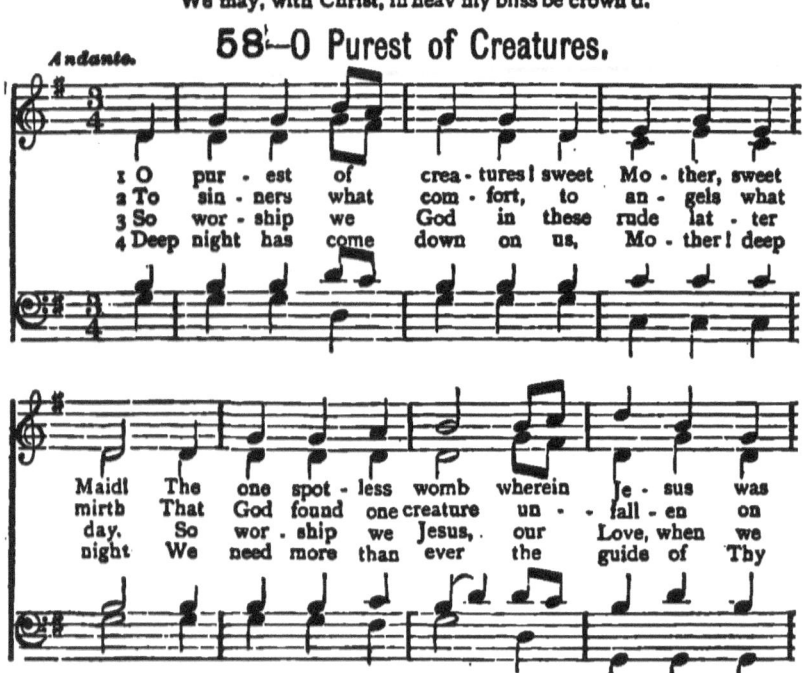

1 O pur-est of crea-tures! sweet Mo-ther, sweet Maid! The one spot-less womb wherein Je-sus was
2 To sin-ners what com-fort, to an-gels what mirth That God found one creature un-fall-en on
3 So wor-ship we God in these rude lat-ter day, So wor-ship we Jesus, our Love, when we
4 Deep night has come down on us, Mo-ther! deep night We need more than ever the guide of Thy

BLESSED VIRGIN MARY.

O PUREST OF CREATURES—Continued.

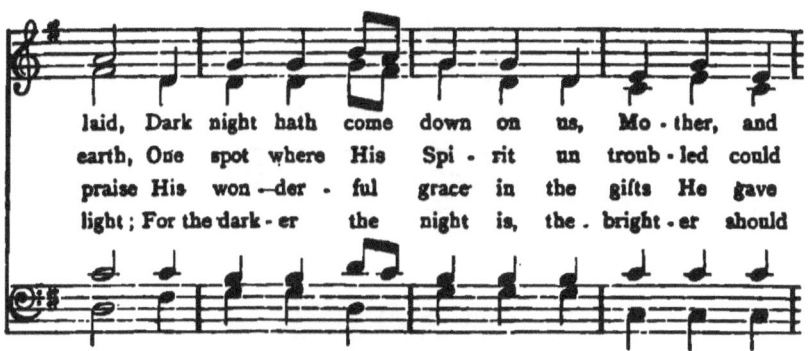

laid, Dark night hath come down on us, Mo-ther, and
earth, One spot where His Spi-rit un troub-led could
praise His won-der-ful grace in the gifts He gave
light; For the dark-er the night is, the bright-er should

we Look out for Thy shin-ing, sweet Star of the Sea.
be, The depth of thy shin-ing, sweet Star of the Sea.
Thee, The gift of clear shin-ing, sweet Star of the Sea.
be Thy beau-ti-ful shin-ing, sweet Star of the Sea.

59—Daily, Daily, Sing to Mary.

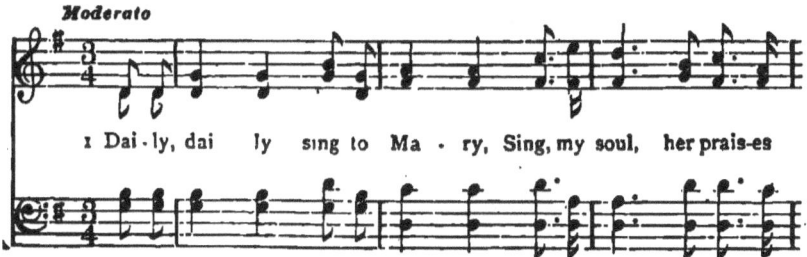

Moderato

1 Dai-ly, dai-ly sing to Ma-ry, Sing, my soul, her prais-es

BLESSED VIRGIN MARY.

DAILY, DAILY SING TO MARY—Continued.

due: All her feasts, her actions wor-ship, With the heart's de-vo-tion true. Lost in wond'ring con-tem-pla-tion, Be her Ma'-jes-ty con-fess'd; Call her Mo-ther, call her Vir-gin, Hap-py Mo-ther, Virgin blest.

She is mighty to deliver;
  Call her, trust her lovingly,
When the tempest rages round thee;
  She will calm the troubled sea.
Gifts of heaven she has given,
  Noble Lady to our race;
She, the Queen, who decks her subjects
  With the light of God's own grace.

3 Sing, my tongue, the Virgin's trophies
  Who for us her Maker bore,
For the curse of old inflicted,
  Peace and blessing to restore.
Sing in songs of peace unending,
  Sing the world's majestic Queen:
Weary not nor faint in telling,
  All the gifts she gives to men.

4 All our joys do flow from Mary;
  All then join her praise to sing:
Trembling sing the Virgin Mother,
  Mother of our Lord and King.
While we sing her awful glory,
  Far above our fancy's reach,
Let our hearts be quick to offer
  Love alone the heart can teach.

BLESSED VIRGIN MARY.

60—O blest for e'er the Mother.

1 O blest for e'er the Mother, And Virgin full of grace, Who bore our God, our brother, The saviour of our race.

CHORUS.—Sweet Jesus, low before Thee, We bend in fear and love, O grant we may adore Thee In Thy bright realms above.

2 Pure as the light of heaven,
In meekness nearest Thee,
'Tis Thou hast Mary given,
Our guide, our friend to be.

CHORUS.—Sweet Mother, tears are falling,
From hearts that love Thy Son,
Then hear thy children calling
On thee, and bless thy own.

61—'Tis the Month of our Mother.

1. 'Tis the month of our Mother, The blessèd and beautiful days, When our lips and our spirits Are glowing with love and with praise.

Chorus. All hail! to dear Mary, The guardian of our way, To the fairest of Queens, Be the fairest of seasons, sweet May.

2 Oh! what peace to her children,
   'Mid sorrows and trials to know,
   That the love of their Mother
   Hath ever a solace for woe.

3 And what joy to the erring,
   The sinful and sorrowful soul;
   That a trust in her guidance
   Will lead to a glorious goal.

4 Let us sing, then, rejoicing,
   That God hath so honour'd our race,
   As to clothe with our nature,
   Sweet Mary, the Mother of grace.

62—Mother Of God We Hail Thy Heart.

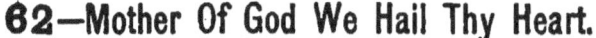

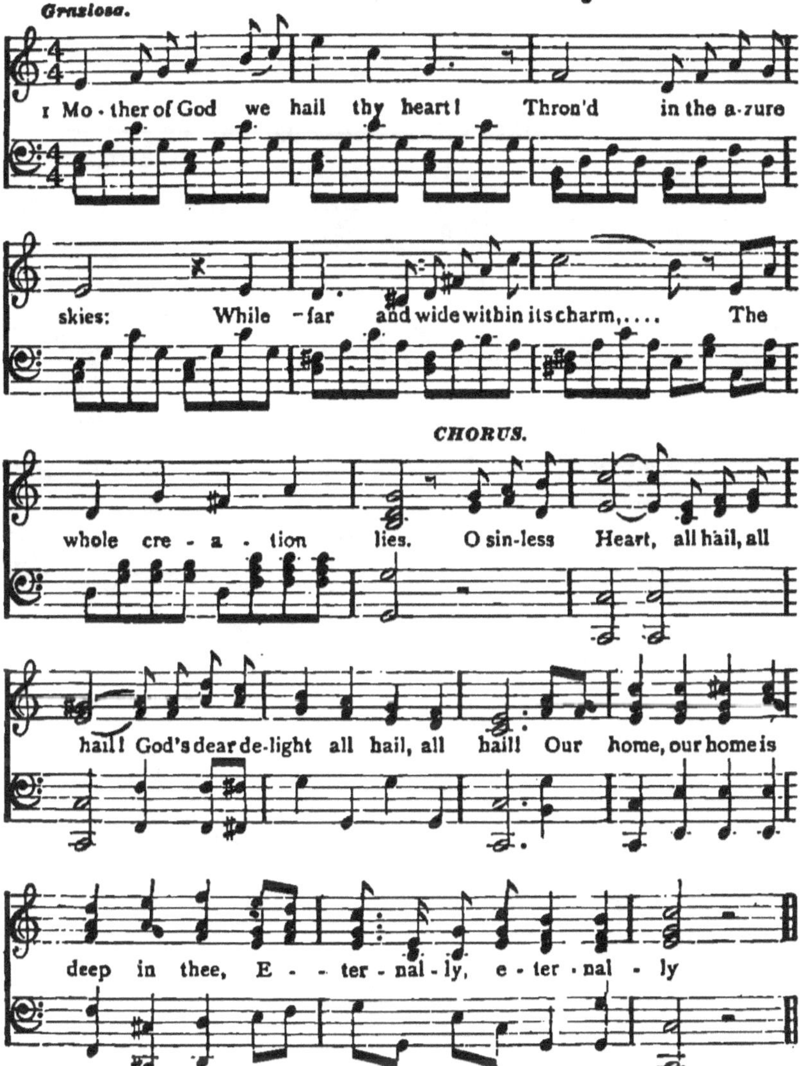
Graziosa.
1 Mo - ther of God we hail thy heart! Thron'd in the a-zure
skies: While - far and wide within its charm,.... The
CHORUS.
whole cre - a - tion lies. O sin-less Heart, all hail, all
hail! God's dear de-light all hail, all hail! Our home, our home is
deep in thee, E - - ter - nal - ly, e - ter - nal - ly

2 Mother of God, from out thy heart
Our Saviour fashioned His;
The fountains of the Precious Blood
Rose in thy depths of bliss.

3 Mother of God, when near thy Heart,
The unborn Saviour lay,
He taught it how to burn with love,
For sinners gone astray.

BLESSED VIRGIN MARY.

MOTHER OF GOD, WE HAIL THY HEART—Continued.

4 Mother of God, He broke thy Heart,
   That it might wider be—
   That in the vastness of its love
   There might be room for me.

5 Mother of God, thy Heart hath height
   On which God loves to dwell,
   And yet the lowliest child on earth
   Is welcome there as well

63—Hail Virgin, Dearest Mary.

LAMBILLOTTE.

1. Hail, Virgin, dearest Mary! Our lovely Queen of May, O spotless blessed Lady, Our lovely Queen of May

1. Thy children humbly bending, surround thy shrine so dear; With heart and voice ascending, Sweet Mary hear our prayer. Hail,

2 Behold earth's blossoms springing
   In beauteous form and hue;—
   All nature gladly bringing
   Her sweetest charms to you.

3 We'll gather fresh, bright flowers,
   To bind our fair Queen's brow;

From gay and verdant bowers
We haste to crown thee now.

4 And now, our blessed Mother,
   Smile on our festal day,
   Accept our wreath of flowers,
   And be our Queen of May.

BLESSED VIRGIN MARY 141

64—Joy of My Heart! O Let Me Pay.

1 Joy of my heart! O let me pay.... To thee thine own sweet month of May. Mary! one gift I beg of thee, My soul from sin and sorrow free, Direct my wand'ring feet a-right, And be thyself my own true light.

CHORUS.

Be love of thee the purging fire, To cleanse for God my heart's desire; Mother, be love of thee a ray From heav'n to show the heav'nward way.

BLESSED VIRGIN MARY.

JOY OF MY HEART! O LET ME PAY—Continued.

2 Mary, make haste thy child to win
From sin and from the love of sin
Mother of God! let my poor love
A mother's prayer and pity move.
O Mary, when I come to die,
Be thou, thy spouse, and Jesus nigh.

CHORUS.
When mute before the Judge I stand,
My holy shield be Mary's hand;
Oh! Mary! let no child of thine,
In hell's eternal exile pine.

3 Be love of thee, my whole life long
A seal upon my wayward tongue.
Write on my heart's most secret core
The five dear wounds that Jesus bore.
O give me tears to shed with thee,
Beneath the Cross on Calvary.

CHORUS.
One more request and I have done;
With love of thee and thy dear Son,
More let me burn, and more each day,
Till love of self is burned away.

65—Glorious Mother! From High Heaven.

1 Glorious Mother! from high heaven Down upon thy children gaze, Gathered in thy own loved season, Thee to bless, and thee to praise.
2 Earth is darksome, we are weary, Satan setteth snares for all; Pray for us, O tender Mary! Pray to Jesus lest we fall.
3 Many call upon thee Mother! Some in manhood, strong in youth; Some in age, in tender childhood, All in loving faith and truth.
4 Bless! O bless us, now and ever, Thou who once the dark earth trod; And when dying, waft our spirits To the bosom of our God.

CHORUS.
See sweet

BLESSED VIRGIN MARY.

GLORIOUS MOTHER ! FROM HIGH HEAVEN—Continued

Ma - ry on thy al - tars Bloom the fairest buds of May; O may we, earth's sons and daugh-ters, Grow by grace, as pure as they.

66—Ah, Her Smile Makes Heav'n Rejoice.

1 Ah, her smile makes heav'n re - joice, Eyes of saints to glisten, Ev-en an - gels at her voice Hush their harps to
2 Christian, though your storm toss'd bark On the sea still linger, Can you call the way too dark, Shown by Ma - ry's

BLESSED VIRGIN MARY.

AH, HER SMILE MAKES HEAV'N REJOICE—Continued

67—Mother Of Mercy, Day By Day

2 Thy love for me I know its worth,
   Oh, it is all in all to me;
  For what did Jesus love on earth
  ||: One half so tenderly as thee:||

3 Get me the grace to love thee more,
   Jesus will give if thou wilt plead;
  And Mother, when life's care are o'er,
  ||: Oh, I shall love thee then indeed·:||

4 Jesus, when His three hours were run,
   Bequeathed thee from the Cross to me,
  And oh! how can I love thy Son,
  ||: Sweet Mother, if I love not thee?:||

68—O Flower Of Grace, Divinest Flower.

1 O flow'r of grace, di-vin-est flow-er! God's light thy life, God's love thy dow'r That all a-lone with vir-gin ray...... Dost.. make in heav'n eternal May: Sweet falls the peerless dig-ni-ty Of God's eternal choice on thee. Help of Christians with mercy lad-en, O Virgin

2 Choice flower that bloomest on the breast Of Je-sus, that is now thy rest, As thine was once the chosen bed...... Of.. His dear Heart and sacred Head; O, Mary! sweet it is to see Thy Son's creation graced by thee. Help of Christians with mercy lad-en, O Virgin

BLESSED VIRGIN MARY.

O FLOWER OF GRACE DIVINEST FLOWER—Continued.

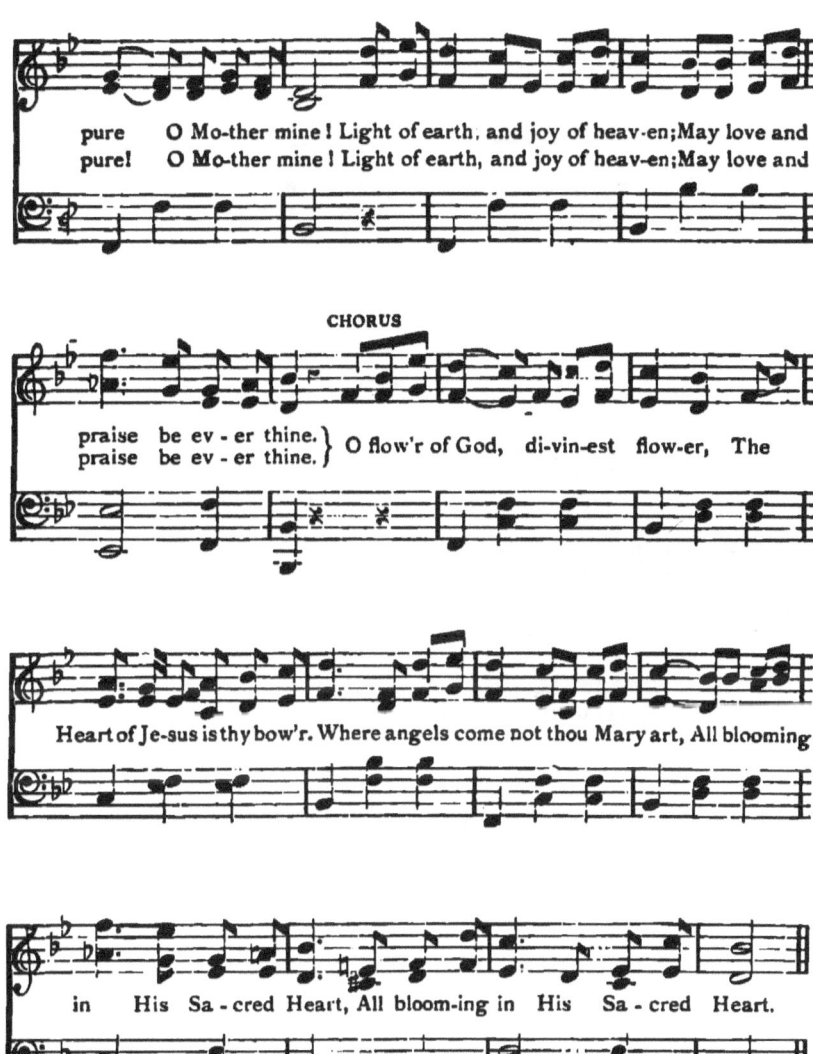

69—Come And Chant The Praises.

2 Oh! teach us love of Jesus,
  Teach us love of thee;
Obedient, patient, pure and mild,
  May we ever be.

3 And when this life is ended,
  Be thou at our side;
As now we fondly trust in thee
  In thee we'll then confide.

BLESSED VIRGIN MARY.

O MATER ADMIRABILIS—Continued.

Ma - ter ad - mi - ra - bi - lis, our life, our hope our joy.

2 O Mater Admirabilis, no language can proclaim
  The rare and wond'rous sweetness, that is blended with thy name.

3 O Mater Admirabilis, protect our lives from sin,
  That in the Heart of Jesus a resting place we win.

71—The Day Is O'er.

Andante.

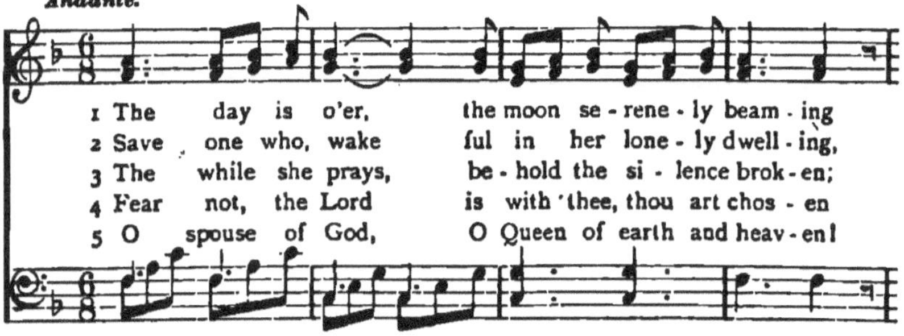

1 The day is o'er, the moon se-rene-ly beam-ing
2 Save one who, wake-ful in her lone-ly dwell-ing,
3 The while she prays, be-hold the si-lence brok-en;
4 Fear not, the Lord is with thee, thou art chos-en
5 O spouse of God, O Queen of earth and heav-en!

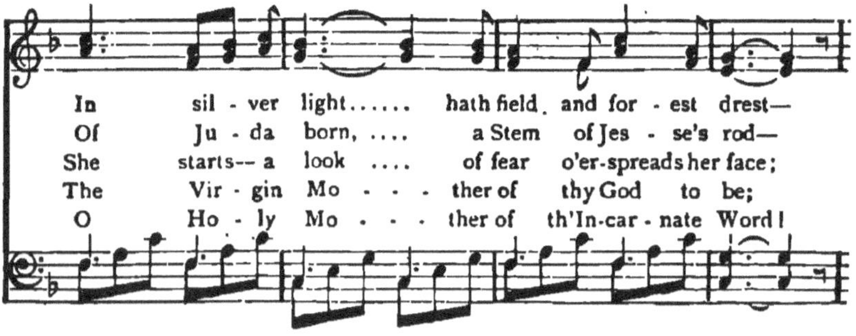

In sil - ver light...... hath field and for - est drest—
Of Ju - da born, ... a Stem of Jes - se's rod—
She starts— a look .... of fear o'er-spreads her face;
The Vir - gin Mo - - - ther of thy God to be;
O Ho - ly Mo - - - ther of th'In-car - nate Word!

2 For on this blesséd day
  She knelt at pray'r,
  When lo! before her shone
  An angel fair.

3 Hail, Mary! infant lips
  Lisp it to-day,
  Hail, Mary! with faint smile,
  The dying say,

4 Hail, Mary! many a heart
  Broken with grief,
  In that angelic prayer
  Has found relief.

BLESSED VIRGIN MARY. 153

73—Ah! What A Joy, Dear Mother.

BLESSED VIRGIN MARY.

AH! WHAT A JOY, DEAR MOTHER—Continued.

2 God's love around thee
  Clothes thee with a splendor
  Eye hath not seen
  Nor heart of man conceived;
  God's blessed angels
  Their fond homage render,
  Sing evermore
  The work in thee achieved.

3 Joy of the ransomed,
  Saints thy love proclaiming,
  See in thy smile
  The love of thy dear Son,
  Love that redeemed them,
  Grace that e'er sustained them.
  Till the long strife
  On earth was hap'ly done.

74—My Own Dear Mother Mary.

BLESSED VIRGIN MARY

MY OWN DEAR MOTHER MARY—Continued.

SOLO.

in my heart it wak - ens, Such ten - der thoughts and blest, My
soul, this world for-sak - ing, Be-fore thy throne .... would rest, Thy
name, Oh, Mo - ther Ma - ry, is mu sic to my soul

2 The cherubim are praising
  Thy beauty and thy grace,
  And heaven is all illumined
  And ravished with thy face!
  Thy name, O, Mother Mary,
  Is music to my soul.

3 Dear Mother, I am weary
  Of daily strife with sin,
  Oh! be with angels near me,
  That I the prize may win.
  Thy name, O, Mother Mary,
  Is music to my soul.

75—Joy! Joy! The Mother Comes.

Allegretto.

1 Joy! joy! the Mo - ther comes,.... And in her arms she

BLESSED VIRGIN MARY.

JOY ! JOY ! THE MOTHER COMES—Continued.

brings,.... The Light of all the world,.... The Christ, the King of kings;.... And in her heart the while.... All si-lent-ly she sings,.... And in her heart the while.. All si-lent-ly she sings.

2 Saint Joseph follows near,
   In rapture lost and love,
While angels 'round about,
   In glowing circles move;
||: And o'er the Mother broods
   The Everlasting Dove. :||.

3 There in the temple court,
   Old Simeon's heart beats high,
And Anna feeds her soul
   With food of prophecy;
||: But, see! the shadows pass,
   The world's true Light draws nigh.:||

4 O Infant God! O Christ!
   O Light most beautiful!
Thou comest, Joy of joys!
   All darkness to annul;
||: And brightest lights of earth,
   Beside Thy Light are dull. :||

BLESSED VIRGIN MARY.

76 – Hail, Thou Star Of Ocean.

1. Hail, thou Star of ocean, God's own Mother blest,..
Ever sinless Virgin, Gate of heav'nly rest.
Taking that sweet Ave Which from Gabriel came,
Peace confirm within us, Changing Eva's name.

2 Break the captive's fetters,
   To the blind give day ;
Chase all evils from us ;
   For all blessings pray.
Show thyself a Mother ;
   May the Word divine,
Born for us thine Infant,
   Hear our prayers through thine.

3 Virgin all excelling,
   Mildest of the mild,
Freed from guilt preserve us,
   Meek and undefiled.
Keep our life all spotless,
   Make our way secure,
Till we find in Jesus
   Joy for evermore.

BLESSED VIRGIN MARY.

77—Mary, Mother; Shield Us Through Life.

2 Star of the main, beneath thy veil
  Clinging to thee, we safely sail.

3 O Mother dear, O Virgin blest,
  Our footsteps guide till death's long rest.

4 Sweet morning Star, when life is o'er
  Then land us on the eternal shore.

BLESSED VIRGIN MARY. 159

ASSUMPTION—AUGUST 15TH.

18—Unfold, Unfold, Ye Golden Gates of Heaven.

Un-fold, un-fold, ye gold-en gates of heav-en, She comes the Queen of all the shin-ing host, The moon be-neath, her crown twelve stars of ev-en, The sun a-bove in her great glo-ry lost. *CHORUS.* The Cher-u-bim and Se-ra-phim and heaven's hosts now swell the glad re-frain, That Ma-ry lov'd Our Mother Ma-ry, Queen of Heaven shall reign, Queen of Heaven shall reign.

BLESSED VIRGIN MARY.

UNFOLD, UNFOLD, YE GOLDEN GATES OF HEAVEN—CONTINUED.

2   Behold her Son, delighted has gone down
    To meet His Mother, taintless from her birth,
    She forward glides, while glory from her crown
    Streams on her exiled children here on earth.

3   Mother of Jesus, hail our heavenly Queen,
    Ten thousand harps swell thro' the azure dome,
    O blessed Earth where one so fair was seen
    More blessed Heav'n, to which our Queen has come.

4   Hail Mary, Queen of mercy, grant our Lord
    May look with pity on thy children here,
    That humbly trusting in His holy word,
    Our souls at last may in thy courts appear.

5   Obtain for us thy rare humility,
    That every act may spring from God's pure Love,
    Then all thy glory we may hope to see,
    Where he assumed thee in His home above.

79—Mother Dear, O Pray For Me.

1 Mother dear, O pray for me! Whilst far from heav'n and thee I wander in a fragile bark, O'er life's tempestuous sea, O

BLESSED VIRGIN MARY. 161

MOTHER DEAR, O PRAY FOR ME—Continued.

Vir-gin Mo-ther, from thy throne, So bright in bliss a-bove, Pro-tect thy child and cheer my path, With thy sweet smile of love.

CHORUS

Mo-ther dear, re-mem-ber me, And nev-er cease thy care, Till in heaven e-ter-nal-ly, Thy love and bliss I share.

2 Mother dear, O pray for me!
   Should pleasure's siren lay,
   E'er tempt thy child to wander far
   From Virtue's path away.
   When thorns beset life's devious way,
   And darkling waters flow,
   Then, Mary, aid thy weeping child,
   Thyself a mother show.

3 Mother dear, O pray for me!
   When all looks bright and fair,
   That I may all my danger see,
   For surely then 'tis near.
   A mother's pray'r how much we need
   If prosp'rous be the ray
   That paints with gold the flow'ry mead,
   Which blossoms in our way.

80—Daughter of a Mighty Father.

1 Daughter of a mighty Father, Maiden patron of the May, Angel forms around thee gather: Macula non est in te. Macula non est in te, Macula non est in te, Macula, non est in te, Macula non est in te.

2 Mother of the Son and Saviour,
Of the Truth, the Life, the Way,
Guide our footsteps, calm our passions.

3 Spouse of the Eternal Spirit,
Blossom which will ne'er decay,
Let us but thy love inherit.

4 Daughter, Mother, Spouse of Heaven,
Listen to our earnest lay,
Sweetest gift to man e'er given.

BLESSED VIRGIN MARY. 163

81—Ave Sanctissima.

1 A - ve Sanc-tis-si-ma, We lift our souls to thee,
2 A - ve Sanc-tis-si-ma, List to thy child-ren's pray'r,

O - ra pro no - bis! 'Tis night-fall on the sea.
Au - di Ma - ri - a! And take us to thy care.

Watch us while sha-dows lie Far o'er the wa-ter spread,
O thou whose vir-tues shine With bright-est pu - ri - ty,

Hear the heart's lone-ly sigh, Thine too hath bled.
Come and each thought re-fine, Till pure like thine.

Thou that hast look'd on death, Aid us when death is near;
O save our souls from ill; Guard thou our lives from fear,

BLESSED VIRGIN MARY.

AVE SANCTISSIMA—Continued.

Whisper of heav'n to faith }
Our hearts with pleasure fill. } Sweet Mother, sweet Mother, hear.

CHORUS.

O ra pro no-bis, The wave must rock our sleep,

O ra Ma-ter, O ra, star of the deep.

82 -O Dearest Mother Of Mercy.

CHORUS.

O dear-est Mo ther of mer cy, Gen-tle and Ho-ly

Queen, Beau-ty bright and se rene, O may we one day in

BLESSED VIRGIN MARY.

O DEAREST MOTHER OF MERCY—Continued.

glo - ry, Bless-ed Mo - ther of grace, Be-hold thy most sweet face, Be-hold thy most sweet face, Be-hold thy most sweet face.

Fine. **SOLO.**

1 All hail our ad - mi - ra - ble Mo - ther, Let an-gels and men sing her praise: None af-ter Je - sus is a - bove her, For her should be the sweetest lays.

D. C. al fine.

2 Protect and hear us, gentlest Mary,
From on high hear our humble cries
On us that mourn and weep in mis'ry,
O turn thy mercy's tender eyes.

3 O clement, sweet and pious Mary,
O thou of whom our Lord was born,
Show us thy Son to make us happy,
When life at last is from us torn.

83 – Mother Mary, At Thine Altar.

Andante.

1. Mother Mary at thine altar We thy loving children kneel; With a faith that cannot falter To thy goodness we appeal. We are seeking for a Mother O'er the earth so waste and wide; And from off the Cross our Brother Points to Mary by His side.

2. Thou wilt love us, thou wilt guide us
With a mother's fondest care;
And our Father, God above us,
Bids us fly for refuge there.
Life's temptations are before us,
We must mingle in the strife;
If thy fondness watch not o'er us,
All unsafe will be our life.

3. So we take thee for our Mother
And we claim the right to be
By the gift of our dear Brother,
Loving children unto thee;
And our humble consecration,
Thou wilt surely not despise,
From thy high and lofty station
Close to Jesus in the skies.

4. Mother Mary, to thy keeping
We ourselves to thee confide,
Toiling, resting, waking, sleeping,
To be ever at thy side.
Cares that vex us, joys that please us,
Life and death we trust to thee;
Thou wilt make them all for Jesus.
And for all eternity.

84—Heart Of Mary, Heart The Purest.

1 Heart of Ma - ry, heart the pur - est, Ev - er shrin'd in mor - tal frame;
Blest a - sy - lum who se - cur - est, All who thy pro - tec - tion claim,
Blest a - sy - lum who se - cur - est, All who thy pro - tec - tion claim.

2 Hear the prayer of one whose weakness
Most demands a Mother's care;
One to whom thy looks, all meekness,
Counsel hope forbid despair'.

3 Round me tempests gath'ring lower.
As I tread life's desert way
And a foe in matchless power,
Marks me for his destined prey.

4 To some spot where ne'er might hover
Danger's shadow, I would flee;
But, ah! where that spot discover,
Where, ah! Mary, but in thee?

85—The Star Of The Ocean Is Risen.

1 The Star of the o - cean is ris - - - en, And
2 Ah! what is this Plan - et so beam - - ing, That
3 Oh! Star of the sea do il - lu - - - mine My

BLESSED VIRGIN MARY.

THE STAR OF THE OCEAN IS RISEN—Continued.

sweet - ly re-flects on the tide;...... Yon bark with a swift gale is
near it the rest die a - way,...... With heav - en - ly lus - tre is
course with this bril-liant ray;...... In thy flame past er - rors con -

driv - - en, And soon it shall reach the green side,........
stream - ing, And chang - es our night in - to day?........
sum - ing, Ah, teach me from thee ne'er to stray.......

To which the bright star seemed to guide it, As
This beau - ti - ful Plan - et is Ma - ry, Who
Thus, thus shall I reach to the hav - en, Where

in - to a hav - en of rest,... Where the wind and the tem - pest that
shines o'er her mar - in - ers here,... Her light is their sure guide to
thy bark just low - ered her sail,.. There en - ter the port - als of

BLESSED VIRGIN MARY.

THE STAR OF THE OCEAN IS RISEN—Continued.

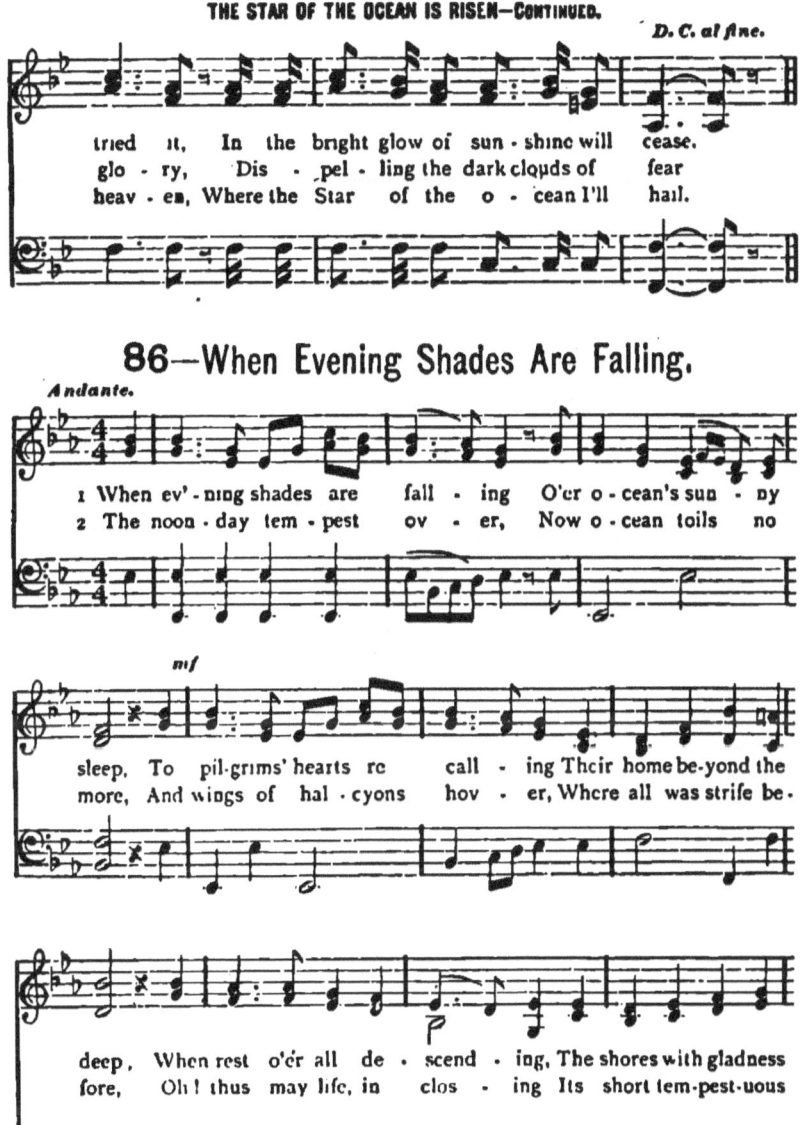

tried it, In the bright glow of sun-shine will cease.
glo-ry, Dis-pel-ling the dark clouds of fear
heav-en, Where the Star of the o-cean I'll hail.

86—When Evening Shades Are Falling.

Andante.

1 When ev'-ning shades are fall-ing O'er o-cean's sun-ny
sleep, To pil-grims' hearts re-call-ing Their home be-yond the
deep, When rest o'er all de-scend-ing, The shores with gladness

2 The noon-day tem-pest ov-er, Now o-cean toils no
more, And wings of hal-cyons hov-er, Where all was strife before, Oh! thus may life, in clos-ing Its short tem-pest-uous

BLESSED VIRGIN MARY. 173

AS THE DEWY SHADES OF EVEN—Continued.

2 Thine own sinless heart was broken,
  Sorrow's sword had pierced its core,
Holy Mother, by that token,
  Now thy pity I implore.
CHORUS.
Queen of heaven, guard and guide me,
  Save my soul from dark despair,
In thy tender bosom hide me,
  Take me, Mother, to thy care.

3 Mother of my Infant Saviour,
  Spouse of God, my plaint, O hear;
Purest Virgin, gracious Matron,
  O relieve me by thy prayer.
CHORUS.
From thy happy seat in Zion,
  Light me through this dark abode,
Smile, oh! gently smile upon me,
  Tell my sorrows to my God.

89—It Is The Name Of Mary.

1 It is the name of Ma - - ry, Which we to-day proclaim: Come all ye Ma-ry's child - ren, To sing that love-ly name. 1 Come sing that name dear child - ren, It is your Mo-ther's own; U-nite your hearts and prais-es, And waft them to her throne.

BLESSED VIRGIN MARY.

IT IS THE NAME OF MARY—Continued.

2 A name of pow'r and sweetness,
　Her name to us so dear,
　A name of awe and grandeur,
　But grandeur free from fear.

3 Sweet name all strong, yet tender,
　That name we love so well,
　The joy of earth and heaven,
　The fear and dread of hell.

4 O name by which we triumph
　O'er hell's embattled foes,
　The victor's mead of glory,
　And solace in his woes.

5 Earth has no name so gentle,
　Nor heaven one so sweet,
　A balm to wounded feelings,
　Bright light to wayward feet.

6 The first word ever spoken
　By Jesus when a child,
　Was thy dear name, O Mother!
　He spoke it and He smiled.

7 O may thy name, dear Mother,
　On life's last fearful day,
　Be my last fervent prayer,
　Be all my hope and stay.

90—Hail, Queen Of The Heavens.

Allegretto.

1 Hail, Queen of the Heavens! Hail, Mistress of earth! Hail, Virgin most pure, Of immaculate birth! Clear Star of the morning in beauty enshrined, O Lady make speed to the help of mankind. Clear Star of the morning, in beauty en-

BLESSED VIRGIN MARY.

HAIL, QUEEN OF THE HEAVENS—Continued.

shrined, O Lady make speed to the help of mankind.

2 Hail, Mother most pure!
  Hail, Virgin renown'd,
  Hail, Queen with the stars,
  As a diadem crown'd
  Above all the angels
  In glory untold,
Standing next to the King in a vesture of
  gold.

3 O Mother of mercy!
  O Star of the wave.
  O Hope of the guilty!
  O Light of the grave!

Thro' thee may we come,
  To the Heaven of rest,
  And see Heaven's King in the courts of
    the blest.

4 These praises and prayers
  I lay at thy feet!
  O Virgin of virgins!
  O Mary most sweet!
  Be thou my true guide
  Thro' this pilgrimage here,
  And stand by my side when death draw-
    eth near.

91—Thro' The World Thy Children Raise.

Words by A. PROCTER. Music by S. N. D.
SOLO.

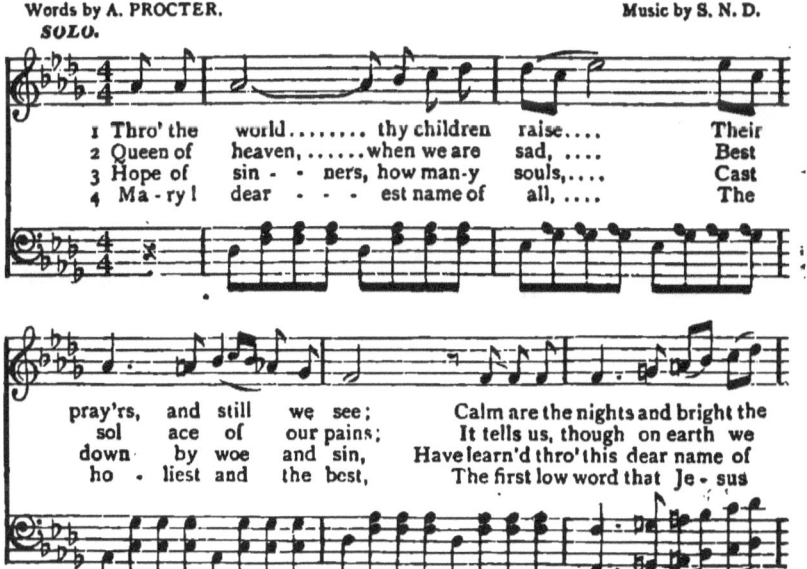

1 Thro' the world........ thy children raise....   Their
2 Queen of heaven,......when we are sad, ...   Best
3 Hope of sin - - ners, how many souls,....   Cast
4 Ma-ry! dear - - - est name of all, ...   The

pray'rs, and still we see;   Calm are the nights and bright the
sol   ace of our pains;   It tells us, though on earth we
down by woe and sin,   Have learn'd thro' this dear name of
ho - liest and the best,   The first low word that Je-sus

BLESSED VIRGIN MARY

THRO' THE WORLD THY CHILDREN RAISE—CONTINUED.

days, Of those who trust in thee.
toil, Our Mo - ther lives and reigns.
thine, A par-don and peace to win.
lisped, Laid on His Mo - ther's breast.

CHORUS. *Animato ad lib.*

Star of the sea, we kneel and pray, When tem - pests raise their voice, Star of the sea, ... the haven reached, We call thee, we call thee and rejoice, Star of the sea, Star of the sea.

92—Mother Dearest, Mother Fairest.

2 Lady, help in pain and sorrow,
　Soothe those rack'd on beds of pain,
　May the golden light of morrow,
　Bring them health and joy again.

3 Help our priests, our virgins holy,
　Help our Pope, long may he reign,
　Pray that we who sing thy praises,
　May in heav'n all meet again.

BLESSED VIRGIN MARY.

93—Mary, Dearest Mother.

1 Mary, dearest Mother, From thy heavenly height
Look on us thy children, Lost in earth's dark night.

CHORUS.

Oh we pray thee lov'd Mary, Mary, fondly we entreat,
Guide us to our sweet Saviour, And leave us at His feet.

Mary, shield us from danger, Keep our souls from sin,

BLESSED VIRGIN MARY.

MARY, DEAREST MOTHER—Continued.

Help thy ex-iled chil-dren, Heav'n at last to win.

2 Oh! we love thee, Mary,
Trusting all to thee;
What is past or present,
What is yet to be.

3 Mother of our Saviour,
Hear our pleading prayer
Take us 'neath thy mantle,
Hide, oh, hide us there.

94—O Heart Of Mary, Pure And Fair

Andante espressivo

1 O heart of Ma-ry, pure and fair, There is no stain in thee; In A - - dam's fall thou hast no share,...... From sin's con-trol thou'rt free.

2 As some fair li - ly midst the thorns, Thou 'mongst Eve's daughters art; Ce - les - tial pur-i-ty a - dorns...... Thy crys-tal depths, chaste heart.

3 Sweet heart, within thy depth so chaste, We'll dwell and ne'er de - part, Till thou our souls hast deeply placed...... In Je - sus' Sa - cred Heart.

4 And when from thy loved heart we'll go, To that of thy dear Son, O shall we leave thee then? Ah, no,...... His Heart and thine are one.

CHORUS.

O heart of Ma-ry, pure and

BLESSED VIRGIN MARY.

O HEART OF MARY, PURE AND FAIR—*Continued.*

fair,........ No beau-ty can with thine compare; From ev'-ry stain of sin thou'rt free; O make us pure in heart like thee.

95—O Mother, Loved.

1. O Mother, loved, Our sweet delight, One glance but cast, So fondly bright.

Watch over us,......watch over us. Watch over us, Watch-over

BLESSED VIRGIN MARY 181

O MOTHER, LOVED—*Continued.*

2 Be love of thee, my whole life long,
My sweetest joy, my only way.
 ||: Watch over us. :||
Shine then brightly, O soft Star,
With thy light driving far
Mists that oft veil my soul,
Clouds that e'er around me roll.

3 Mother of God! our hope, our life,—
Sweet Mother, shield us in the strife.
 ||: Watch over us. :||
From all earthly toils set free,
We'll quickly fly to thee;
Let us rest in thy heart:
From its depths we'll ne'er depart

96—Come Gather Round The Altar.

BLESSED VIRGIN MARY.

COME, GATHER ROUND THE ALTAR—CONTINUED.

2 See, nature has donned all her gayest,
   To greet our Mother Queen,
   And flowers the brightest and fairest,
   Mary's children for her glean.

3 The soft blushing roses are trembling,
   With longings to be placed
   On our Mother's altar impatient
   For her, their soft fragrance to waste

4 Then Mary, our Queen and our Mother,
   Accept the hearts we bring,
   And all through life's stormiest weather,
   Grant that to thee we may cling.

97—Look Down O Mother Mary.

BLESSED VIRGIN MARY.

LOOK DOWN O MOTHER MARY—Continued.

Solo

2 See how ungrateful sinners
We stand before thy Son,
His loving Heart upbraids us
For the evil we have done.

3 Our sins make us unworthy
That title still to bear,
But thou art our Mother
Then show thy love and care.

4 O kindest, dearest Mother,
Thy sinful children save,
Look on us with pity.
Who thy protection crave.

98—Hail, Holy Queen, Loved Mother To Thee.

DUET

1 Hail, holy Queen! loved Mother, to thee We weak erring mortals in safety can flee; O'er sin and temptation salvation is won, Thou interceding with Jesus thy

2 Sweet bells are pealing thro' eve's rosy air, Sancta Regina, oh, list to our prayer; Falling night's shadows o'er valley and sea, Bright Star of evening, our tho'ts turn to

3 Like the lone star whose bright beaming ray Guided the sages their devious way, Where on thy bosom was nestled the dove, While angels rejoicing smiled from a-

BLESSED VIRGIN MARY. 187

AVE MARIA, GUARDIAN DEAR—CONTINUED.

2 Mother, taintless, undefiled
   Sinless let our slumbers be,
   Mother of the sinless Child
   Hear the prayer we raise to thee.

3 Thou hast made our desert bloom;
   Mary deign to hear our prayer;
   If to-night we seek the tomb,
   Shine upon the desert there.

100—Sweet Lady Of The Sacred Heart.

1. Sweet Lady of the Sacred Heart, Thy peerless Virgin charms Moved Jesus from His heav'nly throne To rest within thine arms,

CHORUS.
Jesus from His heav'nly throne, To rest within thine arms Sweet Lady, Sweet Lady, Sweet Lady of the Sacred Heart

2. Sweet Lady of the Sacred Heart,
What joy thy bosom filled,
When close to thine thy Infant's Heart,
In gentle pulses thrilled

3. Sweet Lady of the Sacred Heart,
From Jesus' open side,
On thee the water and the Blood
Flowed as a saving tide

4. Sweet Lady of the Sacred Heart,
Proclaim thy power above,
From Jesus' wounds send piercing darts,
Transfix our souls with love.

BLESSED VIRGIN MARY.

101—Holy Mary, Mother Mild.

1 Holy Mary, Mother mild, O, sweet, sweet Mother! Hear, O hear thy feeble child, O, sweet, sweet Mother! O, exult ye Cherubim! And rejoice ye Seraphim! Praise her! praise her! O praise our spotless Mother!

2 Tossed on life's tempestuous sea,
O, sweet, sweet Mother!
Cast thy tender eyes on me,
O, sweet, sweet Mother!

3 Brightest in the courts above,
O, sweet, sweet Mother!
Joy of angels, Queen of love,
O, sweet, sweet Mother!

4 Maiden Mother! hear my prayer
O, sweet, sweet Mother!
Prove to us thy loving care
O, sweet, sweet Mother!

102—Hail, Queen Of Heaven, The Ocean Star.

1. Hail, Queen of heav'n, the ocean Star, Guide of the wand'rer here below! Thrown on life's surge we claim thy care, Save us from peril and from woe, Mother of Christ, Star of the sea, Pray for the wanderer, Pray for me!

2. O gentle, chaste, and spotless Maid,
We sinners make our prayers thro' thee
Remind thy Son that He has paid
The price of our iniquity,
Virgin most pure, Star of the sea,
Pray for the sinner, O pray for me!

3. Sojourners in this vale of tears,
To thee, blest Advocate, we cry,
Pity our sorrows, calm our fears,
And soothe with hope our misery
Refuge in grief, Star of the sea,
Pray for the mourner, O pray for me!

4. And while to Him who reigns above,
In God-head one, in persons Three,
The source of life, of grace, of love,
Homage we pay on bended knee,
Do thou bright Queen, Star of the sea,
Pray for thy children, pray for me!

103 — O Mother, I Could Weep For Mirth

1 O Mother, I could weep for mirth, Joy fills my heart so fast; My soul to-day is heav'n on earth; Oh! could the transport last! I think of thee and what thou art, Thy majesty, thy state; And I keep singing in my heart, Immaculate, Immaculate.

2 It is this thought to-day that lifts
My happy heart to heaven,
That for our sakes thy choicest gifts
To thee, dear Queen, were given.

3 The angels answer with their songs,
Bright choirs in gleaming rows;
And saints flock round thy feet in throngs,
And heaven with bliss o'erflows.

4 Immaculate Conception! far
Above all graces blest,
Thou shinest like a royal Star
On God's eternal breast!

5 Oh! I would rather, Mother dear,
Thou shouldst be what thou art;
Than sit where thou dost, oh! so near
Unto the Sacred Heart.

BLESSED VIRGIN MARY.

104—Children Of Mary, High Your Voices Raise.

1. Child-ren of Ma-ry, high your voic-es raise,......
   Ye on...... whom she.... casts a ten-der eye;....
   Child-ren of God,... sing her im-mor-tal praise,....
   And all ex-alt her glo-ry to...... the sky........

2. I see as-cend-ing to her glo-rious throne, ...
   The fer-vent prayers of .... ev'-ry faith-ful child;..
   Each heart e-rects an al-tar to her name ....
   Where Ma-ry lives in ev-er-last--ing fame ...

CHORUS.

Chil-dren of Ma-ry, high your voic-es raise,..

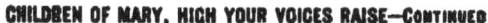

CHILDREN OF MARY, HIGH YOUR VOICES RAISE—CONTINUED

Children of God, sing.... her im-mor-tal praise.

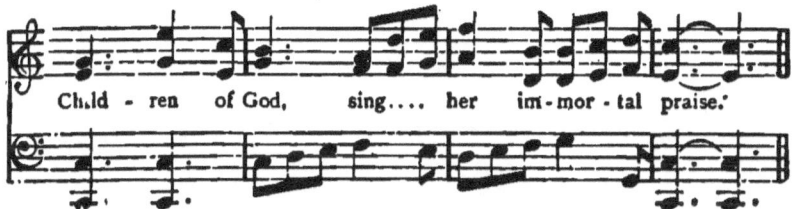

2 I see ascending to her glorious throne,
The fervent prayers of every faithful child;
Each heart erects an altar to her name,
Where Mary lives in everlasting fame,

105—Bring Flowers Of The Rarest.

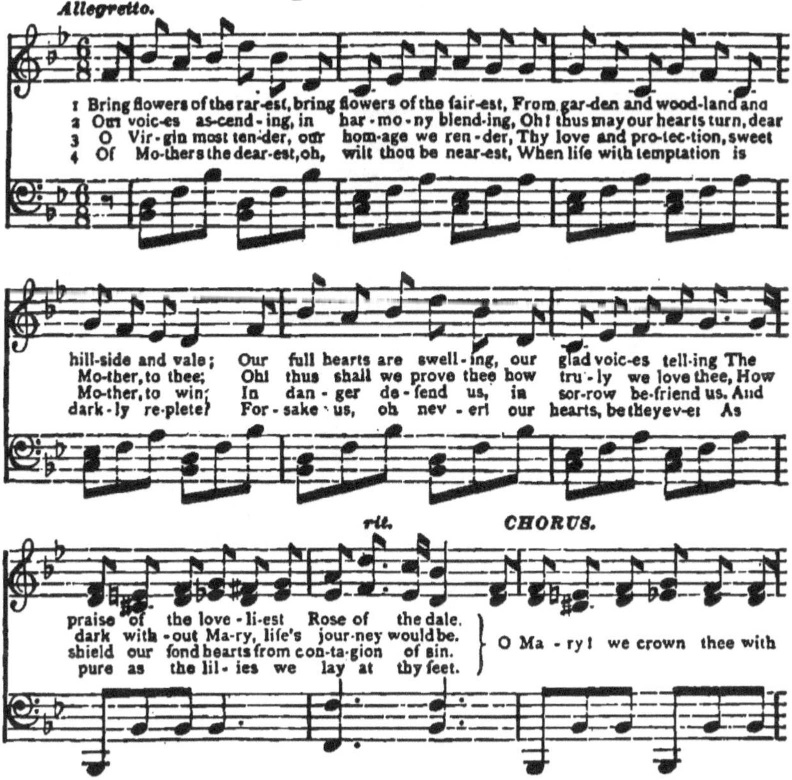
Allegretto.
1 Bring flowers of the rar-est, bring flowers of the fair-est, From gar-den and wood-land and hill-side and vale; Our full hearts are swell-ing, our glad voic-es tell-ing The praise of the love-li-est Rose of the dale.
2 Our voic-es as-cend-ing, in har-mo-ny blend-ing, Oh! thus may our hearts turn, dear Mo-ther, to thee; Oh! thus shall we prove thee how tru-ly we love thee, How dark with-out Ma-ry, life's jour-ney would be.
3 O Vir-gin most ten-der, our hom-age we ren-der, Thy love and pro-tec-tion, sweet Mo-ther, to win; In dan-ger de-fend us, in sor-row be-friend us, And shield our fond hearts from con-ta-gion of sin.
4 Of Mo-thers the dear-est, oh, wilt thou be near-est, When life with temptation is dark-ly replete? For-sake us, oh nev-er! our hearts, be they ev-er As pure as the lil-ies we lay at thy feet.
rit.
CHORUS.
O Ma-ry! we crown thee with

BLESSED VIRGIN MARY.

107—Bright Mother Of Our Maker, Hail.

1 Bright Mother of our Maker, hail! Thou Virgin ever blest; The ocean's Star by which we sail, And gain the port of rest. 2 While we this A-ve thus to thee From Gabriel's mouth rehearse, Prevail that peace our lot may be, And E-va's name reverse.

3 Release our long entangled mind
   From all the snares of ill;
With heavenly light instruct the blind,
   And all our vows fulfil.

4 Exert for us a Mother's care,
   And us thy children own:
Prevail with Him to hear our prayer,
   Who chose to be thy Son.

5 O spotless Maid! whose virtues shine
   With brightest purity,
Each action of our lives refine,
   And make us pure like thee.

BLESSED VIRGIN MARY.

108—Wilt Thou Look Upon Me, Mother.

2 Wilt thou, Mother, hover ever
   On my pathway still to guide,
   Wilt thou whisper kind directions
   To the angel by my side?
3 Wilt thou pray for me to Jesus,
   That His will I e'er may know;

Wilt thou tell me then His pleasure
   That I e'er may to it bow?
4 Oh then Mother, I petition,
   And I know thy aid will come;
   Angels praise thee for it, Mother,
   In thy everlasting home.

BLESSED VIRGIN MARY.

109—Rose Of The Cross.

2 A wanderer here, thro' many a wild—
  Where few their way can see—
||: Bloom with thy fragrance on thy child,
  O Mary! remember me. :||

3 Let me but stand where thou hast stood,
  Beside the crimson tree;
||: And by the water and the Blood,
  O Mary! remember me. :||

4 There let me wash my sinful soul,
  And be from sin set free,
||: Drawn by thy love, by grace made whole;
  O Mary! remember me. :||

110—The Clouds Hang Thick O'er Israel's Camp.

BLESSED VIRGIN MARY.

THE CLOUDS HANG THICK O'ER ISRAEL'S CAMP—*Continued.*

2. The weapon which our Father gave
  Each hand shall fearless wield;
 Who bear our Lady's Rosary
  Need neither sword nor shield:
 With dauntless faith the ranks they face
  Of error and of sin,
 And, armed with those blest beads alone,
  The victory they win.

3. See o'er Lepanto's waters spread
  The Moslem's dark array;
 A voice to Christendom went forth,
  And gave the word to pray:

Jesus and Mary! names of strength
 Invoked, and not in vain;
They conquered in the hour of need,
 And conquer shall again.

4. As Pius then to Europe spake,
  So Leo speaks once more;
 The rosary our weapon still,
  To wield in holy war:
 Ave Maria! from each tongue
  Shall rise the pleading word;
 Oh! doubt not that the prayer of faith
  Will now, as then, be heard.

111—Mother Mary, Queen Most Sweet.

BLESSED VIRGIN MARY.

MOTHER MARY, QUEEN MOST SWEET—*Continued.*

Solo

2 Sweetest Mary, bend thine ear,
   Thou my own dear Mother art,
||: Therefore shall thy name be dear,
   Never from my lips depart. :||

3 When the demon hosts invade,
   When the tempest rages high,
||: Crying "Mary, Mother, aid,"
   I will make temptation fly. :||

4 Mother, Mary, Queen most sweet,
   When the hour of death draws nigh
||: Help me, Mary, to repeat
   Thy dear name and then to die. :||

BLESSED VIRGIN MARY.

112—O Sanctissima, O Piissima.

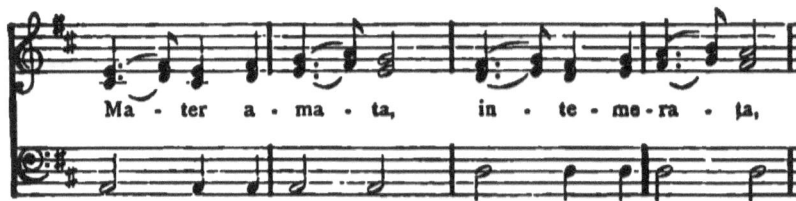

2 Tota pulchra es, O Maria,
  Et macula non est in te;
  Mater amata, intemerata,
  Ora, ora pro nobis.

3 Sicut lilium, inter spinas,
  Sic Maria inter filias.
  Mater amata, intemerata,
  Ora, ora pro nobis.

4 In miseria, in angustia,
  Ora Virgo, pro nobis.
  Pro nobis ora, in mortis hora.
  Ora, ora pro nobis.

BLESSED VIRGIN MARY.

113—O Mother Blest.

2 O heavenly Mother, Mistress, sweet,
   It never yet was told
   That suppliant sinner left thy feet
   Unpitied, unconsoled.

3 O Mother pitiful and mild,
   Cease not to pray for me:
   For I do love thee as a child,
   And sigh for love of thee.

4 Most pow'rful Mother, all men know
   Thy Son denies thee nought;
   Thou askest, wishest it, and lo!
   His power thy will has wrought.

5 O Mother blest, for me obtain,
   Ungrateful though I be,
   To love that God who first could deign
   To show such love to me.

BLESSED VIRGIN MARY.

114 – As The Gentle Spring Uncloses.

SOLO. Andante.

1 As the gentle Spring uncloses' And the winter fades away, Sunlight glistens, lilies blow, As we greet the month of May; As we hail its peerless Queen, Mary, Mother of delight, In her own especial season, Sing her

AS THE GENTLE SPRING UNCLOSES—Continued.

CHORUS.

praise from morn till night. Ma-ry, Mother sweet, Mary, Mother fair, Virgin Queen of May, hear our prayer. Un-to Je-sus pray, that each day, We may grow like thee, Our Queen of May.

2 May is Mary's—she is ours—
　Thus the month is doubly dear,
　As we crown her with our flowers,
　Angels gladly hover near,
　And the blessed Jesus smiles
　On each humble votary,
　And our homage to His Mother
　Will requite most graciously.

3 Dearest Mother! we remember
　How, at one request of thine,
　Jesus at the marriage feast
　Changed the water into wine;
　At our feast, Ah! let the flood
　Of our tears thy pity move,
　Beg, oh! beg thy Son to change it
　To the wine of perfect love.

4 Take us all 'neath thy protection,
　Heart and soul and senses take!
　Tell dear Jesus we are thine,
　And He'll bless us for thy sake,
　And the treasures of our Mary
　Up in heaven we shall store,
　Naught shall steal them, naught corrode them,
　They shall last for evermore.

BLESSED VIRGIN MARY.

115 — On this Day, O Beautiful Mother.

2 Queen of angels deign to hear,
Lisping children's humble pray'r;
Young hearts gain, O Virgin pure,
Sweetly to thyself allure.

3 Rose of Sharon, lovely flow'r,
Beauteous bud of Eden's bow'r;
Cherished lily of the vale,
Virgin Mother, Queen we hail.

4 In vain the flow'rs of love we bring,
In vain sweet music's note we sing,
If contrite heart and lowly prayer,
Guide not our gifts to thy bright sphere.

5 Fast our days of life we run,
Soon the night of death will come;
Tower of strength in that dread hour,
Come with all thy gentle power.

116—To Love Thee, O Mary.

To love thee, O Mary! Is our only joy,
Mother pure, thy glory Shall our lips employ.
1 See! the storm is raging, Clouds above us lower,
All our thoughts engaging— Save us by thy power.

2 Gloomy clouds above us
  Hide thee from our eyes;
  Let us feel thou lov'st us—
  Brighten now our skies.

3 Thy sweet light brings gladness,
  Gentle Star of morn;
  Take from earth its sadness—
  Darkest skies adorn.

BLESSED VIRGIN MARY.

117—O! When Shall We With Angels Bright.

2 O! if 'tis now so sweet to love,
   And oft to breathe thy holy name,
What will it be in realms above—
   Where seraphs' ardour hearts inflame?

3 But hark! a voice from starry skies,
   Those gentler tones our hearts will know

Our Mother loved has heard our sighs,
   She sees us languish here below.
4 Her children there she'll kindly cheer,
   She'll fold them in her fond embrace;
From ev'ry eye she'll wipe the tear,
   And from sad hearts all sorrow chase.

118—Hail! All Hail, Sweet Notre Dame De Lourdes.

2 Blessed thou above all others,
  Mary, Mistress of the spheres,
  Star of hope serenely beaming
  Through this darksome vale of tears,

3 Happy angels joy to own thee,
  O'er their choirs exalted high,
  Thron'd in blissful light and beauty
  Empress of the starry sky.

BLESSED VIRGIN MARY.

119—Hail, Rose of Mystic Beauty.

Hail, Rose of Mys-tic beauty! Bright flower in heaven's field, Far sweeter is thy fragrance Than earthly flowers can yield. Of creatures thou art purest, None love-li-er can there be, All heaven resounds with prais-es, Sweet Mystic Rose, to thee.

2 Within Thee, peerless flower,
Did Jesus once repose,
For Thou alone art worthy
To be His Mystic Rose.
Too pure for this world's garden,
Sweet Rose of priceless worth,
From Heaven God sent His angels,
Who took Thee from the earth.

3 Enraptured with Thy beauty,
My soul with love o'erflows;
I long to be in heaven
With Thee, sweet Mystic Rose.
O Mary, Rose of Heaven!
Hear Thou our earnest prayer;
Protect us all from danger
And take us to Thy care.

120—Mary! How Sweetly Falls That Word.

Andantino.

1. Mary! How sweet-ly falls that word On my en-raptured ear!...... Oft do I breathe in ac-cents low, That sound when none are near........

CHORUS. *Animato.*

Sing, O my lips, and loud-ly pro-claim: O Ma-ry, O Ma-ry, how sweet is thy name!

BLESSED VIRGIN MARY.

MARY! HOW SWEETLY FALLS THAT WORD—Continued.

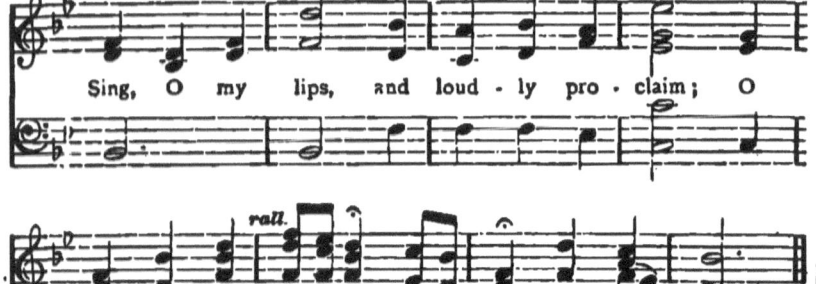

2 Sweet as the warbling of a bird,
Sweet as a mother's voice;
So sweet to me is that dear name,
It makes my soul rejoice.

3 Bright as the glittering stars appear,
Bright as the moonbeams shine,

So bright in my mind's eye is seen
Thy loveliness divine!

4 Through thee I offer my requests,
And when my prayer is done,
In ecstasy sublime I see
Thee seated near thy Son.

121 — The Sun Is Shining Brightly.

1 The sun is shin-ing bright-ly, The trees are clothed with green. The beauteous bloom of flow-ers On ev'-ry side is there,
2 There's mu-sic in the heav-ens, For birds are sing-ing And na-ture's songs and prais-es Are sounding through the
3 And when night clos-es o'er us, And twink-ling stars ap-pear; The chaste moon calm-ly reign-eth, In skies so bright and

BLESSED VIRGIN MARY.

122—Ave Maria, Bright and Pure.

1. A-ve Maria! bright and pure, Hear, O hear me when I pray; Pains and pleasures try the pilgrim On his long and dreary way; Fears and perils are around me. A-ve Maria, bright and pure, O-ra pro me, O-ra pro me.

2 Ave Maria, Queen of heaven,
Teach, O teach me to obey;
Lead me on through fierce temptations,
Stand and meet me in the way.
When I fail and faint, my Mother,
Ave Maria, bright and pure, Ora pro me,
Ora pro me.

3 Then shall I, if Thou, O Mary,
Art my strong support and stay,
Fear nor feel the three-fold danger,
Standing forth in dread array.

Now and ever shield and guard me,
Ave Maria, bright and pure, Ora pro me,
Ora pro me.

4 When my eyes are slowly closing,
And I fade from earth away,
And when Death, the stern destroyer,
Claims my body as his prey,
Claims my soul, O then, sweet Mary,
Ave Maria, bright and pure. Ora pro me,
Ora pro me.

123 — O Mary, Dear Mother, How Fondly I Flee.

1. O Mary, dear Mother, how fondly I flee
In dark hours of peril, sweet Refuge, to thee!
When danger is greatest, the world most unkind,
My safety, my solace, beside thee I find.

2. In thy blessed keeping my soul is secure,
Though foes gather round to affright or allure,
I fear not the devil, his might nor his charms,
When cheered by thy presence, upheld by thy arms.

3. I fear not the wicked, their weapons, their skill;
I fear not the world, let it rage as it will;
I fear not my passions, though wayward and wild,
If thou, Help of Christians, wilt shelter thy child.

4. In moments of sorrow, in anguish of heart,
In pain, in affliction, my comfort thou art;
When coldly repulsed and abandoned by all,
Thou still standeth by me, thou hearest my call.

5. O, help me in life, in its work and its woes,
To carry my crosses, to conquer my foes!
O, help me in death, that my soul be set free
To fly unto Jesus, thy Son, and to thee.

ST. JOSEPH. 217

HOLY PATRON! THEE SALUTING—*Continued.*

of man-kind; Hear thy chil-dren thee im-plor-ing, May we thy pro-tec-tion find.

125—Joseph, Pure Spouse.

1. Jo-seph, pure spouse of that im-mor-tal bride
Who shines in ev-er vir-gin glo-ry bright,
Thy praise let all the earth re-echo-ing send

ST. JOSEPH.

JOSEPH, PURE SPOUSE—*Continued.*

Back to the realms, back to the realms, of light.

2 Thine arms embraced thy Maker newly born,
   With Him to Egypt's desert didst thou flee;
   Him in Jerusalem didst seek and find.
   Oh, day of joy; oh, day of joy to thee!

3 Not until after death their blissful crown
   Others obtain; but unto thee was given

In thine own lifetime to enjoy thy God,
As do the blest, as do the blest in heaven.

4 Grant us, great Trinity, for Joseph's sake,
   The heights of immortality to gain,
   There with glad tongues Thy praise to celebrate
   In one eternal, one eternal strain.

126—Holy Joseph, Dearest Father.

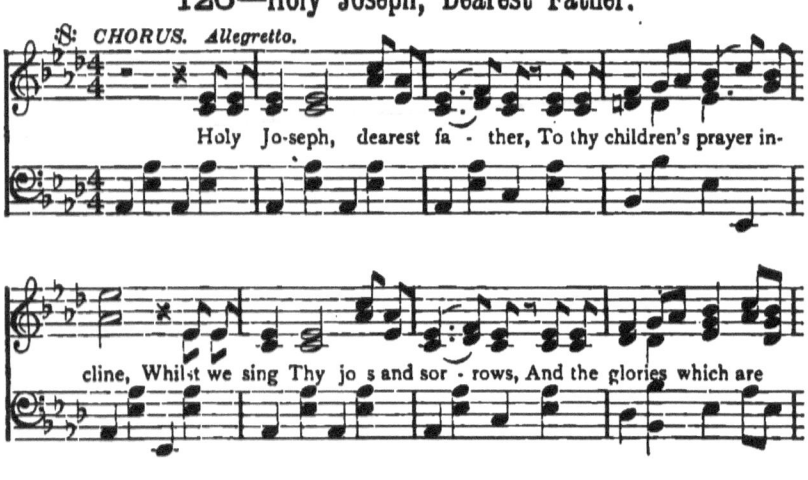

Holy Joseph, dearest father, To thy children's prayer incline, Whilst we sing Thy joys and sorrows, And the glories which are thine.

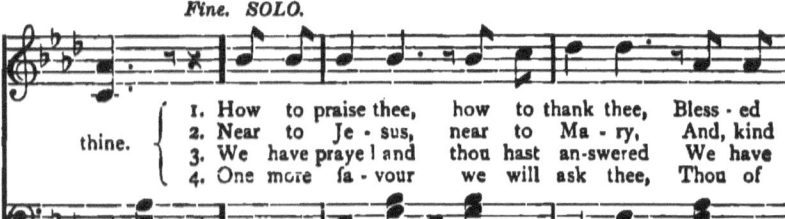

1. How to praise thee, how to thank thee, Bless-ed
2. Near to Jesus, near to Mary, And, kind
3. We have prayed and thou hast answered We have
4. One more favour we will ask thee, Thou of

ST. JOSEPH.   219

HOLY JOSEPH, DEAREST FATHER—*Continued.*

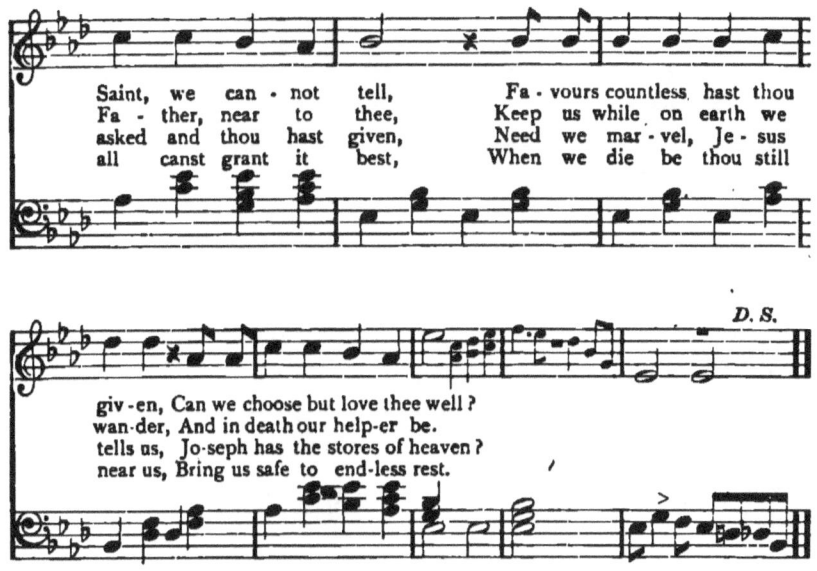

Saint, we can-not tell,   Fa-vours countless hast thou
Fa-ther, near to thee,   Keep us while on earth we
asked and thou hast given,   Need we mar-vel, Je-sus
all canst grant it best,   When we die be thou still

giv-en, Can we choose but love thee well?
wan-der, And in death our help-er be.
tells us, Jo-seph has the stores of heaven?
near us, Bring us safe to end-less rest.

127—With Tender Love.

Words with kind permission of J. FISCHER BROS.

1. With ten-der love we come to thee, Dear guide and friend, Saint Jo - seph; With heart and voi-ces joy - ous - ly, Our words of praise we

ST. JOSEPH.

WITH TENDER LOVE—*Continued.*

sing, Saint Joseph, dear, when life is dark, When waves of sin and sorrow

rise, Guide thou our frail and trembling bark, Safe to the port beyond the skies.

2 Kind Father, from thy throne above,
Look down upon thy children,
And help our wayward hearts to love
The hidden life so dear.

3 O favor'd Saint ; O lily fair,
That bloomed in fullest beauty,
Impart to us the perfume rare
Of thy humility.

128—Dear Guardian of Mary.

1. Dear Guardian of Mary! dear nurse of her child! Life's ways are full weary, the desert is
2. For thou to the pilgrim art father and guide, And Jesus and Mary felt safe at thy
3. O blessed Saint Joseph! how great was thy worth, The one chosen shadow of God up-on
4. When the treasures of God were unsheltered on earth, Safe keeping was found for them both in thy

ST. JOSEPH. 221

DEAR GUARDIAN OF MARY—Continued.

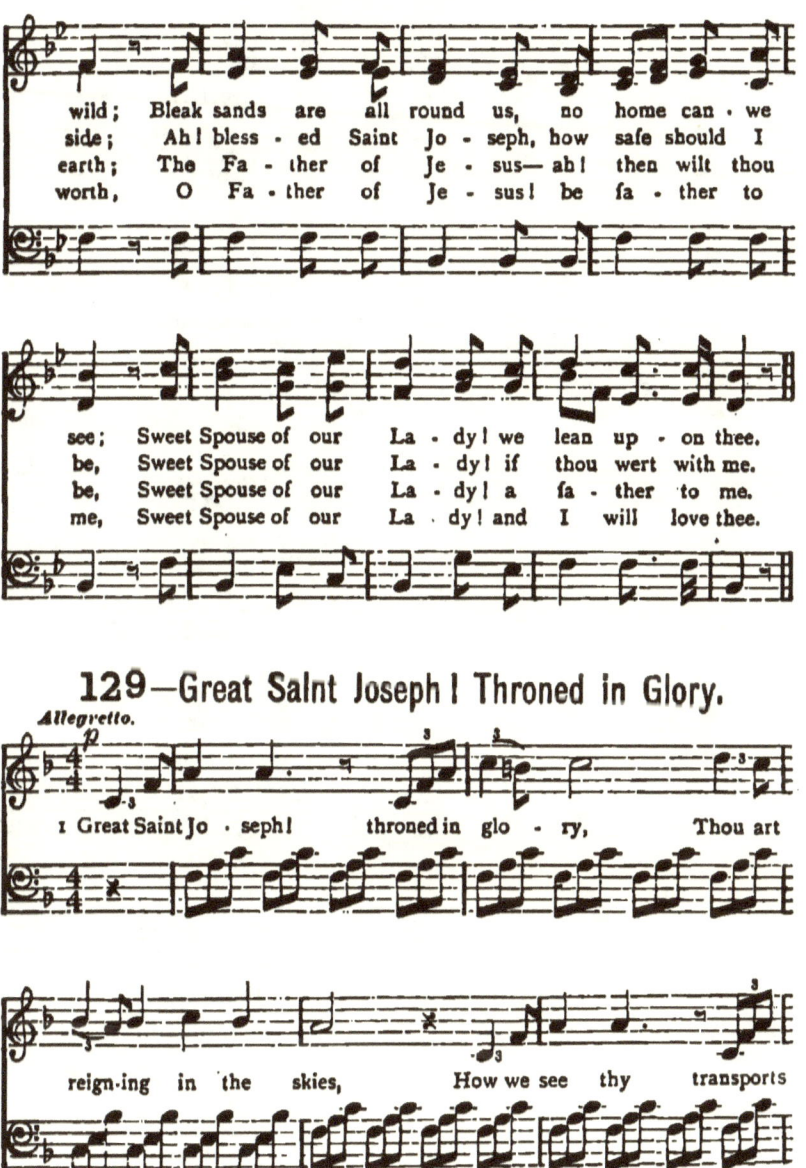

wild; Bleak sands are all round us, no home can we
side; Ah! bless-ed Saint Jo-seph, how safe should I
earth; The Fa-ther of Je-sus—ah! then wilt thou
worth, O Fa-ther of Je-sus! be fa-ther to

see; Sweet Spouse of our La-dy! we lean up-on thee.
be, Sweet Spouse of our La-dy! if thou wert with me.
be, Sweet Spouse of our La-dy! a fa-ther to me.
me, Sweet Spouse of our La-dy! and I will love thee.

129—Great Saint Joseph! Throned in Glory.

Allegretto.

1 Great Saint Jo-seph! throned in glo-ry, Thou art reign-ing in the skies, How we see thy transports

ST. JOSEPH.

GREAT SAINT JOSEPH! THRONED IN GLORY—Continued.

2 Thou wert as a shadow tender,
 Of the great Eternal One,
Shielding from the world's rude tempests,
 Mary, Mother of His Son.

3 Ah, when life's long scene is closing,
 Holy Patron then be nigh,
In that hour of bitter anguish,
 Teach, oh! teach us how to die.

ST. JOSEPH. 223

130—Great St. Joseph, Meek and Lowly.

Music and words by Sisters of Mercy,
St. Xavier's, Chicago, Ill.

Andante.

1. Great St. Jo-seph, meek and low - ly, Guardian of our Lord, All-ho - ly, Hail this glorious day, While our voic-es blithely sound - ing, Lov - ing hearts in rap - ture bound - ing, List our prayer to thee............ Make us ho - ly be.

2. Great St. Jo-seph, Christ-like, tend - er, Fos - ter-fath-er and de-fend - er Of our Heavenly King, Pa - tient, gen - tle, humble, fer - vent, Hap - py, si - lent, faith - ful serv - ant, Hear us while we pray............ Guard our souls this day.

ST. JOSEPH.

GREAT ST. JOSEPH, MEEK AND LOWLY—*Concluded*

high we raise, Thy glo-ries now we sing. Our hearts in praise, on
high we raise, Thy glo-ries now we sing, Saint
Jo-seph, dear-est saint, Saint Jo-seph, dear-est saint.

131—Dear St. Joseph,

Words set of "Visits to St. Joseph."   NAZARETH CONVENT, Rochester, N. Y.

Dear St. Jo-seph, oh, re-
Bring to me, my dear-est
Glori-ous Jo-seph, deign to

ST. ROSE OF LIMA.

132—First Flow'ret of the Desert.

ARR. BERTINI.

1. First flow'ret of the des-ert wild, Whose leaves the sweets of grace ex-hale, We greet thee, Lima's sainted child, Rose of A-mer-i-ca, all hail! When first appeared the in-fant smile Beam-ing up-on thy features meek, It seemed as if there blushed the while, The rose-bud on thy vir-gin cheek. We greet thee, sainted child, Rose of A-mer-i-ca, all hail! Li-ma's sainted child, Rose of A-mer-i-ca, all hail!

2. And once a-mid thy raptures prayer, Thy heavenly Spouse him-self came down, Most sweet-ly breathing in thy ear, "Rose of my heart, receive thy crown," And whilst a-mid His glo-ries now Thou seest Him face to face, O deign, St. Rose, to bear thy suppliants' vow, That grace and glo-ry we may gain.

ST. ANNE.

133—To Kneel At Thine Altar.

2 Of old when our fathers touch'd Canada's shore,
They named thee its Patron and Saint evermore.

3 To all who invoke thee thou lendest an ear,
Thou soothest the sorrows of all who draw near.

4 Saint Anne, we implore thee to list to our pray'r
In time of temptation, take us in thy care.

5 In this life obtain for us that which is best,
And bring us at length to our heavenly rest.

ST. ANNE. 229

134—O Lady High In Glory Raised.

O Lady high in glory raised, Whose daughter ever blest, ... The Sovereign of the skies hath laid On her maternal breast. 1 What we had lost in hapless Eve, Thy Virgin Child restores. Op'ning to us in Christ anew, The everlasting doors.

2 O gain celestial light and grace,
Dear heir of endless fame,
For us and all who memory keep
Of thy immortal name.

3 To Him, the Saviour of the world,
Whom Anna's daughter bore,
Be with the Sire and Paraclete
All glory evermore.

ST. PATRICK.

135—Hibernia's Champion Saint, All Hail!

B. S.

1. Hi-ber-nia's Champion Saint, all hail! With fadeless glo-ry crown'd; The off-spring of your ar-dent zeal, This day your praise shall sound.

CHORUS.

Great and glo-rious St. Pat-rick, Pray for that dear coun-try,

Great and glo-rious St. Pat-rick, Hearken to the pray'r of thy children.

2 Borne on the wings of charity,
 To Erin's coast you flew;
 Bade Satan from her valleys flee,
 And his dark shrines o'erthrew.

3 Wand'ring thro' error's gloomy night,
 Our sires did lose their way;
 You cheer'd their hearts with heavenly
 With truth's consoling ray. [light,

4 Sickness flies, his voice obeying,
 Sightless eyes behold the day,
 And the pow'r of God displaying,
 Death unwilling yields his prey.

5 Mortals, with amazement seeing
 Senseless idols prostrate fall,
 Own the author of their being,
 And proclaim Him Lord of all.

ST. PATRICK.

136—All Praise To Saint Patrick.

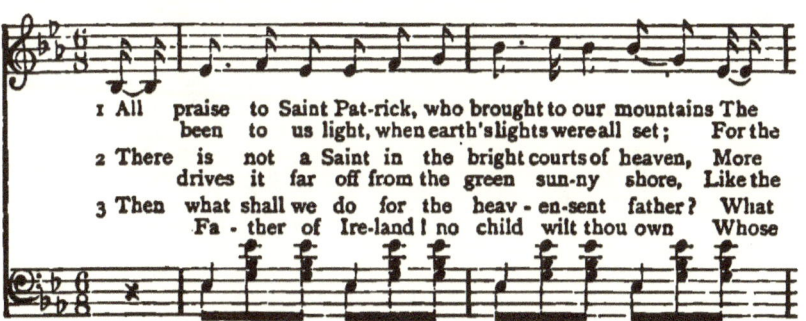

1 All praise to Saint Pat-rick, who brought to our mountains The
    been to us light, when earth's lights were all set; For the
2 There is not a Saint in the bright courts of heaven, More
    drives it far off from the green sun-ny shore, Like the
3 Then what shall we do for the heav-en-sent father? What
    Fa-ther of Ire-land! no child wilt thou own Whose

1 gift of God's faith, the sweet light of His love! All praise to the Shepherd who
    glo-ries of faith they can nev-er de-cay, And the best of our glories is
2 faith-ful than he to the land of his choice; Oh, well may the na-tion to
    rep-tiles that fled from his curse in dis-may, And Erin, when error's proud
3 shall the proof of our loy-al-ty be? By all that is dear to our
    life is not light-ed by grace on its way; For they are true Irish, ah

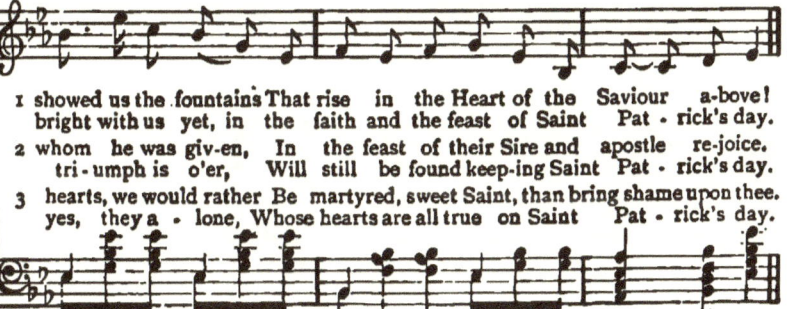

1 showed us the fountains That rise in the Heart of the Saviour a-bove!
    bright with us yet, in the faith and the feast of Saint Pat-rick's day.
2 whom he was giv-en, In the feast of their Sire and apostle re-joice.
    tri-umph is o'er, Will still be found keep-ing Saint Pat-rick's day.
3 hearts, we would rather Be martyred, sweet Saint, than bring shame upon thee.
    yes, they a-lone, Whose hearts are all true on Saint Pat-rick's day.

ST PATRICK

ALL PRAISE TO SAINT PATRICK--Continued.

For hundreds of years, In smiles and in tears, Our Saint hath been with us, our
In glo-ry a-bove   True to his love,   He keeps the false faith from
But oh, he will take The promise we make, So to live that our lives, by

shield and our stay;   All else may have gone, Saint Patrick alone—He hath
his chil-dren away— The dark false faith   Far worse than death, Oh he
God's help, may display The light that he bore To E-rin's shore. Oh Yes!

137—Hail, Patron Of Erin.

Andante grazioso.

1 Hail, Patron of Erin! bright Star of the West, What land has not heard of thy fame? Dear, dear to my soul are the souls thou hast blest, And dearer, if aught, be thy name. To

ST. DOMINIC.
HAIL, PATRON OF ERIN—Continued.

millions in darkness 'twas thine to give light, That light which can never de-cay, The Gospel soon banished i-dol-a-try's night, And Christians bask'd in its ray...

2 On thy steps, great Saint! all blessings awaited,
  Though slav'ry has since been our doom;
  Yet the light of thy doctrine ne'er has abated,
  'Twas the lamp that cheer'd through the gloom.
3 Like the light, that illumes the billowy sea,
  When darkness o'ershadows its breast,
  To guide the toss'd mariners, wan with dismay,
  To the haven of safety and rest.

ST. DOMINIC.
138—Thou, Who Hero-Like, Hast Striven.

Maestoso.

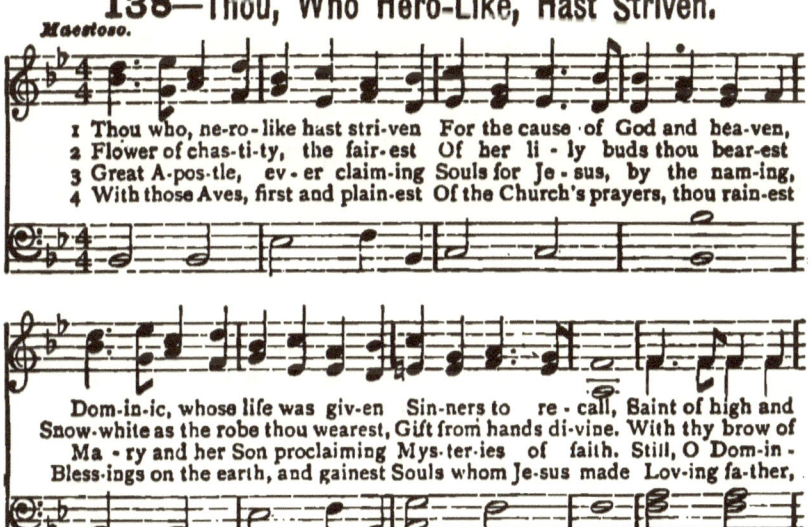

1 Thou who, ne-ro-like hast stri-ven For the cause of God and hea-ven, Dom-in-ic, whose life was giv-en Sin-ners to re-call, Saint of high and
2 Flower of chas-ti-ty, the fair-est Of her li-ly buds thou bear-est Snow-white as the robe thou wearest, Gift from hands di-vine. With thy brow of
3 Great A-pos-tle, ev-er claim-ing Souls for Je-sus, by the nam-ing, Ma-ry and her Son proclaiming Mys-ter-ies of faith. Still, O Dom-in-
4 With those Aves, first and plain-est Of the Church's prayers, thou rain-est Bless-ings on the earth, and gainest Souls whom Je-sus made Lov-ing fa-ther,

ST. STANISLAUS KOSTKA

THOU, WHO HERO-LIKE, HAST STRIVEN—Continued.

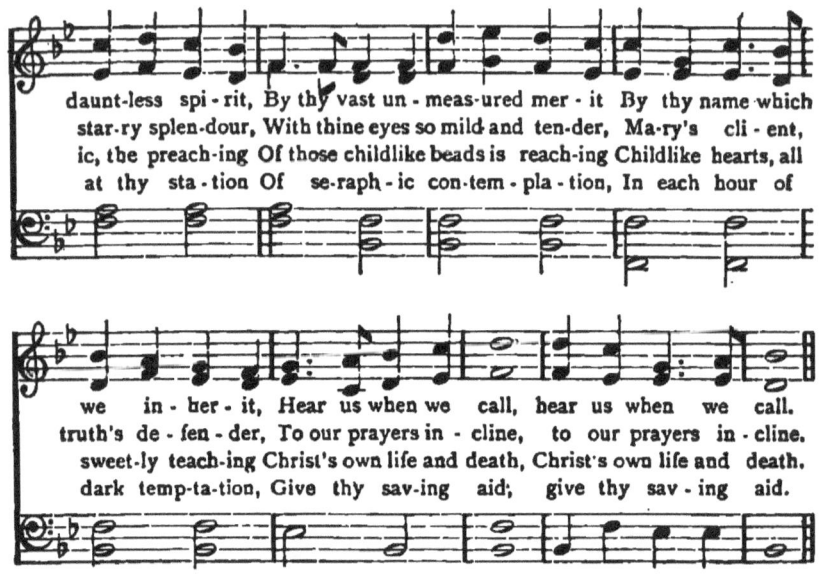

daunt-less spi-rit, By thy vast un-meas-ured mer-it By thy name which
star-ry splen-dour, With thine eyes so mild and ten-der, Ma-ry's cli-ent,
ic, the preach-ing Of those childlike beads is reach-ing Childlike hearts, all
at thy sta-tion Of se-raph-ic con-tem-pla-tion, In each hour of

we in-her-it, Hear us when we call, hear us when we call.
truth's de-fen-der, To our prayers in-cline, to our prayers in-cline.
sweet-ly teach-ing Christ's own life and death, Christ's own life and death.
dark temp-ta-tion, Give thy sav-ing aid; give thy sav-ing aid.

ST. STANISLAUS KOSTKA.

139—Dear Saint, Who On Thy Natal Day.

Animato.

1 Dear Saint, who on thy na-tal day, To
Ma-ry's ten-der care was given, And didst be-neath her

ST. THERESA.

DEAR SAINT, WHO ON THY NATAL DAY—Continued.

2 Sweet flow'r, that loved to bloom unknown,
A Saint 'mid worldly pomp and pride;
Who at the footstep of a throne
Knew naught but Jesus crucified.

3 Blest youth, who cast a crown away,
To be with Christ despised and poor;
Teach us to walk our lowly way,
Content, though humble be our store.

4 Teach us, like thee, to shrink from sin,
Like thee to love sweet purity;
That we from Mary's heart may win
The love she once bestowed on thee!

5 Thus safe beneath her gentle sway,
Oh, may the grace to us be given
To pass from earth some happy day,
And join thee in the courts of heaven

ST. THERESA.

140 Faithful To Thy Spouse And Love.

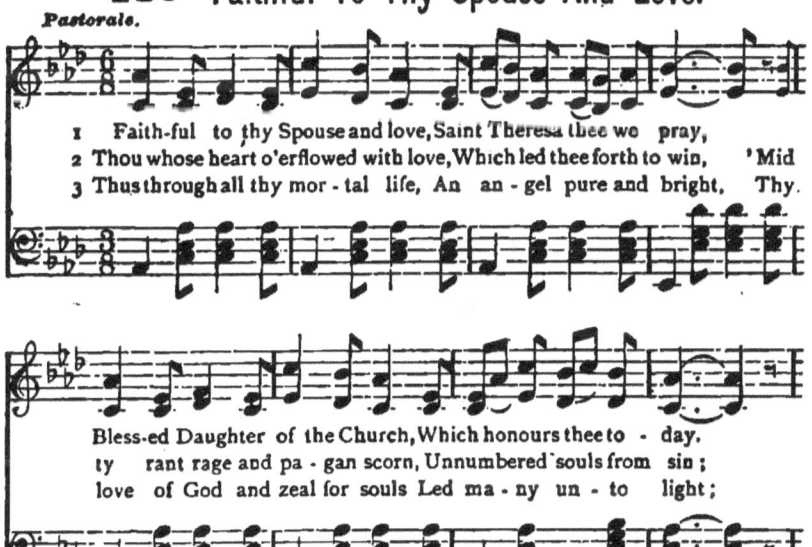

1 Faithful to thy Spouse and love, Saint Theresa thee we pray,
Blessed Daughter of the Church, Which honours thee to-day.

2 Thou whose heart o'erflowed with love, Which led thee forth to win,
'Mid tyrant rage and pagan scorn, Unnumbered souls from sin;

3 Thus through all thy mortal life, An angel pure and bright,
Thy love of God and zeal for souls Led many unto light;

ST. THERESA.

FAITHFUL TO THY SPOUSE AND LOVE—Continued.

Thou didst serve thy God in truth, And he 'mid death and shame,
All the fad-ing joys of earth Were worthless in thine eye;
When thy time of tri-umph came, Thy blood bedewed the sod;

Gave thee strength to meet the strife, And conquer in his Name.
For oh! immortal was the crown A-wait-ing thee on high!
O hap-py name, but happier fate, To yield thy life for God!

CHORUS.

Blest Saint Theresa, pray that we May ne'er our God de-ny, But
meek of heart and firm of faith, May for Him live and die!

141 — We Come To Thee, O Happy Saint.

ST. AGATHA.

Allegretto.

1. We come to thee, O happy Saint, To claim thy care and love...... To beg thy guidance thro' this life, To endless bliss above. O pray for us Saint Agatha, For
2. While in the rosy dawn of youth, To God thy heart was given,.... And true thro' life thy spotless soul 'Mid suff'ring soared to heaven. Thy purity has won for thee A
3. O pray for us, O martyred Saint, While on the sea of life,...... We struggle with the wind and waves, O aid us 'mid the strife. And when we've triumphed o'er sin And

142—Veni Sponsa Christi.

Quartette for Female voices

Sisters of St. Joseph, Nazareth Convent, Rochester. N.Y.

VENI SPONSA CHRISTI —Continued.

num, Quam ti-bi Do-mi-nus, Præ-par-a-vit in æ-ter-

num. Ve-ni, Cæ-ci-lia, Ve-ni, Cæ-ci - - li-a.

143—O, Turn to Jesus, Mother, Turn.

Adagio.

1. O turn to Je-sus, Moth-er, turn, And call Him by His tend'rest
2. Ah! they have fought a gal-lant fight; In death's cold arms they per-se-
3. They are the children of thy tears; Then has-ten, Moth-er! to their

names; Pray for the ho-ly souls that burn This hour a-mid the cleansing flames.
vered; And af-ter life's un-cheer-y night, The har-bor of their rest is neared.
aid; In pit-y think each hour appears An age, while glo-ry is delayed.

ALL SOULS.

144—Pray for the Dead.

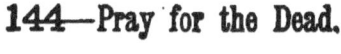

Pray for the dead! at noon and eve, Lift up to God thy fond request, Implore his goodness to relieve The suff'ring souls and grant them rest.

1. Pray for the dead! though faithful they, Yet while the penalties remain, Must suffering purge the debt away, And penance cleanse the sinful stain.
2. Pray for the dead! thy pray'rs, tho' weak, May yet be heard and bring them ease, For God will hear thy sigh, if meek—Thy tears if offered up for peace.
3. Pray for the dead! in holy fear, Pray that their stains may be forgiv'n, That thou thy-self may leave the bier, To enter pure at once in heav'n.

ALL SOULS.

145 — O Dearest Lord, We Humbly Crave.

1. O dearest Lord, we humbly crave Thy mercy for the holy dead who suffer in the burning wave The rigours of Thy justice dread, O Jesus unto our request In pity let Thy Heart incline! And grant them, Lord, eternal rest—Let light forever on them shine.

2. Behold how patiently they bear
The flames that cleanse, the pangs that thrill,
And bless and praise Thee, even there
Submissive to Thy holy will.
O, by the pains that racked Thy breast
From life's first dawn to life's decline,
Grant—grant them, Lord, eternal rest—
Let light forever on them shine.

3. They've conquered in the holy fight—
The shock of earth and hell withstood
They are the heroes of Thy might,
They are the purchased of Thy blood.
Then clasp them, Jesus, to Thy breast;
For though they suffer, they are Thine.
And grant them, Lord eternal rest—
Let light forever on them shine.

4. O, listen to those piteous cries
They waft to Thee by night, by day;
The sobs of love that vainly tries
To rush unto its God away!
By absence, more than pain, distressed,
With love they burn, with love they pine,
Then grant them, Lord, eternal rest—
Let light forever on them shine.

ADVENT. 243

146—See, He Comes

1 See, He comes! whom ev'ry nation, Taught of God, de-sired to see;.... Filled with hope and ex-pec-ta-tion, That He would their Sav-iour be. Sing, O! sing with ex-ult-a-tion, Haste we to our Fa-ther's Home..... Peace, re-demp-tion,

ADVENT.

SEE, HE COMES—Continued.

joy, sal-va-tion, Now from Heaven to earth are come.

See, He comes! whom kings and sages,
  Prophets, patriarchs of old,
Distant climes and countless ages,
  Waited eager to behold.
Sing, oh! sing with exultation,
  Haste we to our Father's home;
Peace, redemption, joy, salvation,
  Now from heaven to earth are come.

3 See, the Lamb of God appearing,
    God of God from Heaven above!
  See the Heavenly Bridegroom cheering
    His dear Bride with words of love!
  Glory to th' Eternal Father,
    Glory to th' Incarnate Son,
  Glory to the Holy Spirit,
    Glory to the Three in One.

147—Like The Dawning Of The Morning.

1 Like the dawn-ing of the morn-ing, On the moun-tains gold-en
2 Thou wert hap-py, bless-ed Moth-er, With the ve - ry bliss of
3 Thou hast wait-ed, child of Da - vid, And thy wait - ing now is

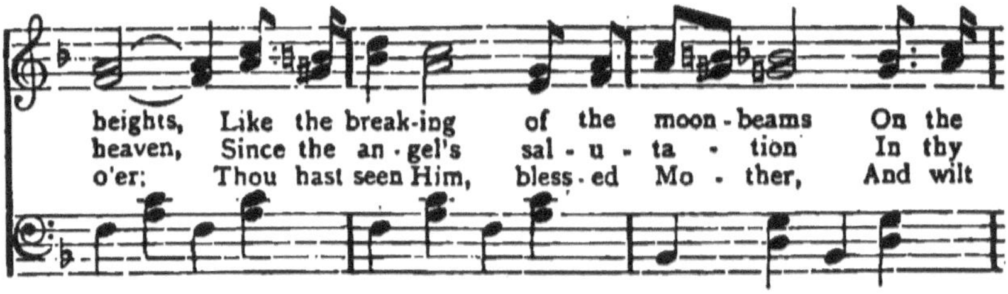

heights, Like the break-ing of the moon-beams On the
heaven, Since the an-gel's sal-u-ta-tion In thy
o'er; Thou hast seen Him, bless-ed Mo-ther, And wilt

gloom of cloud-y nights, Like a se-cret told by
rap-tured ear was given; Since the A-ve of that
see him ev - er - more. Oh, his hu-man face and

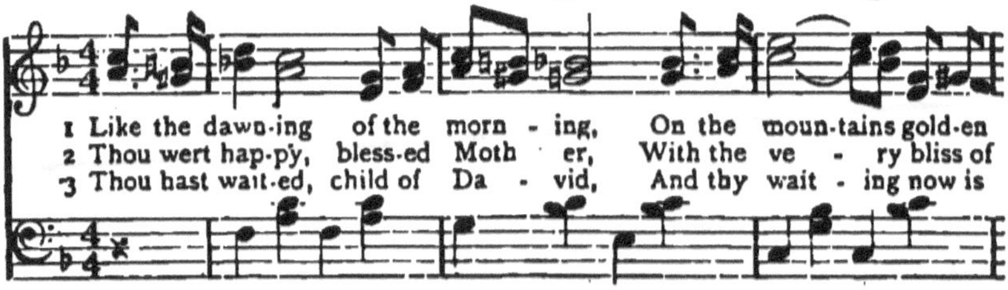

ADVENT

LIKE THE DAWNING OF THE MORNING—Continued

an - gels,   Get - ting known up - on   the earth,   Is the
mid - night   When thou wert a - noint - ed Queen, Like a
fea - tures, They were pass - ing sweet   to see;   Thou be-

Mo-ther's ex-pec-ta-tion   Of Mes - si - ah's speed-y birth
riv - er o-ver - flow - ing Hath the grace within thee been.
hold-est them this mo - ment; Mo-ther show them now to me.

148—Hark! An Awful Voice Is Sounding.

Moderato.

1 Hark! an aw-ful voice is sounding; "Christ is nigh!" it seems to say,

"Cast a-way the dreams of darkness, O ye chil-dren of the day!"

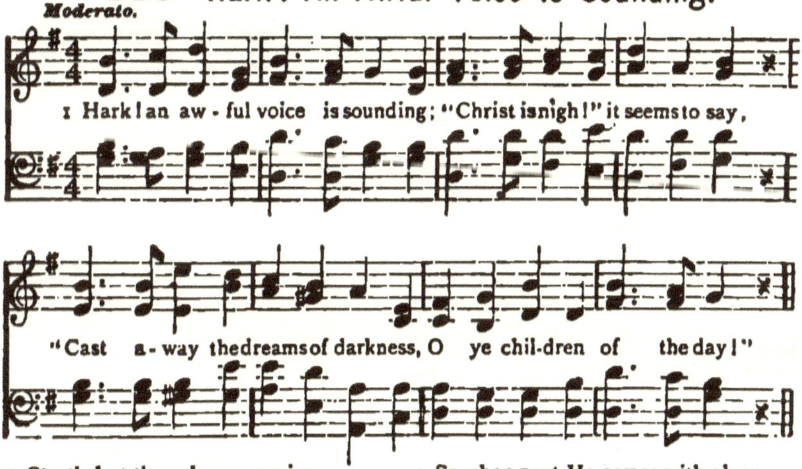

2 Startled at the solemn warning,
   Let the earth-bound soul arise,
  Christ her Sun, all sloth expelling,
   Shines upon the morning skies.

3 Lo, the Lamb so long expected,
   Comes with pardon down from heaven;
  Let us haste with tears of sorrow,
   One and all to be forgiven.

4 So when next He comes with glory,
   Wrapping all the earth in fear,
  May He then, as our defender,
   On the clouds of heaven appear.

5 Honour, glory, virtue, merit,
   To the Father and the Son,
  With the co-eternal Spirit,
   While eternal ages run.

149 — Hark! What Mean Those Holy Voices.

1. Hark! what mean those ho-ly voic-es, Sweet-ly sound-ing through the skies?.... Lo, th' an-gel-ic host re-joic-es,
2. Peace on earth, good-will from heav-en, Reach-ing far as man is found; .. Souls re-deemed and sins for-giv-en,
3. Christ is born: the great A-noint-ed! Heav-en and earth His praises sing!.... O re-ceive whom God ap-point-ed
4. Hast-en, mor-tals, to a-dore Him; Learn His Name to mag-ni-fy,....... Till in heav'n ye sing be-fore Him,

CHORUS.

Heav'nly al-le-lu-ias rise.
Loud our golden harps shall sound.
For you Prophet, Priest and King!
Glo-ry be to God most high."

Lis-ten to the won-drous sto-ry, Which they chant in hymns of joy— "Glo-ry in the

CHRISTMAS.

HARK! WHAT MEAN THOSE HOLY VOICES—CONTINUED.

high-est, glo-ry! Glo-ry be to God most high!"

150 —Adeste Fideles

WITH HEARTS TRULY GRATEFUL

1 A-des-te fi-de-les, Læ-ti tri-um-phantes, Ve-ni-te, ve-ni - te in
2 De-um de De-o, Lu-men de lu-mi-ne, Ges-tant pu-el - læ
3 Can tet nunc I - o Chorus an-ge-lo-rum, Can-tet nunc au - la cœ
3 Er-go qui na-tus Di-e ho-di-er-na, Je-su ti-bi sit

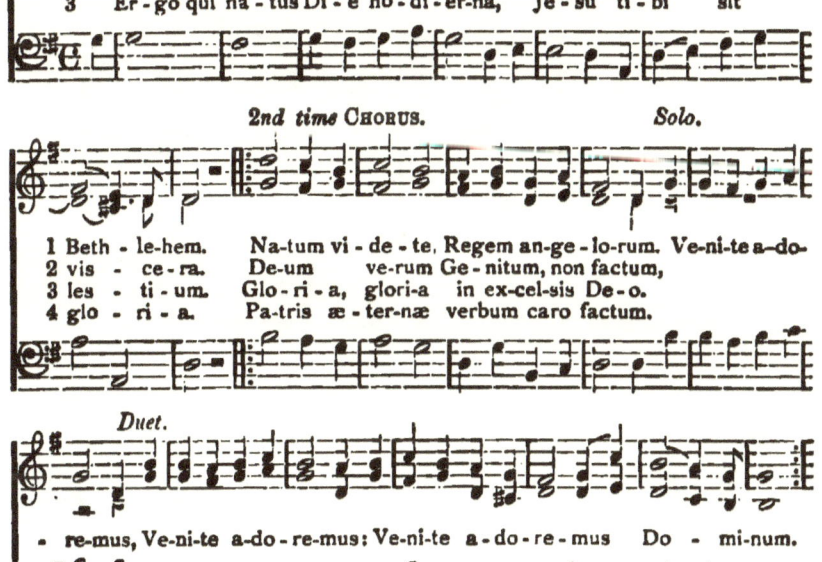

1 Beth - le-hem. Na-tum vi - de - te, Regem an-ge - lo-rum. Ve-ni-te a-do-
2 vis - ce-ra. De-um ve-rum Ge-nitum, non factum,
3 les - ti-um. Glo-ri- a, glori-a in ex-cel-sis De-o.
4 glo - ri - a. Pa-tris æ - ter-næ verbum caro factum.

- re-mus, Ve-ni-te a-do-re-mus; Ve-ni-te a-do-re-mus Do - mi-num.

CHRISTMAS.

WITH HEARTS TRULY GRATEFUL—Continued.

1 With hearts truly grateful,
   Come all ye faithful,
   To Jesus, to Jesus in Bethlehem;
   See Christ your Saviour,
   Heaven's greatest favour.
Chorus ||:Let s hasten to adore Him:||
   Our God and King.

2 God to God equal Light of Light e-
   Carried in Virgin's ever   [ternal;
      spotless womb.
   He all preceded,
   Begotten not created.

3 Angels now praise Him,
   Loud their voices raising,
   The heavenly mansions
      with joy now ring.
   Praise, honor, glory,
   To Him who is most holy.

4 To Jesus, born this day,
   Grateful homage repay;
   To Him who all heavenly
      gifts doth bring.
   Word uncreated,
   To our flesh united.

151—Oh! Lovely Infant, Dearest Saviour.

Oh! Love-ly In-fant dearest Saviour, Je-sus friend we love Thee best; See we all in-vite Thee kind-ly Oh, come with-in our hearts to rest. Oh, come with-in our hearts to rest, Glo-ri-a, Glo-ri-a in ex-cel-sis De-o

CHRISTMAS

OH! LOVELY INFANT, DEAREST SAVIOUR. —CONTINUED.

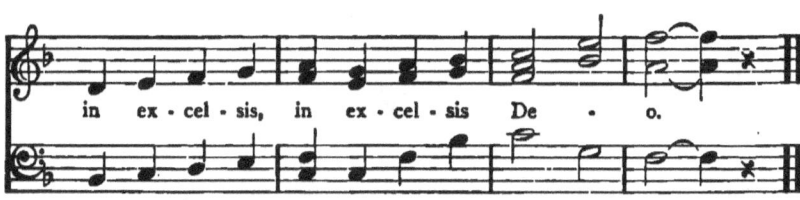

2 Linger not in Thy poor stable,
Stay not in the freezing cold;
Our warm hearts are warmly opened
Thee, sweet Infant, Thee to enfold.

3 Oh we know Thee, King of Heaven,
Tho' we see Thee weak and small,

And we say with hearts confiding,
Thou comest here to save us all-

4 See, I came my heart to offer,
Make it now a crib for Thee,
Come O Jesus, lovely Infant,
Come, enter in and stay with us.

152—Sleep, Holy Babe!

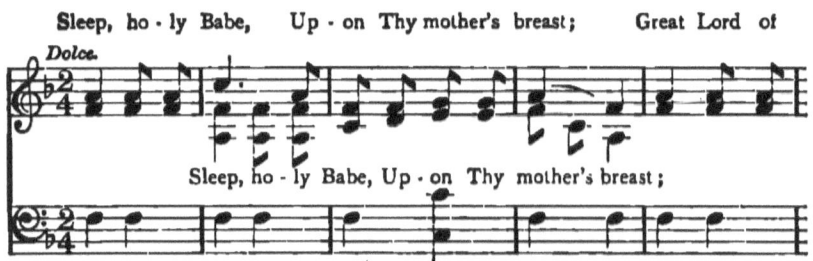

2   Sleep, holy Babe!
       Thine angels watch around;
    All bending low, with folded wings,
    Before the Incarnate King of kings,
       In reverent awe profound.
    Sleep, holy Babe! sleep, holy Babe!

3   Sleep, holy Babe!
       While I with Mary gaze
    In joy upon that face awhile,
    Upon the loving infant smile
       Which there divinely plays.
    Sleep, holy Babe! sleep, holy Babe!

4   Sleep, holy Babe!
       Ah, take thy brief repose;
    Too quickly will Thy slumbers break,
    And Thou to lengthened pains awake,
       That death alone shall close.
    Sleep, holy Babe! sleep, holy Babe!

CHRISTMAS. 251

153—See! Amid the Winter's Snow.

1. See! amid the winter's snow, Born for us on earth below; See! the tender Lamb appears, Promised from eternal years.

ff CHORUS.

Hail! thou ever blessed morn! Hail! Redemption's happy dawn! Sing through all Jerusalem, Christ is born in Bethlehem.

2 Lo! within a manger lies,
He who built the starry skies;
He who, throned in height sublime,
Sits amid the cherubim.

3 Say, ye holy shepherds, say
What your joyful news to-day?

Wherefore have ye left your sheep,
On the lonely mountain steep!

4 "As we watched at dead of night,
Lo! we saw a wondrous light;
Angels singing, ' Peace on earth,'
Told us of the Saviour's birth."

154—Angels We Have Heard.

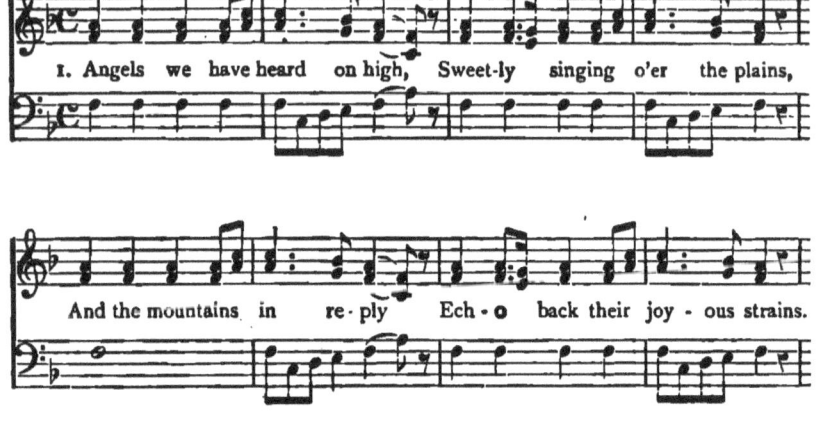

2 Shepherds, why this jubilee?
   Why your rapturous strains prolong?
   Say what may the tidings be,
   Which inspire your heavenly song.

3 Come to Bethlehem, come and see,
   Him whose birth the angels sing;
   Come adore on bended knee,
   The Infant Christ, the new-born King.

4 See within a manger laid,
   Jesus, Lord of heaven and earth!
   Mary, Joseph, lend your aid,
   With us sing our Saviour's birth.

155—Dear Little One, How Sweet Thou Art!

2 When Mary bids Thee sleep Thou
  sleep'st,
  Thou wakest when she calls;
  Thou art content upon her lap,
  Or in the rugged stalls.
  Simplest of Babes! with what a grace,
  Thou dost Thy mother's will,
  Thine infant fashions all betray
  The God-head's hidden skill.

3 When Joseph takes Thee in his arms,
  And smooths Thy little cheek,
  Thou lookest up into his face
  So helpless and so meek.
  Yes! Thou art what Thou seem'st to be,
  A thing of smiles and tears;
  Yet Thou art God, and heav'n and
  earth,
  Adore Thee with their fears.

156—Stars Of Glory Shine More Brightly

2 See a beauteous angel soaring
　In the bright celestial blaze,
On the shepherds low adoring
　Rest his mild effulgent rays.
"Fear not"—cries the heavenly stranger—
"Him whom ancient seers foretold,
Weeping in a lonely manger,
　Shepherds, haste ye to behold"

1 See the shepherds quickly rising,
　Hastening to the humble stall,
And the new-born Infant prizing,
　As the mighty Lord of all.

Lowly now they bend before Him
　In His helpless infant state,
Firmly, faithful they adore Him,
　And His greatness celebrate,

4 Hark the swell of heavenly voices
Peal along the vaulted sky;
Angels sing, while earth rejoices—
"Glory to our God on high;
Glory in the highest heaven,
　Peace to humble men on earth;
Joy to these and bliss is given,
　In the great Redeemer's birth."

EPIPHANY.

THE HEAVENS BEND TO KISS THE EARTH—Continued.

2 The palm to-day rules o'er the sword,
   The Truth has dawned on earth,
   Idolatry has died the death,
   Religion has its birth.
   Across the arch of night God views
   Fair Bethlehem beneath,
   Where Angel choirs weave for His Son
   This joyous choral wreath.

3 We sing of Him Who'll null death's sway
   And heal the withered hand,
   Who'll turn the demon's power away
   And give kind Peace our land.
   We sing of Him Who'll walk the sea
   And calm the raging wind,
   We sing of Him Who is to be
   The Saviour of mankind.

158—A Glorious Voice Sounds Through the Night.

1 A glorious voice sounds through the night, And chides the dark-ness in-to light; The mists of sleep are driv'n a-far, And Christ shines forth the Morn-ing Star.
2 Now from the tor-por leaps the mind, And leaves all taint of earth be-hind; The new-born plan-et flames on high, And bids all care and sor-row fly.
3 Now from a-bove the Lamb is sent, To pay the debt, O pen-i-tent! Weep! and with tears thy praise up-lift, In thanks for so su-preme a gift.
4 To Fa-ther, Son and Ho-ly Ghost The King of Heaven's im-mor-tal host, May men and an-gels praise out-pour, For-ev-er and for-ev-er more.

EPIPHANY. 257

159 What Beauteous Sun-Surpassing Star.

Moderato.

1 What beauteous sun-sur-pass-ing Star O'er Bethlehem's lonely road, Reveals a ris-ing bright-er far, And shows the cra-dled God. The Star from Ja-cob see a-rise, By pro-phets long fore-told; Ye East-ern na-tions, in the skies, His mes-sen-ger be-hold

2 While thus the Star its light imparts,
  A ray within doth shine,
Which leads a few but faithful hearts
  To seek the glorious sign.
No dangers can their purpose shake
  Love suffers no delay ;
Home, kindred, country, they forsake,
  God calls, and they obey.

3 Jesus, bright morning Star, our hearts
  Cleanse with Thy light within,
And suffer not the tempter's arts
  To lure us back to sin.
The Light of Gentile lands adore,
  The Day-spring from on high,
Alike the Father evermore,
  And Spirit magnify.

LENT

160—Parce Domine.

Par - ce, Do - mi - ne,.... par - ce po - pu - lo,.... tu - o - ne in æ - ter - num i - ras - ca - ris.... no - bis.

161—Miserere.

1 Mi - se - re - re .... me - - i, De - us,* secundum magnam mi - se - ri - cor - di - am tu - am
2 Et se - cun - dum multitudinem mise-} ra - ti - o - num tu - a - rum. dele. i - ni - qui - ta - tem me - am.

3 Amplius lava me ab iniqui - ta - te me - a, * et a pecca - to me - o mun - da me.

4 Quoniam iniquitatem meum e - go <g> - nos - co, * et peccatum meum con - • me - est - sem - per.

5 Tibi soli peccavi, et malum co - ram te - fe - ci; * ut justificeris in sermonibus tuis, et vincas cum - jud - i - ca - ris

6 Ecce enim in iniquitatibus - con-cep-tus sum, * et in peccatis concepit me ma - ter me - a.

LENT.

MISERERE—Continued

7 Ecce enim veritatem-dil - ex - is - ti,
* incerta et occulta sapientiæ tuæ mani -
fes - tas - ti mi - hi.
8 Asperges me hyssopo-et-mun - da
bor: * lavabis me, et super ni - vem de
al - ba - bor.
9 Auditui meo dabis gaudium et-læ
ti - ti - am; * et exultabunt ossa hu - mi -
li - a - ta.
10 Averte faciam tuam a pec - ca - tis
me - is, * et omnes iniquita - tes me - as
de - le.
11 Cor mundum crea in-me De - us, *
et spiritum rectum innova in viscer - i
bus me - is.
12 Ne projicias me a fa - cie tu - a, *
et Spiritum Sanctum tuum ne au-fer - as
a me.
13 Redde mihi lætitiam salu - ta - ris
tu - i, * et spiritu principa - li con - fir -
ma me.

14 Docebo iniquos-vi - as tu - as, * et
impii ad te-con - ver - ten - tur.
15 Libera me de sanguinibus, Deus,
Deus sal - u - tis me - æ, * et exultabit
lingua mea justi - ti - am tu - am.
16 Domine, labia me - a a - pe - ries, *
et os meum annuntia bit-lau-dem tu-am.
17 Quoniam si voluisses, sacrificium
de - dis - sem u - tique; * holocaust - is
non de-lec - ta - beris.
18 Sacrificium Deo spiritus contri -
bu - la - tus; * cor contritum et humila-
tum, Deus, non de - spi - cies.
19 Benigne fac, Domine, in bona voluntate - tu - a Si - on, * ut ædificentur
mu - ri Je - ru - salem.
20 Tunc acceptabis sacrificium justitiæ, oblationes et ho - lo - caus - ta; *
tunc imponent super alta - re tu-um vi -
tulos
21 Gloria Patri, etc.

162 Benedictus.

1 Be - ne - dic - tus Do - mi - nus De - us Is - ra - el,
quia visitavit, et fecit redemptionem ple - bis su - æ:

2 Et erexit cornu sal - u - tis no - bis - *
in domo David pu - er - i su - i.
3 Sicut locutus est per - os sancto -
rum, * qui a sæculo sunt, prophe - ta -
rum e - jus.
4 Salutem ex ini-mi - cis nos - tris, *
et de manu omnium qui-o - der - unt nos.
5 Ad faciendam misericordiam cum-
pa - tribus nos - tris, * et memorari tes-
tamenti-su - i sanc - ti.

6 Jusjurandum quod juravit ad Abra-
ham-pa - trem nos - trum, * datu - rum
se no - bis.
7 Ut sine timore, de manu inimicorum
nostrorum-li - bera - ti, * servi - a - mus
il - li.
8 In sanctitate, et justitia co - ram
ip so, * omnibus di - e - bus nos - tris.
9 Et tu, puer, propheta Altissi - mi
vo - ca - beris,* præibis enim ante faciem
Domini parare-vi - as e - jus:

LENT.

BENEDICTUS—CONTINUED.

10 Ad dandam scientiam salutis plebi ejus; * in remissionem peccatorum eorum:

11 Per viscera misericordiæ Dei nostri: * in quibus visitavit nos oriens ex alto

12 Illuminare his, qui in tenebris, et in umbra mortis sedent: * ad dirigendos pedes nostros in viam pacis.

13 Gloria Patri, etc:

162* O Cor Jesu.

O Cor Jesu Sacratissimum
O Cor Mariæ Immaculatum
O Cor Joseph Purissimum
Miserere nobis.
Ora pro nobis.
Ora pro nobis.

163—Now Are The Days Of Humblest Prayer.

Slowly.

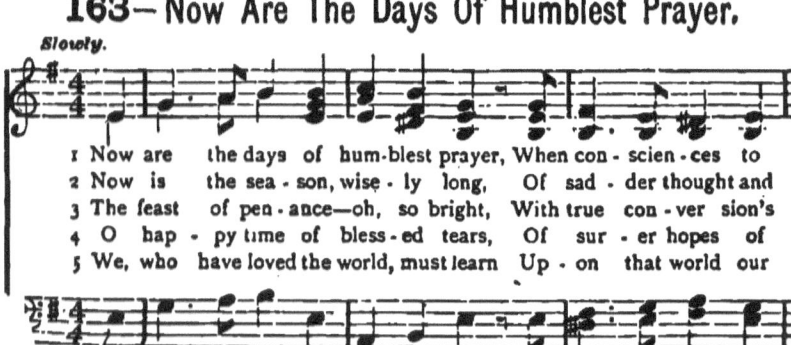

1 Now are the days of humblest prayer, When consciences to
2 Now is the season, wisely long, Of sadder thought and
3 The feast of penance—oh, so bright, With true conversion's
4 O happy time of blessed tears, Of surer hopes of
5 We, who have loved the world, must learn Upon that world our

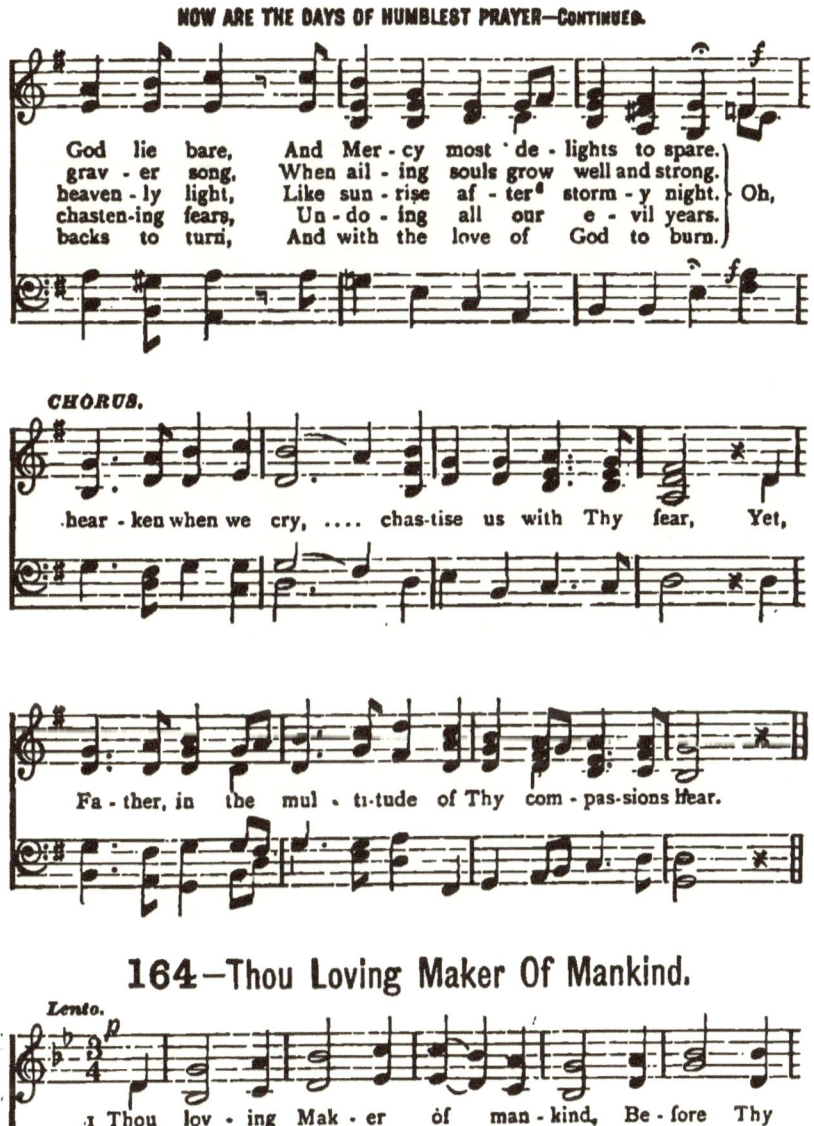

LENT

NOW ARE THE DAYS OF HUMBLEST PRAYER—Continued.

God lie bare, And Mer-cy most de-lights to spare.
grav-er song, When ail-ing souls grow well and strong.
heaven-ly light, Like sun-rise af-ter storm-y night.
chasten-ing fears, Un-do-ing all our e-vil years.
backs to turn, And with the love of God to burn.

Oh,

CHORUS.

.hear-ken when we cry, ... chas-tise us with Thy fear, Yet, Fa-ther, in the mul-ti-tude of Thy com-pas-sions Hear.

164—Thou Loving Maker Of Mankind.

Lento.

1 Thou lov-ing Mak-er of man-kind, Be-fore Thy

THOU LOVING MAKER OF MANKIND—Continued.

Throne we pray and weep; O strengthen us with grace divine, Duly this sacred time to keep

2 Great Judge of hearts, Thou dost discern
Our ills, and all our weakness know;
Again to Thee with tears we turn,
Again to us Thy mercy show.
3 Much have we sinned; but we confess
Our guilt, and all our faults deplore;
O, for the praise of Thy great Name,
Our fainting souls to health restore.

4 And grant us, while by fasts we strive
This mortal body to control,
To fast from all the food of sin
And so to purify the soul.
5 Hear us, O Trinity thrice blest;
Sole Unity, to Thee we cry;
Vouchsafe us from these fasts below
To reap immortal fruit on high.

165—Christians, Who Of Jesus' Sorrows.

Larghetto.

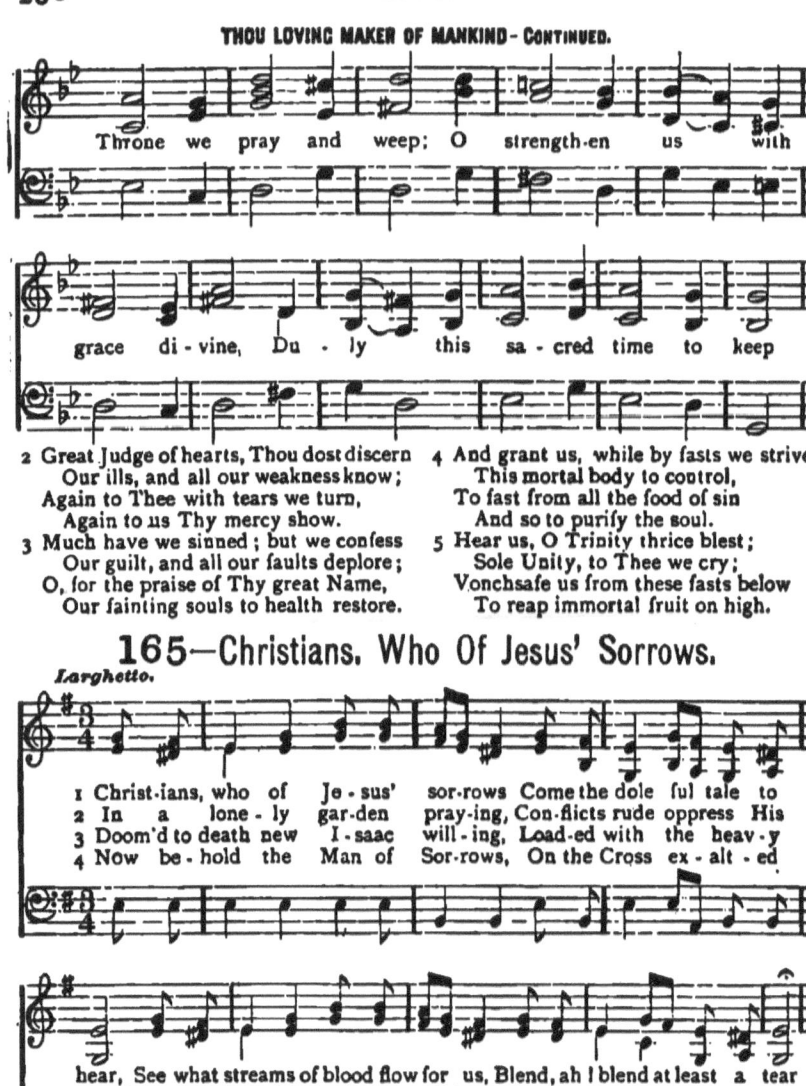

1 Christians, who of Jesus' sorrows Come the doleful tale to hear, See what streams of blood flow for us, Blend, ah! blend at least a tear
2 In a lonely garden praying, Conflicts rude oppress His soul, Fear and hope His soul assailing Strive by turns His will to rule.
3 Doom'd to death new Isaac willing, Loaded with the heavy tree, In His heart our sins bewailing, He ascends Mount Calvary.
4 Now behold the Man of Sorrows, On the Cross exalted high; Suff'ring, bleeding, dying for us, Now behold salvation nigh

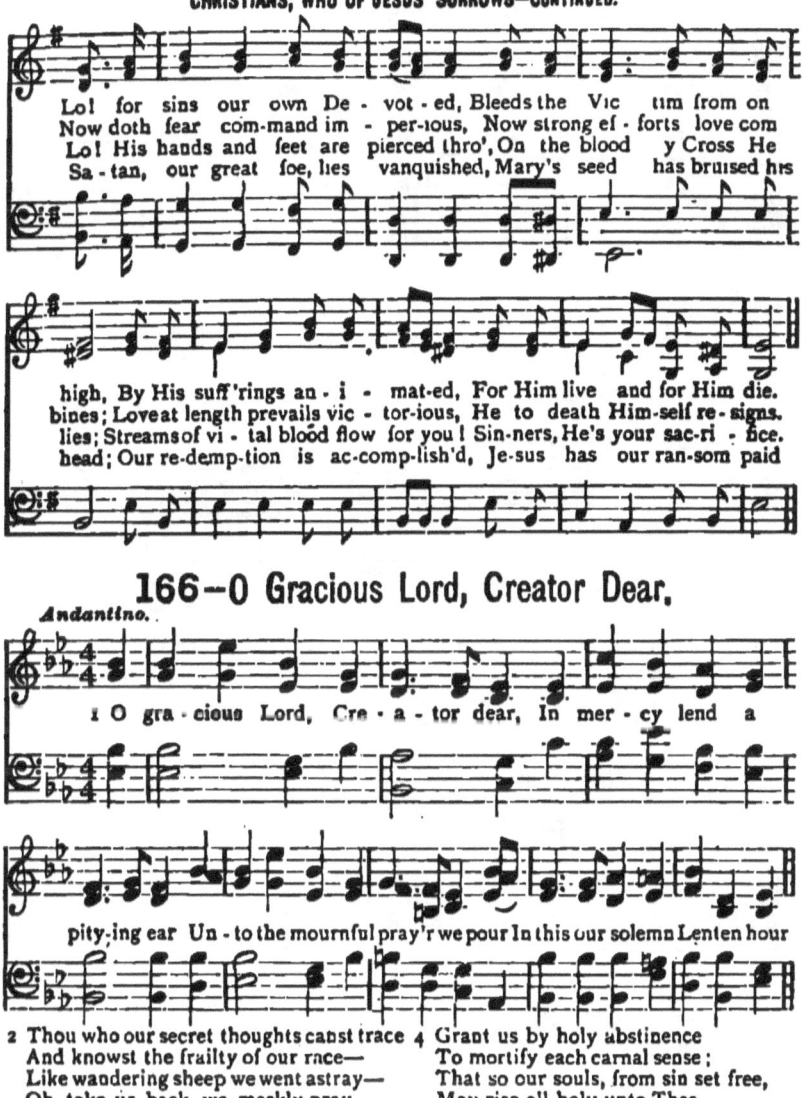

LENT.

CHRISTIANS, WHO OF JESUS' SORROWS—Continued.

Lo! for sins our own De-vot-ed, Bleeds the Vic-tim from on high, By His suff'rings an-i-mat-ed, For Him live and for Him die.
Now doth fear com-mand im-per-ious, Now strong ef-forts love com-bines; Love at length prevails vic-tor-ious, He to death Him-self re-signs.
Lo! His hands and feet are pierced thro', On the blood-y Cross He lies; Streams of vi-tal blood flow for you! Sin-ners, He's your sac-ri-fice.
Sa-tan, our great foe, lies vanquished, Mary's seed has bruised his head; Our re-demp-tion is ac-comp-lish'd, Je-sus has our ran-som paid

166—O Gracious Lord, Creator Dear.

Andantino.

1 O gra-cious Lord, Cre-a-tor dear, In mer-cy lend a pity-ing ear Un-to the mournful pray'r we pour In this our solemn Lenten hour.

2 Thou who our secret thoughts canst trace
And knowst the frailty of our race—
Like wandering sheep we went astray—
Oh, take us back, we meekly pray

3 Black is our guilt and great our shame;
But for, the glory of Thy Name,
Forgive the wickedness we own,
And heal the wounds for which we groan.

4 Grant us by holy abstinence
To mortify each carnal sense ;
That so our souls, from sin set free,
May rise all-holy unto Thee.

5 Blest Three in One, with grief sincere,
Before thy footstool we appear;
Oh, bless our fast, that it may prove
The source of pardon, peace, and love.

LENT.

168—O, Come And Mourn With Me Awhile.

2 Come, take thy stand beneath the Cross,
And let the Blood from out that Side
Fall gently on thee drop by drop;
Jesus, our Love, is crucified!

3 O Love of God! O Sin of Man!
In this dread act your strength is tried;
And victory remains with love,
For He, our Love, is crucified!

169—What A Sea Of Tears And Sorrow.

Lento

1. What a sea of tears and sor-row
Did the soul of Ma-ry toss
To and fro up-on its bil-lows,
While she wept her bit-ter loss,
In her arms her Je-sus hold-ing,
Torn so new-ly from the cross.

2. Oh that mournful Virgin-Mother!
See her tears, how fast they flow
Down upon His mangled body,
Wounded side, and thorny brow;
While His hands and feet she kisses,—
Picture of immortal woe.

3. Oft and oft His arms and bosom
Fondly straining to her own;
Oft her pallid lips imprinting
On each wound of her dear Son
Till at last, in swoons of anguish,
Sense and consciousness are gone.

4. Gentle Mother, we beseech thee.
By thy tears and troubles sore;
By the death of thy dear Offspring
By the bloody wounds He bore,
Touch our hearts with that true sorrow
Which afflicted thee of yore.

LENT.
170—Stabat Mater.

1. Sta-bat Ma-ter do-lo-ro-sa, Jux-ta, Cru-cem
la-cry-mo-sa, Dum pen-de-bat Fi-li-us.
2. Cu-jus a-ni-mam ge-men-tem, Con-tris-ta-tam
et do-len-tem, Per-tran-si-vit gla-di-us.

3. O quam tristis et afflicta
Fuit illa benedicta
Mater Unigeniti!

4. Quæ mœrebat, et dolebat,
Pia Mater, dum videbat
Nati pœnas inclyti.

5. Quis est homo, qui non fleret,
Matrem Christi si videret
In tanto supplicio?

6. Quis non posset contristari,
Christi Matrem contemplari
Dolentem cum Filio?

7. Pro peccatis suæ gentis
Vidit Jesum in tormentis,
Et flagellis subditum.

8. Vidit suum dulcem Natum
Moriendo desolatum,
Dum emisit spiritum.

9. Eja Mater fons amoris,
Me sentire vim doloris
Fac, ut tecum lugeam.

10. Fac, ut ardeat cor meum
In amando Christum Deum
Ut sibi complaceam.

11. Sancta Mater, istud agas,
Crucifixi fige plagas
Cordi meo valide.

12. Tui Nati vulnerati,
Tam dignati pro me pati,
Pœnas mecum divide.

13. Fac me tecum pie flere,
Crucifixo condolere,
Donec ego vixero.

14. Juxta Crucem tecum stare,
Et me tibi sociare
In planctu desidero.

15. Virgo virginum præclara,
Mihi jam non sis amara;
Fac me tecum plangere.

16. Fac ut portem Christi mortem,
Passionis fac consortem,
Et plagas recolere.

17. Fac me plagis vulnerari,
Fac me Cruce inebriari,
Et cruore Filii.

18. Flammis ne urar succensus,
Per te Virgo sim defensus
In die Judicii.

19. Christe, cum sit hinc exire,
Da per Matrem me venire
Ad palmam victoriæ.

20. Quando corpus morietur,
Fac ut animæ donetur
Paradisi gloria. Amen.

℣. Ora pro nobis, Virgo dolorosissima. ℟. Ut digni efficiamur promissionibus Christi.

171—Lord of Mercy and Compassion.

Lord of mercy and compassion, Look with pity down on me,
Father let me call Thee Father, 'Tis Thy child return'd to Thee.

Chorus.
Jesus Lord I ask for mercy, Let me not implore in vain,
Pardon for my sins, and grace, Never more to sin again.

2 See! our Saviour bleeding, dying,
   On the cross of Calvary,
To that cross my sins have nailed Him
   And He bleeds and dies for me.

3 By my sins I have abandon'd,
   Right and claim to Heav'n above,
Where the saints rejoice for ever,
   In a boundless sea of love.

EASTER.

172 All Hail, Dear Conqueror! All Hail.

1. All hail! dear Conqueror, all hail! Oh what a vic-to-ry is Thine! How beau-ti-ful Thy strength ap-pears, Thy crimson wounds how bright they shine! Thou cam-est at the dawn of day. Arm-ies of souls a-round Thee were, Blest spir-its thronging to a-dore Thy Flesh, so marvelous, so fair

2 The everlasting God-head lay
 Shrouded within those Limbs Divine,

3 And Thou too, Soul of Jesus! Thou
 Towards the sacred Flesh didst yearn.

EASTER.

173 — Alleluia! Alleluia! Let The Holy Anthem Rise.

1 Alleluia! Alleluia! let the holy anthem rise, And the choirs of heaven chant it in the temple of the skies; Let the mountains skip with gladness, and the joyful valleys ring With Hosannas in the Highest to our Saviour and our King.

2 Alleluia! Alleluia! He endured the knotted whips,
And the jeering of the rabble, and the scorn of mocking lips,
And the terrors of the gibbet upon which He would be slain;
But His death was only slumber—He is risen up again.

3 Alleluia! Alleluia! like the sun from out the wave,
He has risen up in triumph from the darkness of the grave,
He's the Splendour of the Nations, He's the lamp of endless day,
He's the very Lord of Glory who is risen up to-day.

4 Alleluia! Alleluia! He has burst our prison bars,
He has lifted up the portals of our home beyond the stars;
He has won for us our freedom—'neath His feet our foes are trod;
He has purchased back our birthright to the Kingdom of our God.

5 Alleluia! Alleluia! Blessed Jesus, make us rise
From the life of this corruption to the life that never dies.
May we share with Thee Thy glory, when the days of time are past,
And the dead shall be awakened by the trumpet's mighty blast.

EASTER.

THE DAWN WAS PURPLING O'ER THE SKY—Continued.

Fa - thers forth, In - to the beam of life and day
from the dead, And death is slain no more to rise."
clete be praise While age on end - less ag - es flows.

175—Christ The Lord is Risen To-day.

With spirit.

1 Christ the Lord is ris'n to-day; Christians haste your vows to pay;
Of - fer ye your prais-es meet, At the pas - chal Victim's feet
For the sheep the Lamb hath bled, Sin - less in the sin-ner's stead,
Christ the Lord is ris'n on high, Now He lives no more to die!

EASTER.

CHRIST THE LORD IS RIS'N TO-DAY—Continued.

2 Christ, the Victim, undefiled
Man to God hath reconciled,
When in strange and awful strife,
Met together death and life.
Christians, on this happy day,
Haste with joy your vows to pay;
Christ the Lord is ris'n on high,
Now He lives no more to die!

3 Christ who once for sinners bled,
Now the first-born from the dead,
Thron'd in endless might and pow'r,
Lives and reigns for ever more.
Hail, eternal Hope on high!
Hail, Thou King of victory!
Hail, Thou Prince of Life ador'd!
Help and save us, gracious Lord!

176—To-Day He's Risen.

1 To-day He's ri-sen, death no more Shall bind Him to the grave; No more can hell or sin's fell pow'r O'er Him Do-min-ion have.........

2 O death! where is thy mor-tal sting? Where's now thy vic-to-ry? To-day His glo-rious praise we sing, Who tri-umphed ov-er thee.........

3 I know that my Re-deem-er lives, And reigns a-bove the skies; He will re-vive my dust a-gain, And bid my bod-y rise.........

177—Haec Dies.

EASTER.

By L. BORDES.

EASTER.

HAEC DIES—Continued.

EASTER. 277

HAEC DIES—*Continued.*

Do - mi - nus: Al - le - lu - - - ia, Al - le-
lu - - ia, Al - le - lu - ia, Al - le-
lu - ia, Al - le - lu - ia.

178—O Filii et Filiae.

Al - le - lu - ia, al - le - lu - ia, al - le - lu - ia!

2. Et Maria Magdalene—Et Jacobi et Salome—Venerunt corpus ungere. Alleluia!
3. A Magdalena moniti—Ad ostium monumenti—Duo currunt discipuli. Alleluia!
4. Sed Joannes Apostolus—Cucurrit Petro citius:—Ad sepulchrum venit prius. Alleluia!
5. In albis sedens Angelus—Respondit mulieribus—Quia surrexit Dominus. Alleluia!
6. Discipulis adstantibus—In media stetit Christus—Dicens: Pax vobis omnibus. Alleluia!

EASTER. 279

O FILII ET FILIAE—Continued.

7. Postquam audivit Didymus—Quia surrexerat Jesus—Remansit fide dubius. Alleluia!
8. Vide, Thoma, vide manus—Vide pedes, vide latus: Noli esse incredulus. Alleluia!
9. Quando Thomas Christi latus—Pedes vidit atque manus—Dixit: Tu es Deus meus. Alleluia!
10. Beati qui non viderunt—Et firmiter crediderunt—Vitam aeternam habebunt. Alleluia!
11. In hoc festo sanctissimo—Sit laus et jubilatio: Benedicamus Domino. Alleluia!
12. De quibus nos humillimas—Devotas atque debitas—Deo dicamus gratias. Alleluia!

179—Hail the Holy Day of Days!

B. L.

1. Hail! the holy day of days, High the song of triumph raise,
   To the Saviour glory tell, How the cross hath vanquished hell.
   By the prec'ous blood are we Now re-deemed of Christ and free.
   High thanks-giv-ing therefore raise, Sing the great Re-deem-er's praise.

2. Now the glorious vic-t'ry won, Thou the ev-er-last-ing Son,
   With the Fath-er thron'd on high, Rul-est all be-low the sky.
   King of kings, Thy saints u-nite To the choir of an-gels bright,
   Al-le-lu-ia, Lord we sing, Je-sus Christ, Re-deem-er, King.

ASCENSION.

180—Thy Sacred Race, O Lord, Is Run.

Moderato.

1 Thy Sa-cred race, O Lord is run, Thy work is wrought, Thy vict'ry won The glo-ry Thou didst leave requires Thy presence in su-per-nal choirs. The clouds Thy chariot, earth a-far Be-neath Thy feet, a lit-tle star; Ten thousand thousand angels sing To welcome their re-turn-ing King.

2 The gates of heaven obey the call
And open to the Lord of all;
His throne receives the eternal Son,
Both God and Man for ever one.
Thou Mediator and High-Priest,
Fresh from the sacrifice released,
By love constrained dost hither bring
Thy smitten Heart's best offering.

3 And she who from Thy open side
Her being took, Thy holy Bride,
*Still nourish*ed from Thy side survives,
And life and all from Thee derives.

Hence in the thickest of the fight,
Thy warriors win their heavenly might,
And hence, Thy martyrs sing their psalms,
And joyous wave triumphal palms.

4 Where Thou, the head, art gone Thy voice
Calls all Thy members to rejoice;
Ah, let them cleave the shining way,
Thy footprints through the ether fray.
To Thee be glory, conquering King,
Who unto heaven Thy way dost wing,
Great Son of the eternal Sire,
Whose Spirit is our one desire.

ASCENSION.

181—O Thou Eternal King Most High.

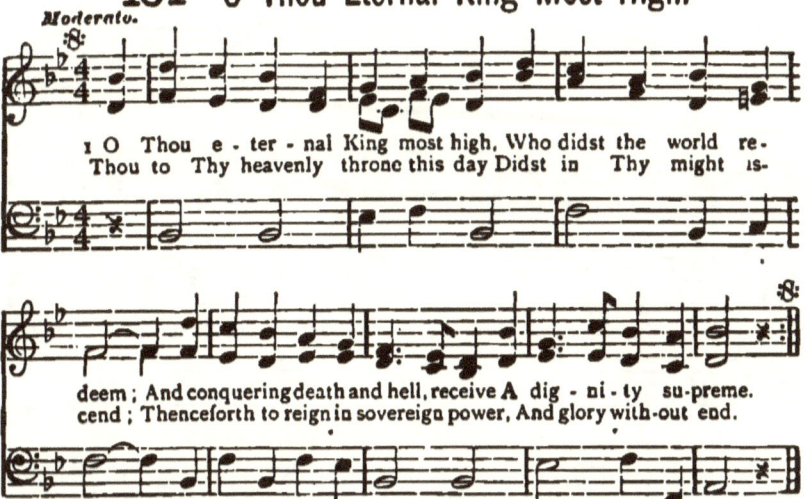

1 O Thou e-ter-nal King most high, Who didst the world re-deem; And conquering death and hell, receive A dig-ni-ty su-preme.

Thou to Thy heavenly throne this day Didst in Thy might as-cend; Thenceforth to reign in sovereign power, And glory with-out end.

2 There seated in Thy majesty,
To Thee submissive bow,
The spacious earth, the highest heaven,
The depths of hell below.
There, waiting for Thy faithful souls,
Be Thou to us, O Lord,
Our peerless joy while here we stay,
In Heav'n our great reward.

3 Renew our strength; our sins forgive
Our miseries efface;
And lift our souls aloft to Thee,
By Thy celestial grace.
So, when Thou shinest on the cloud,
With Thy angelic train,
May we be saved from vengeance due,
And our lost crowns regain.

182—Our Lord is Risen.

1 Our Lord is ris-en from the dead, Our Je-sus is gone up on high, The pow'rs of hell are cap-tive

282 PENTECOST.

OUR LORD IS RISEN—Continued.

2 There His triumphal chariot waits.
  And angels chant the solemn lay,
  Lift up your heads, ye heavenly gates,
  Ye everlasting doors give way.

3 Loose all your bars of massive light,
  And wide unfold th' ethereal scene
  He claims these mansions as His right
  Receive the King of glory in.

PENTECOST

183—Veni Creator Spiritus.

PENTECOST. 283

184—See the Paraclete Descending.

2 Men in every danger fearing,
　Now the greatest danger scorn;
　Amidst tortures perserving,
　Show themselves in Christ new-born

3 Source of love, our hearts inflaming
　With true zeal and virtue pure.
　Grant we may in heaven reigning,
　Sing Thy praise for evermore.

PENTECOST.

185—Holy Spirit, Come And Shine.

1 Holy Spirit, come and shine
On our souls with beams divine,
Issuing from Thy radiance bright,
Come, O Father of the poor,
Ever bounteous of Thy store,
Come, our hearts' unfailing light

2 Come, Consoler, kindest, best,
Come, our bosoms' dearest guest,
Sweet refreshment, sweet repose.
Rest in labour, coolness sweet,
Tempering the burning heat,
Truest comfort of our woes.

3 O divinest Light, impart
Unto every faithful heart
Plenteous streams from love's bright flood
But for Thy blest Deity,
Nothing pure in man could be;
Nothing harmless, nothing good.

PENTECOST.

HOLY SPIRIT, COME AND SHINE—Continued.

4 Wash away each sinful stain,
Gently shed Thy gracious rain
On the dry and fruitless soul.
Heal each wound and bend each will,
Warm our hearts benumbed and chill,
All our wayward steps control

5 Unto all Thy faithful just,
Who in Thee confide and trust,
Deign the seven-fold gift to send.
Grant us virtue's best increase
Grant a death of hope and peace.
Grant the joys that never end

186—Creator-Spirit, All-Divine.

1 Cre-a-tor-Spir-it, all-Di-vine, Come vis-it ev-ery soul of Thine And fill with Thy ce-les-tial flame The hearts which Thou Thyself didst frame. O gift of God, Thine is the sweet Con-sol-ing name of Par-a-clete—And spring of life and fire and love, And unc-tion flow-ing from a-bove.

3 The mystic seven-fold gifts are Thine,
Finger of God's right hand divine;
The Father's promise sent to teach
The tongue a rich and heavenly speech.

4 Kindle with fire brought from above
Each sense, and fill our hearts with love;
And grant our flesh, so weak and frail,
The strength of Thine which ne'er may fail.

5 Drive far away our deadly foe,
And grant us Thy true peace to know;

So we, led by Thy guidance still,
Safely may pass through every ill.

6 To us, through Thee, the grace be shown
To know the Father and the Son;
And Spirit of them both, may we
Forever rest our faith in Thee.

7 To Sire and Son be praises meet,
And to the holy Paraclete;
And may Christ send us from above
That Holy Spirit's gift of love. Amen.

PENTECOST 287

188.—Come, Holy Ghost, Creator Blest.

TRINITY.

COME, HOLY GHOST, CREATOR BLEST—CONTINUED.

D.C. al Fine.

and Fire of love, And sweet a-noint-ing from a-bove.

3 O Holy Ghost, thro' Thee alone,
   Know we the Father and the Son
   Be this our never-changing creed,
   ‖: That Thou Dost from them both
        [proceed :‖

4 Praise we the Father and the Son,
   And Holy Spirit with them One;
   And may the Son on us bestow
   ‖: The gifts that from the Spirit flow :‖

TRINITY.

189—Have Mercy On Us, God Most High.

Moderato.

1 Have mer-cy on us, God Most High! Who lift our hearts to
2 When heav'n and earth were yet un-made, When time was yet un-
3 O! lis-ten, then most pit-i-full To Thy poor creature's

Thee,   Have mer-cy on us worms of earth, Most Ho-ly Trin-i-
known,   Thou in Thy bliss and ma-jes-ty, Didst live and love a-
heart,   It bless-es Thee that Thou art God, That Thou art what Thou

ty! Most an-cient of all mys-te-ries, Before Thy throne we lie; Have
lone! Thou wert not born, there was no fount From which Thy being flowed; There
art! Most an-cient of all mys-te-ries, Still at Thy feet we lie; Have

CORPUS CHRISTI.

HAVE MERCY ON US, GOD MOST HIGH—Continued.

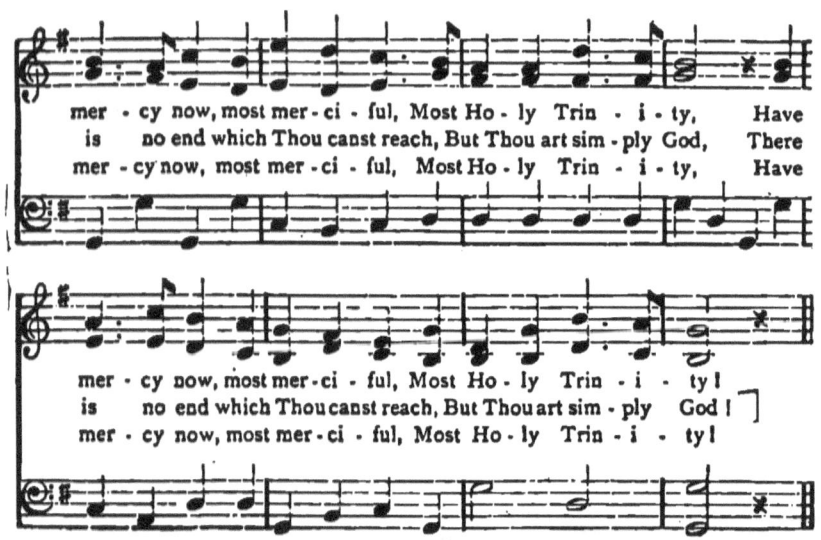

mer - cy now, most mer - ci - ful, Most Ho - ly Trin - i - ty, Have
is no end which Thou canst reach, But Thou art sim - ply God, There
mer - cy now, most mer - ci - ful, Most Ho - ly Trin - i - ty, Have

mer - cy now, most mer - ci - ful, Most Ho - ly Trin - i - ty!
is no end which Thou canst reach, But Thou art sim - ply God!
mer - cy now, most mer - ci - ful, Most Ho - ly Trin - i - ty!

CORPUS CHRISTI.

190—Sing, My Joyful Tongue, The Mystery.

Maestoso.

1 Sing, my joy - ful tongue, the mys - te - ry,
Of the glo - rious Bo - dy slain, And the

CORPUS CHRISTI.

SING, MY JOYFUL TONGUE, THE MYSTERY—Continued.

Blood all pure and prec-ious Shed a lost world

to re-gain, By the King of na-tions.

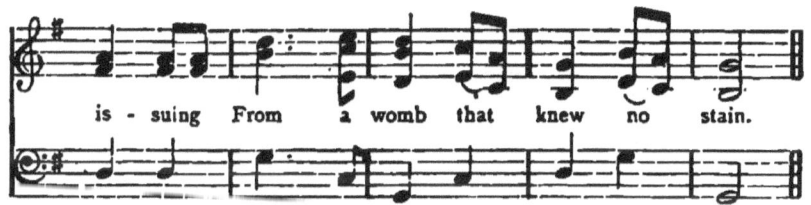
is-suing From a womb that knew no stain.

2 Born unto us of a Virgin
 Purer than the purest snow,
And amongst mankind conversing
 Seeds of heavenly truth to sow,
He at lenght in wondrous order,
 Closed His sojourn here below,

3 Seated, with His brethren round Him,
 On the night when last they met,
For the law's complete fulfilment

When the Lamb was duly ate,
 Then before the twelve disciples
For their food Himself He set,

4 By a word the Word Incarnate
 Simple bread to Flesh divine,
 Simple wine to Blood converteth ;
But, if sense to doubt incline,
 Under faith's sufficient teaching
 Simple hearts all doubts resign

191—Lauda Sion.

1 Lau-da, Si-on, Sal-va-to-rem, Lau-da Du-cem et Pas-
Quan-tum po-tes, tan-tum au-de; Qui-a ma-jor om-ni

CORPUS CHRISTI.

LAUDA SION—Continued.

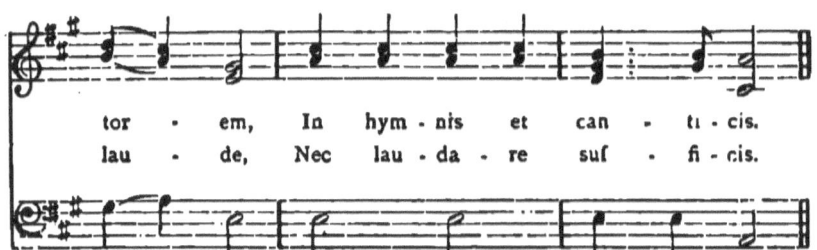

    tor - em, In hym - nis et can - ti - cis.
    lau - de, Nec lau - da - re suf - fi - cis.

2 Laudis thema specialis,
    Panis vivus et vitalis
      Hodie proponitur.
    Quem in sacræ mensa cœnæ,
    Turbæ fratrum duodenæ,
      Datum non ambigitur.

3 Sit laus plena, sit sonora,
    Sit jucunda, sit decora,
      Mentis jubilatio.
    Dies enim solemnis agitur,
    In qua mensæ prima recolitur
      Hujus institutio.

4 In hac mensa novi Regis,
    Novum Pascha novæ legis,
      Phase vetus terminat.
    Vetustatem novitas,
    Umbram fugat veritas,
      Noctem lux eliminat.

5 Quod in cœna Christus gessit,
    Faciendum hoc expressit
      In sui memoriam.
    Docti sacris institutis,
    Panem, vinum in salutis
      Consecramus hostiam.

6 Dogma datur Christianis,
    Quod in carnem transit panis,
      Et vinum in sanguinem.
    Quod non capis, quod non vides,
    Animosa firmat fides,
      Præter rerum ordinem.

7 Sub diversis speciebus,
    Signis tantum et non rebus,
      Latent res eximiæ.
    Caro, cibus, sanguis, potus;
    Manet tamen Christus totus
      Sub utraque specie.

8 A sumente non concisus,
    Non confractus, non divisus,
      Integer accipitur.
    Sumit unus, sumunt mille
    Quantum isti, tantum ille :
      Nec sumptus consumitur.

9 Sumunt boni, sumunt mali :
    Sorte tamen inæquali,
      Vitæ, vel interitus.
    Mors est malis, vita bonis :
    Vide paris sumptionis
      Quam sit dispar exitus.

10 Fracto demum Sacramento,
    Ne vacilles, sed memento,
    Tantum esse sub fragmento,
      Quantum toto tegitur.
    Nulla rei fit scissura,
    Signi tantum fit fractura :
    Qua nec status, nec statura
      Signati minuitur.

11 Ecce panis Angelorum,
    Factus cibus viatorum :
    Vere panis filiorum,
      Non mittendus canibus.
    In figuris præsignatur,
    Cum Isaac immolatur :
    Agnus Paschæ deputatur,
      Datur manna patribus.

12 Bone pastor, panis vere,
    Jesu nostri miserere :
    Tu nos pasce, nos tuere
    Tu nos bona fac videre
      In terra viventium.
    Tu, qui cuncta scis et vales,
    Qui nos pascis hic mortales :
    Tuos ibi commensales,
    Cohæredes, et sodales,
      Fac sanctorum civium.
      Amen. Alleluia.

EVENING.

192—Sweet Saviour! Bless Us Ere We Go.

1 Sweet Sa-viour, bless us ere we go,.... Thy word in-to our minds in-stil, And make our luke-warm hearts to glow, With low-ly love and fer-vent will.

CHORUS.
Through life's long day and death's dark night, O gen-tle Je-sus be our light, O gen-tle Je-sus be our light.

2 The day is done, its hour has run;
And Thou hast taken count of all
The scanty triumphs grace hath won,
The broken vow, the frequent fall.

3 Grant us, dear Lord! from evil ways,
True absolution and release,
And bless us more than in past days,
With purity and inward peace.

4 Do more than pardon; give us joy;
Sweet fear and sober liberty;
And simple hearts without delay,
That only long to be like Thee.

5 Sweet Saviour! bless us, night is come,
Mary and Joseph near us be
Good angels watch about our home,
And we are one day nearer Thee.

EVENING.

193—Hear Thy Children, Gentle Jesus.

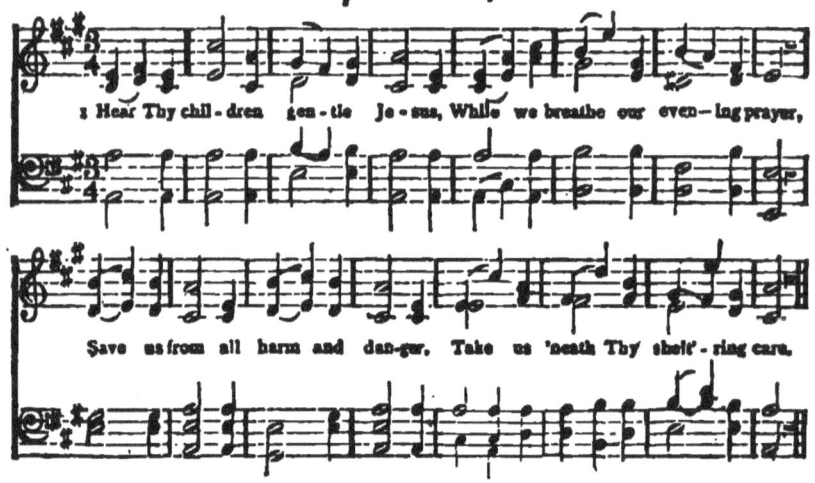

2. Save us from the wiles of Satan,
   'Mid the lone and sleepful night,
   Sweetly may our Guardian Angels,
   Keep us 'neath their watchful sight.

3. Gentle Jesus, look in pity,
   From Thy glorious throne above,

All the night Thy heart is wakeful
In Thy sacrament of love.

4. Shades of even fast are falling,
   Day is fading into gloom;
   When the shades of death fall round us,
   Lead Thine exiled children home.

OCCASIONAL.

194—Lead, Kindly Light, Amid The Encircling Gloom.

1 Lead Kind-ly Light, a-mid th' en-cir-cling gloom,......
2 I was not ev - er thus, nor pray'd that Thou......
3 So long Thy power hath blest me, sure it still........

OCCASIONAL.

195—Faith Of Our Fathers.

FAITH OF OUR FATHERS—Continued.

196—Yes, Heaven Is The Prize.

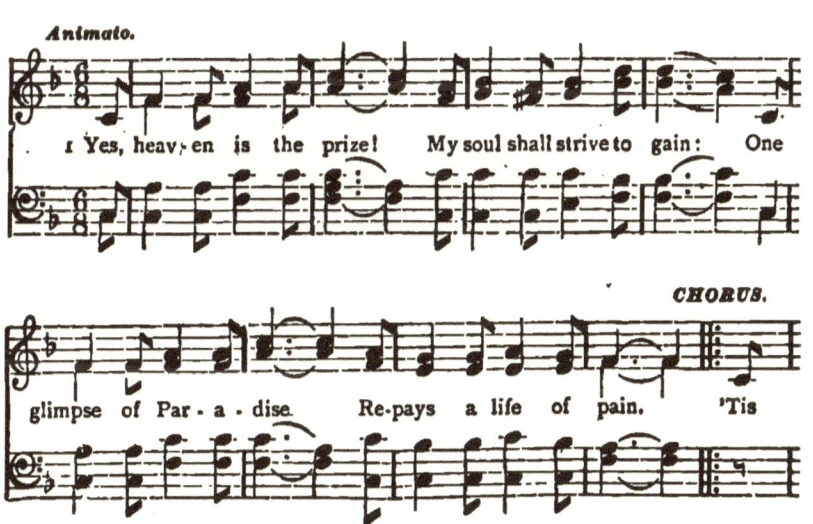

OCCASIONAL.

YES, HEAVEN IS THE PRIZE—Continued.

2 Yes, heaven is the prize!
   When sorrows press around,
Look up beyond the skies,
   Where hope and strength are found.

3 Yes, heaven is the prize!
   Oh! 'tis not hard to gain;

He surely wins who tries,
   For hope can conquer pain.

4 Yes, heaven is the prize!
   Death opens wide the door;
And then the spirit flies
   To God for evermore.

197—Pity, My God, 'Tis For Our Loved Land.

300 OCCASIONAL.

VENI JESU AMOR MI—Continued.

200—At the Commencement.

B.BS.

1. On bended knee a guilty race, Before Thee we appear; O grant us, Lord, Thy saving grace, Our sighs of sorrow hear. That we're unworthy, Lord, we own, But let Thy mercy still be shown, And on us sinners pity take, For Thine and our sweet Jesus' sake, For Jesus' sake, For Jesus' sake, For Thy sweet Jesus' sake.

2. Full grievously we've sinned we know, Far, far from duty swerved; But yet, kind Lord, hold back the blow, Too well by sin deserved, Forget not all the blood He shed, Thy Son, our Brother, on whose head Thou once didst lay that guiltiness, Which now in sorrow we confess, We now confess, We now confess, In sorrow we confess.

304 GUARDIAN ANGEL.

AT THE SANCTUS—Continued.

"Ho-ly! Ho-ly! Ho-ly! Art Thou, Lord God of Hosts!" The
bless-ed He who com-eth In Thy Name, might-y Lord." Ho-

star-ry sky a-round us, The shin-ing earth be-low, The
san-na in the high-est! To Da-vid's Son in-tone; Thus

great-ness of Thy glo-ry, In bright ef-ful-gence show
may we sing in glo-ry, For ev-er round His throne.

GUARDIAN ANGEL.

203—Dear Angel, Ever At My Side.

1 Dear an-gel, ev-er at my side, How

GUARDIAN ANGEL.

DEAR ANGEL, EVER AT MY SIDE—CONTINUED.

love - ly must Thou be, To leave thy home in heaven, to guide a lit - tle child like me,........ a lit - tle child like me.

2 Thy beautiful and shining face
   I see not, tho' so near;
   The sweetness of thy soft low voice,
   I am too deaf to hear.

3 I cannot feel thee touch my hand,
   With pressure light and mild,
   To check me as my mother did,
   When I was but a child.

4 But I have felt thee in my thoughts,
   Fighting with sin for me;
   And when my heart loves God I know
   The sweetness is from thee.

5 And when, dear spirit, I kneel down
   Morning and night to prayer
   Something there is within my heart,
   Which tells me thou art there.

6 Yes! when I pray, thou prayest too;
   Thy prayer is all for me;
   But when I sleep, thou sleepest not,
   But watchest patiently

7 Then love me, love me, Angel dear!
   And I will love thee more;
   And help me, when my soul is cast
   Upon th' eternal shore.

204—Bless Me, Befriend Me.

Semplice

1 Bless me, be - friend me, Sweet an - gel, I pray;
2 Beam on my glad - ness, Thy joy I shall share;
3 An - gel so ho - ly! Whom God sends to me,
4 O, may I nev - er For - get thou art near;
5 Till my last sor - row I'll walk in thy light;

ST. MICHAEL.
MICHAEL, PRINCE OF HIGHEST HEAVEN—Continued.

les-tial ranks, Low-ly sing-ing in thine honour, Bring we now our meed of thanks, Bring we now our meed of thanks. 1 Mighty vic-tor all re-splen-dent Next to Ma-ry thou dost reign, Come and bless us with thy pres-ence, Bring with thee thy heaven-ly train

2 Gabriel, silver-tongued and glorious,
   Raphael, healer of our woes;
Blessed angels, gentle guardians,
   Be our aid, repel our foes.

3 Breathe into our hearts your sweetness,
   Fill our souls with love divine,
May your gracious presence ever
   Round your charge protecting shine

4 We will honour, we will love you,
   Blesssd spirit, more and more,
Our devotion still increasing,
   As your favours on us pour.

5 Till with you forever singing,
   In a glad unending strain.
God the Father, Son and Spirit,
   Where the blessed ever reign.

206—Know Ye that Angels Silently Glide.

1. Know ye that an-gels si-lent-ly glide, From their blest mansions, down to our side?
Know ye their bright eyes watch night and day, Lest evil spirits make you their prey?
Beau-ti-ful angels keep watch and ward O-v r the chil - dren dear to the Lord.
By your sweet presence render us still Steadfast in goodness, proof against ill.

2 Blessings precede them while they ad-
Satan in terror lowers his lance; [vance,
All the dark legions flee in dismay,
Melting like morning vapors away.

3 Often their gentle voice from above
Touches our heart-strings, teaches us love,
Leads us to worship happily here,
Even as Angels in their bright sphere.

ANGELS.

207—O God! How Ought My Grateful Heart.

O God! how ought my grate-ful heart To praise Thy bount-eous

hand, Who send'st Thy An-gel from the skies, To

be my guide and friend, To be my guide and friend.

2 My soul is surely something great,
　Meant for Eternity;
　That Angels thus should be employed
‖ In watching over me. ‖

3 And when the morning from the east
　Sends forth her golden rays;
　Teach me to raise my heart to God,
‖ And sing His glorious praise. ‖

4 In evening, when the cooling breeze
　Invites to sweet repose,
　May I in grateful thanks to Him
‖ My weary eyelids close. ‖

5 Celestial Guardian, thus with Thee,
　And by Thy constant care,
　May I the world's corruption flee,
‖ And heavenly blessings share. ‖

ANGELS.

208—Hark, Hark, My Soul.

1. Hark, hark, my soul, an-gel-ic songs are swelling O'er earth's green fields and o cean's wave-beat shore; How sweet the truth those blessed strains are tell-ing, Of that new life when sin shall be no more.
2. On-ward we go, for still we hear them singing, "Come, weary souls, for Je-sus bids you come!" And through the dark, its ech-oes sweet-ly ring-ing, The mu-sic of the gos-pel leads us home.
3. Far, far a-way, like bells at evening pealing, The voice of Je-sus sounds o'er land and sea, And lad-en souls, by thousands meekly steal-ing, Kind Shepherd turn their wear-y steps to Thee.
4. Rest comes at length, tho' life be long and drear-y, The day must dawn and darksome night be past: All jour-neys end in welcomes to the wear-y, And heav'n, the heart's true home, will come at last.

Maestoso Chorus.

An-gels of Je-sus, an-gels of light, Sing-ing to wel-come

ANGELS.

HARK, HARK, MY SOUL—*Continued.*

LITANY OF BLESSED VIRGIN.

209—Litany. No. 1.

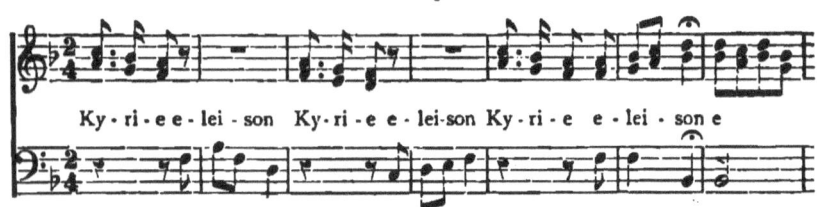

Ky-ri-e e-lei-son Ky-ri-e e-lei-son Ky-ri-e e-lei-son e

1. Pa-ter de cœ-lis De-us Fi-li Redemptor mundi De-us

1st & 2nd. Mi-se-re-re no-bis mi-se-re-re

2 Sancta Trinitas, unus Deus miserere nobis.
3 Sancta Maria,
4 Sancta Dei Genitrix,
5 Sancta Virgo Virginum,
6 Mater Christi,
7 Mater divinæ gratiæ,
8 Mater purissima,
9 Mater castissima,
10 Mater inviolata,
11 Mater intemerata,
12 Mater amabilis,
13 Mater admirabilis,
14 Mater boni consilii,

} *Ora pro nobis.*

15 Mater Creatoris,
16 Mater Salvatoris,
17 Virgo prudentissima,
18 Virgo veneranda,
19 Virgo prædicanda,
20 Virgo potens,
21 Virgo clemens,
22 Virgo fidelis,
23 Speculum justitiæ,
24 Sedes sapientiæ,
25 Causa nostrae lætitiæ,
26 Vas spirituale,
27 Vas honorabile,
28 Vas insigne devotionis,

} *Ora pro nobis.*

Ag-nus De-i qui tol-lis pec-ca-ta mundi. Par-ce no-bis, par-ce

2. Exaudi nos ex-au-
3. Mi-se-re-re mi-se

LITANY OF BLESSED VIRGIN. 313

LITANY—*Concluded.*

le - i - son. Chris - te au - di nos Chris - te ex - au - di nos.

Spi-ri-tus Sancte De - us mi-se-re-re nobis miserere no - bis.

no-bis mise-re-re no-bis mise-re-re mise-re-re no - bis.

29 Rosa mystica,	41 Regina Patriarcharum,
30 Turris Davidica,	42 Regina Prophetarum,
31 Turris eburnea,	43 Regina Apostolorum,
32 Domus aurea,	44 Regina Martyrum,
33 Fœderis arca,	45 Regina Confessorum,
34 Janua cœli,	46 Regina Virginum,
35 Stella matutina,	47 Regina Sanctorum omnium,
36 Salus infirmorum,	
37 Refugium peccatorum,	48 Regina sine labe originali concepta,
38 Consolatrix afflictorum,	
39 Auxilium Christianorum	49 Regina sanctissimi Rosarii.
40 Regina Angelorum,	

Ora pro nobis. *Ora pro nobis.*

no - bis, par-ce no-bis Do-mi-ne. Christe au-di nos, Christe ex-au-di nos.

di nos ex-au-di nos Do-mi-ne.
re - re mi-se-re-re no - bis.

12

Litanies.

No. 5.

No. 6. St. Xavier's Litany of the B. V. M.

Arranged by S. M. A

210—Litany of the Sacred Heart.

BY KIND PERMISSION OF THE APOSTLESHIP OF PRAYER.

Soprano. Alto, *ad lib*
Con moto. *p*
LUDWIG BONVIN, S. J. Op. No. 58.

Ky - ri - e, e - le - i - son. Chris - te, e - le - i - son.

Ky - ri - e, e - le - i - son. Chris - te au - di nos. Chris - te, ex - au - di - son.

1 Pater de coelis   De - us   Mi - se - re - re   no - bis.
2 Fili Redemptor mundi   De - us   Mi - se - re - re   no - bis.
3 Spiritus Sancte   De - us   Mi - se - re - re   no - bis.
4 Sancta Trinitas unus   De - us   Mi - se - re - re   no - bis.

Cor Je - su, Filii Patris æ - ter - ni, Mi - se - re - re no - bis.
Cor Je - su, in sinu Virginis
         Matris a Spiritu Sancto for - ma - tum, Mi - se - re - re no - bis.
Cor Je - su, Verbo Dei substantialiter u - ni - tum, Mi - se - re - re no - bis.
Cor Je - su, Maiestatis in fi - ni - tae, Mi - se - re - re no - bis.
Cor Je - su, Templum De - - - i sanc - tum, Mi - se - re - re no - bis.
Cor Je - su, Tabernaculum Al - tissi - mi, Mi - se - re - re no - bis,
Cor Je - su, Domus Dei et por - ta coe - li, Mi - se - re - re no - bis.
Cor Je - su, fornax ardens ca - ri - ta - tis, Mi - se - re - re no - bis.
Cor Je - su, justitiæ et amoris re - cep - ta - culum, Mi - se - re - re no - bis.
Cor Je - su, bonitate et amo - - re - ple - num, Mi - se - re - re no - bis
Cor Je - su, virtutum omnium - ab - ys - sus Mi - se - re - re no - bis

LITANY.

LITANY OF THE SACRED HEART—Continued.

211. Litany of the Saints.

(To be sung at the Forty Hours' Exposition of the Most Blessed Sacrament.)

Edit. Ratisbon.

Ky - ri - e e - le - i - son. Chris - te e - le - i - son.

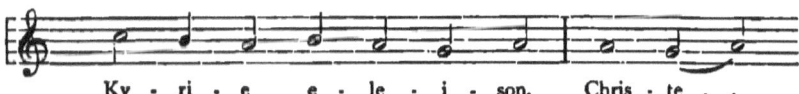

Ky - ri - e e - le - i - son. Chris - te . .

au - di nos. Chris - te ex - au - di nos.

Pater de cœlis De - us. Mi - se - re - re no - bis.
Fili, Redemptor mundi De - us. Mi - se - re - re no - bis.
Spiritus sancte De - us. Mi - se - re - re no - bis.
Sancta Trinitas, unus De - us. Mi - se - re - re no - bis.

Sancta Ma - ri - a. O - ra pro no - bis.

Sancta Dei Genitrix. Ora, etc.
Sancta Virgo Virginum. Ora, etc.
Sancte Michael. Ora, etc.
Sancte Gabriel. Ora, etc.
Sancte Raphael. Ora, etc.
Omnes sancti Angeli et Archangeli.
  Orate, etc.

Omnes sancti beatorum Spirituum ordines. Orate, etc.
Sancte Joannes Baptista. Ora, etc.
Sancte Joseph. Ora, etc.
Omnes sancti Patriarchæ et Prophetæ.
  Orate, etc.

LITANY OF THE SAINTS.

LITANY OF THE SAINTS—*Continued.*

Sancte Pe - tre. O - ra pro no - bis.

Sancte Paule.
Sancte Andrea.
*Sancte Jacobe.
Sancte Joannes.
*Sancte Thoma.
*Sancte Jacobe.
*Sancte Philippe.
*Sancte Bartholomæe.
*Sancte Matthæe.
*Sancte Simon.
*Sancte Thaddæe.
*Sancte Matthia.
*Sancte Barnaba.
*Sancte Luca.
*Sancte Marce.
Omnes sancti Apostoli | et Evangelistæ. Orate, etc.
Omnes sancti Discipuli Domini. Orate, etc.
*Omnes sancti Innocentes. Orate, etc.
Sancte Stephane.
Sancte Laurenti.
Sancte Vincenti.
*Sancti Fabiane et Sebastiane. Orate, etc.
*Sancti Joannes et Paule. Orate, etc.
*Sancti Cosma et Damiane. Orate, etc.
*Sancti Gervasi et Protasi. Orate, etc.
Omnes sancti Martyres. Orate, etc.

Sancte Silvester.
Sancte Gregori.
*Sancte Ambrosi.
Sancte Augustine.
*Sancte Hieronyme.
*Sancte Martine.
*Sancte Nicolæ.
Omnes sancti Pontifices | et Confessores. Orate, etc.
Omnes sancti Doctores. Orate, etc.
Sancte Antoni.
Sancte Benedicte.
Sancte Bernarde.
Sancte Dominice.
Sancte Francisce.
Omnes sancti Sacerdotes et Levitæ. Orate, etc.
Omnes sancti Monachi et Eremitæ. Orate, etc.
Sancta Maria Magdalena.
Sancta Agatha.
Sancta Lucia.
Sancta Agnes.
Sancta Cæcilia.
Sancta Catharina.
Sancta Anastasia.
Omnes sanctæ Virgines et Viduæ. Orate, etc.

Omnes Sancti et Sanctæ De - i, In - ter - ce - di - te pro no - bis.

LITANY OF THE SAINTS—Continued.

Pro - pi - ti - us es - to, Par - ce no - bis, Do - mi - ne.

Propitius esto, exaudi nos, Domine.
Ab omni malo,
Ab omni peccato,
Ab ira tua,
A subitanea et improvisa morte,

Ab insidiis diaboli,
Ab ira et odio et omni mala voluntate,
A spiritu fornicationis,
A fulgure et tempestate,
A flagello terræmotus,
A peste, fame, et bello

} *Libera nos, Domine.*

A morte perpetua,
Per mysterium sanctæ incarnationis tuæ,
Per adventum tuum,
Per nativitatem tuam,
Per baptismum, et sanctum jejunium tuum,
Per crucem et passionem tuam,
Per mortem et sepulturam tuam,
Per sanctam resurrectionem tuam,
Per admirabilem ascensionem tuam,
Per adventum Spiritus sancti Paracliti,
In die Judicii.

} *Libera nos, Domine.*

Pec - ca - to - res. R. Te ro - gam - us au - di nos.

Ut nobis parcas,
Ut nobis indulgeas,
Ut ad veram pœnitentiam nos perducere digneris,
Ut ecclesiam tuam sanctam regere, et conservare digneris,

Ut domnum apostolicum, et omnes ecclesiasticos ordines in sancta religione conservare digneris,
Ut inimicos sanctæ ecclesiæ humiliare digneris,

Ut regibus, et principibus Christianis pacem, et veram concordiam donare digneris,
Ut cuncto populo Christiano pacem, et unitatem largiri digneris,

} *Te rogamus, audi nos.*

Ut nosmetipsos in tuo sancto servitio confortare, et conservare digneris,
Ut mentes nostras ad cœlestia desideria erigas,
Ut omnibus benefactoribus nostris sempiterna bona retribuas,
Ut animas nostras fratrum, propinquorum, et benefactorum nostrorum ab æterna damnatione eripias
Ut fructus terræ dare, et conservare digneris,

Ut omnibus fidelibus defunctis requiem æternam donare digneris,
Ut nos exaudire digneris,

Fili Dei,

} *Te rogamus, audi nos.*

LITANY OF THE SAINTS.

LITANY OF THE SAINTS—*Continued.*

A - gnus De - i, qui tol - lis pec - ca - ta
A - gnus De - i, qui tol - lis pec - ca - ta
A - gnus De - i, qui tol - lis pec - ca - ta

mun - di. R. Par - ce no - bis, Do - mi - ne.
mun - di. Ex - au - di nos, Do - mi - ne.
mun - di. Mi - se - re - re, no - bis.

Chri - ste, au - di nos. Chri - ste, ex - au - di nos.

Ky - ri - e e - le - i - son. Chri - ste e -

le - i - son. Ky - ri - e e - - -

CELEBRANT.

le - i - son.— Pa - ter no - ster.

V. Et ne nos inducas in tentati - - - o - nem.
R. Sed libera nos a........................ma - lo.

LITANY OF THE SAINTS.

LITANY OF THE SAINTS—*Continued.*

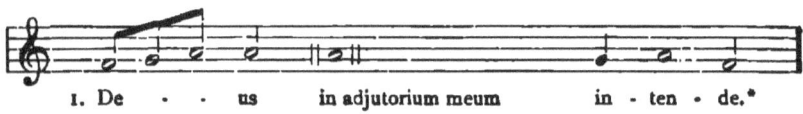

1. De — — us in adjutorium meum in - ten - de.*

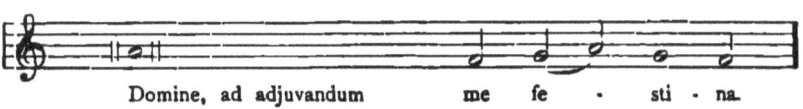

Domine, ad adjuvandum me fe - sti - na.

2. Confundantur, et revereantur, *qui quaerunt animam meam.
3. Avertantur retrorsum, et erubescant, *qui volunt mihi mala.
4. Avertantur statim erubescentes, *qui dicunt mihi : Euge, euge !
5. Exultent, et laetentur | in te omnes, | qui quaerunt te : *et dicant semper : | Magnificetur Dominus, | qui diligunt salutare tuum.
6. Ego vero egenus, et pauper sum: *Deus, adjuva me.
7. Adjutor meus, et liberator meus es tu : *Domine, ne moreris.
8. Gloria Patri, et Filio, *et Spiritui sancto.
9. Sicut erat in principio, | et nunc, et semper, *et in saecula saeculorum. Amen.

V. Salvos fac servos tuos.
R. Deus meus, sperantes in te.
V. Esto nobis, Domine, turris fortitudinis.
R. A facie inimici.
V. Nihil proficiat inimicus in nobis.
R. Et filius iniquitatis non apponat nocere nobis.
V. Domine, non secundum peccata nostra facias nobis.
R. Neque secundum iniquitates nostras retribuas nobis.
V. Oremus pro Pontifice nostro, N.
R. Dominus conservet eum, et vivificet eum, et beatum faciat eum in terra, et non tradat eum in anima inimicorum ejus.
V. Oremus pro benefactoribus nostris.
R. Retribuere dignare, Domine, omnibus nobis bona facientibus propter nomen tuum, vitam æternam. Amen.
V. Oremus pro fidelibus defunctis.
R. Requiem æternam dona eis Domine ; et lux perpetua luceat eis.
V. Requiescant in pace.
R. Amen.
V. Pro fratribus nostris absentibus.
R. Salvos fac servos tuos, Deus meus sperantes in te.
V. Mitte eis Domine auxilium de sancto.
R. Et de Sion tuere eos.
V. Domine, exaudi orationem meam
R. Et clamor meus ad te veniat.
V. Oremus.*
R. Amen.
V. Dominus vobiscum.
R. Et cum spiritu tuo.
V. Exaudiat nos omnipotens et misericors Dominus.
R. Et custodiat nos semper. Amen.

212—Te Deum Laudamus.

TE DEUM LAUDAMUS.

TE DEUM LAUDAMUS—Continued.

TE DEUM LAUDAMUS.

TE DEUM LAUDAMUS—Continued.

1 Choir.
Et lau-da-mus no-men tu-um in sae - cu-lum:

2 Choir.
et in sae-cu-lum sae-cu-li. Dig-na-re Do-mi-ne di-e is-to:

1 Choir.
si-ne pec-ca-to nos cus-to-di-re. Mi-se-re-re no stri Do-mi-ne:

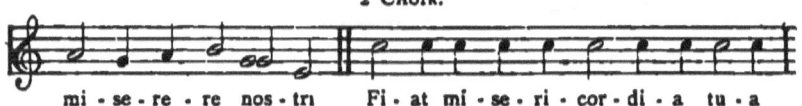

2 Choir.
mi-se-re-re nos-tri Fi-at mi-se-ri-cor-di-a tu-a

Do-mi-ne su-per-nos; quem-ad-modum spe-ra-vi-mus in te.

1 Choir. 1 and 2 Choirs.
In te Do-mi-ne, spe-ra-vi: non con-fun-dar in ae-ter-num.

℣. Benedictus es, Domine, Deus Patrum nostrorum.
℟. Et laudabilis, et gloriosus in saecula.
℣. Benedicamus Patrem, et Filium
cum Sancto Spiritu
℟. Laudemus, et superexaltemus Eum
in saecula.
℣. Benedictus es, Domine Deus, in
firmamento cœli.

℟. Et laudabilie, et gloriosus, et super
exaltatus in saecula.
℣. Benedic anima mea Domino.
℟. Et noli oblivisci omnes retribu-
tiones ejus.
℣. Domine exaudi orationem meam.
℟. Et clamor meus ad te veniat
℣. Dominus vobiscum,
℟. Et cum Spiritu tuo,

OREMUS

213 — Vidi Aquam.
For Easter.

214 Asperges Me.

Sung before Mass, from Trinity to Palm Sunday inclusive.
2 VOICES & BASS AD LIB.

Repeat the "Asperges me," to the Psalm "Miserere."

The Priest having returned to the foot of the Altar, sings:

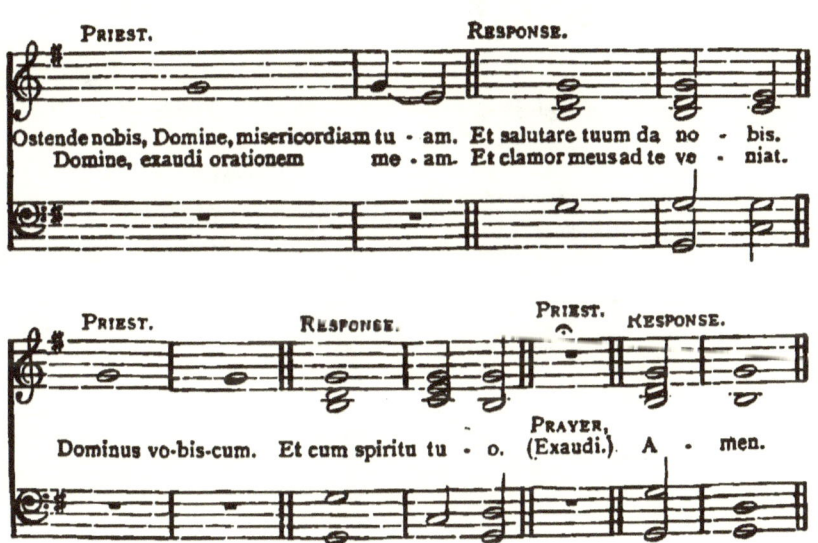

215 — Missa De Angelis.

KYRIE.

336   MISSA DE ANGELIS.

GLORIA.

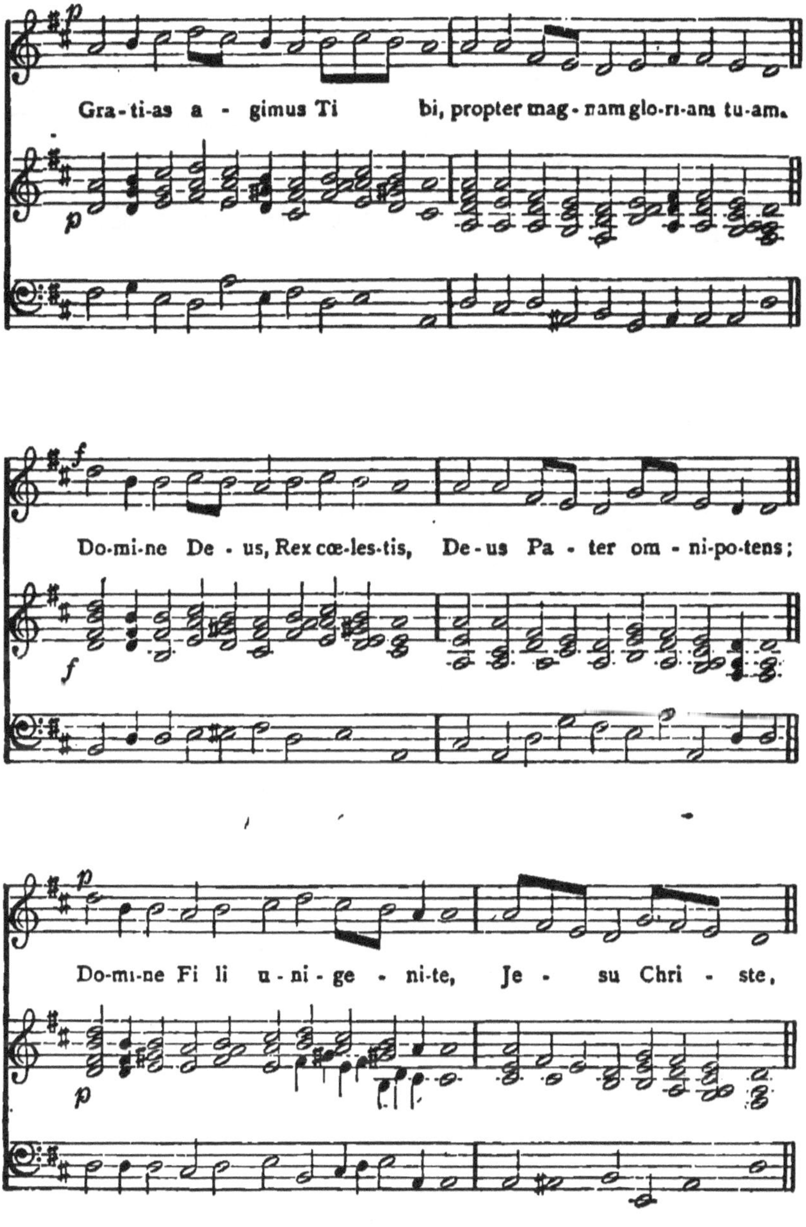
Gra-ti-as a - gimus Ti bi, propter mag - nam glo-ri-am tu-am.
Do-mi-ne De - us, Rex cœ-les-tis, De - us Pa - ter om - ni-po-tens;
Do-mi-ne Fi li u - ni - ge - ni-te, Je - su Chri - ste,

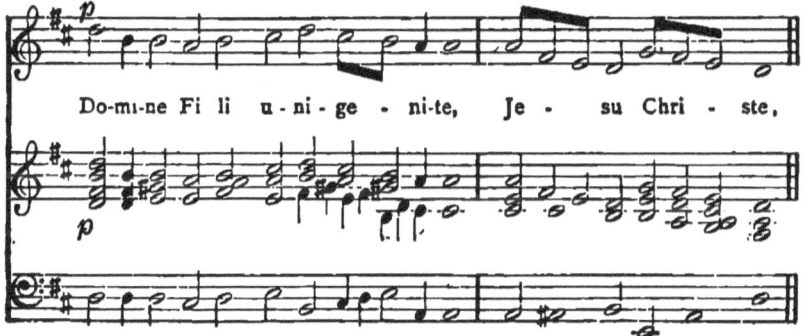

MISSA DE ANGELIS.

MISSA DE ANGELIS.
CREDO.

MISSA DE ANGELIS.

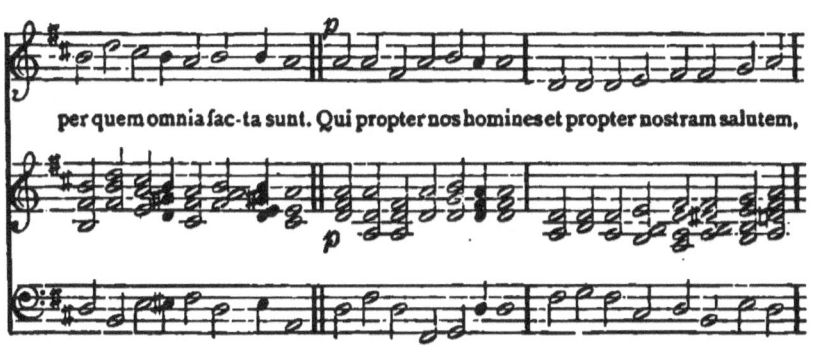

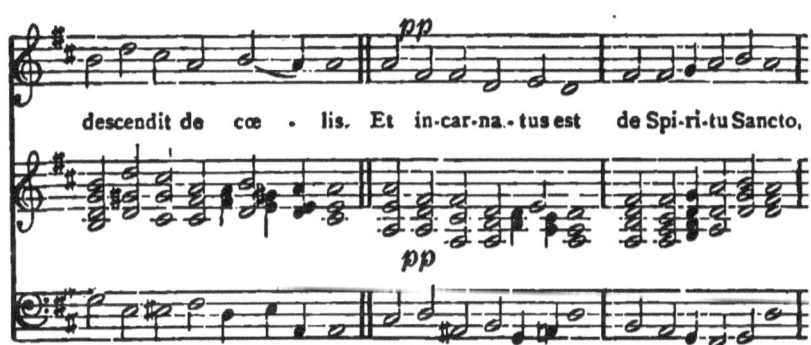

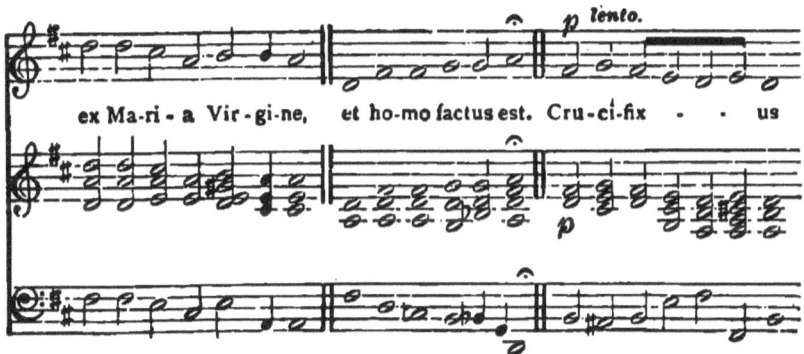

SANCTUS.

MISSA DE ANGELIS.

MISSA DE ANGELIS.

MISSA DE ANGELIS.

AGNUS DEI.

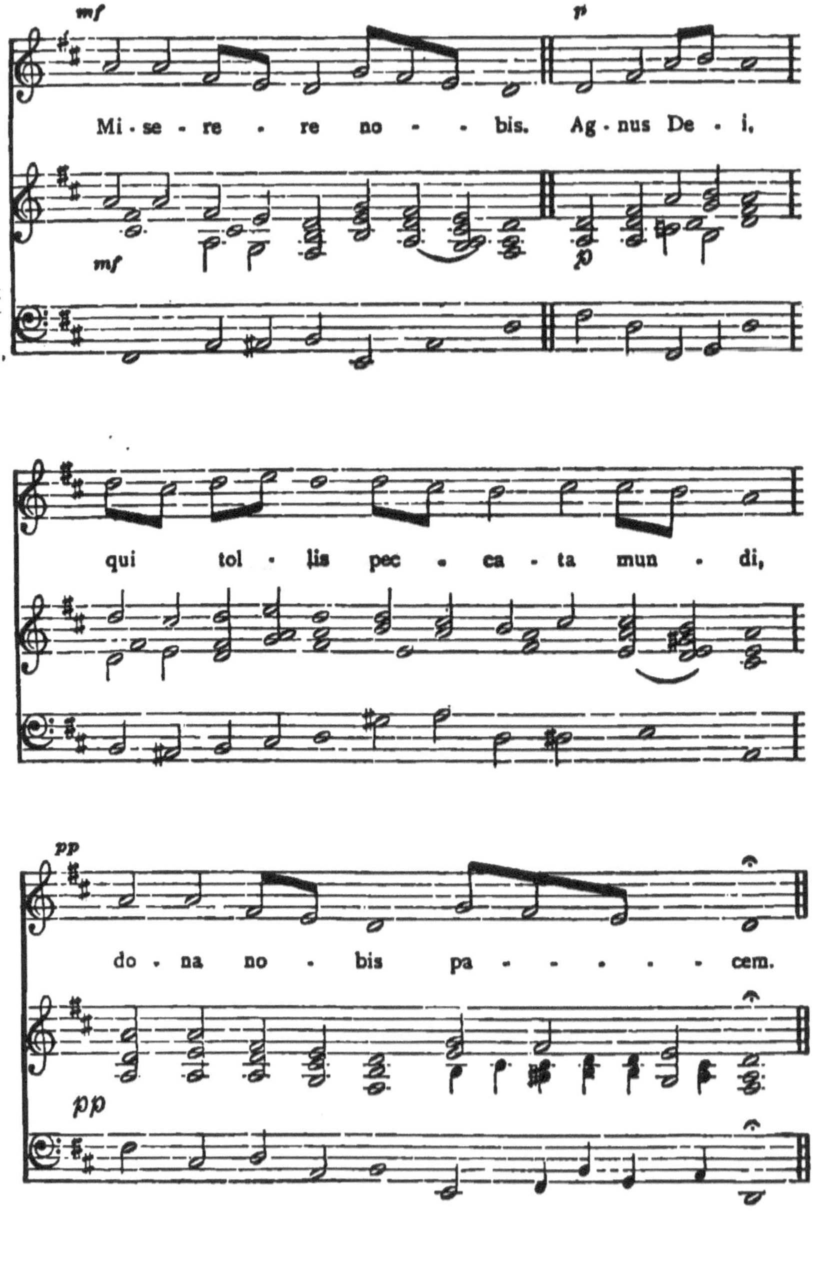
mf
p
Mi - se - re - re no - - bis. Ag - nus De - i,
mf
p
qui tol - lis pec - ca - ta mun - di,
pp
do - na no - bis pa - - - - - - cem.
pp

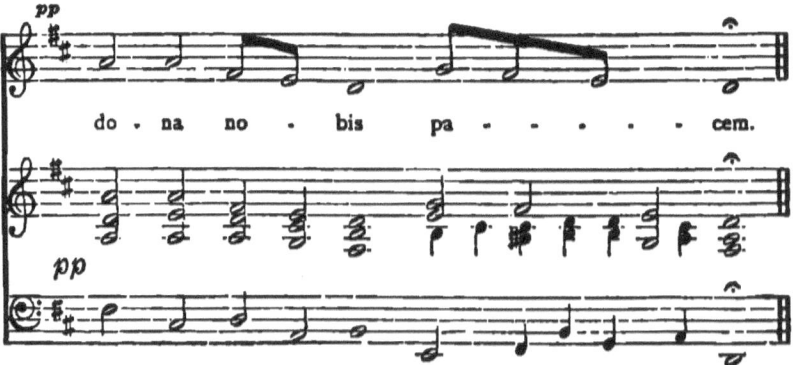

216—Short Choral Mass in E flat.
Kyrie.

MASS.

KYRIE—Continued.

Gloria in Excelsis Deo.

Benedictus.

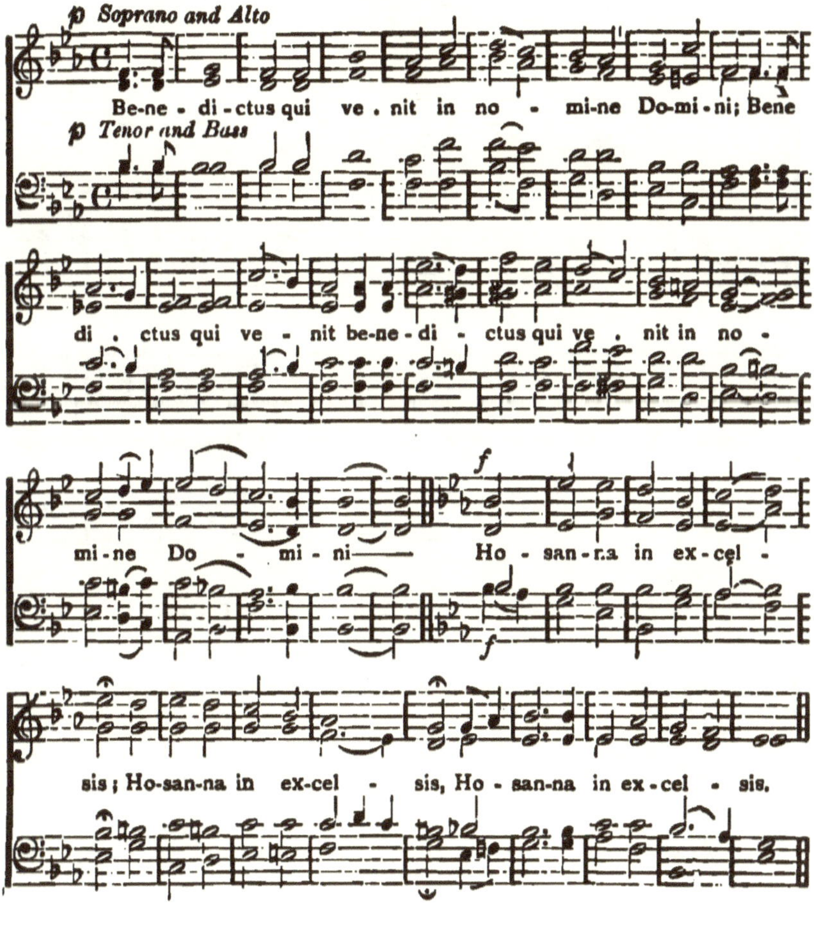

Agnus Dei

By permission of Dittson Co. (from Peter's Sodality Hymn Book)
SISTERS OF NOTRE DAME.

217—Responses at High Mass.

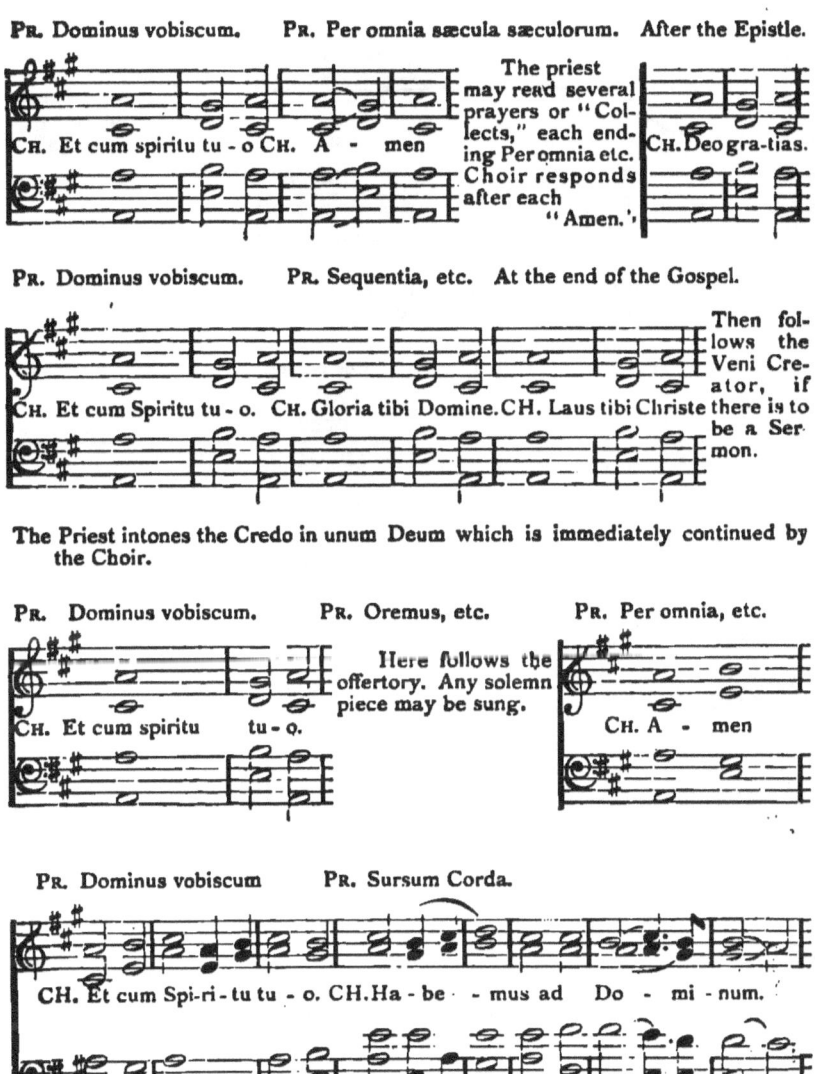

RESPONSES AT HIGH MASS.

Pr. Gratias agamus, etc.

Ch. Dig - - num et jus - tum est.

Then follows the Preface, chanted by the Priest, at the end of which the bell is rung, and the Choir sings the Sanctus.

As soon as the bell is sounded for the Elevation, the Choir must be silent till the Elevation is over, then sing the Benedictus.

Pr. Per omnia, etc., At the end of the Pater noster.   Pr. Per omnia, etc.

Ch. A-men. Ch. Sed li - be - ra nos a ma - lo. Ch. A - men

Pr. Pax Domini sit semper vobiscum.   Pr. Dominus vobiscum.

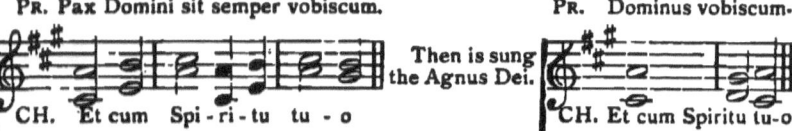

Ch. Et cum Spi - ri - tu tu - o   Then is sung the Agnus Dei.   Ch. Et cum Spiritu tu-o

Pr. Per omnia, etc. Pr. Dominus vobiscum, Pr. Ite missa est, or Benedica-
[mus Domino.

Ch. A - - men. Ch. Et cum Spiritu tu - o, Ch. Deo Gra - - tias.

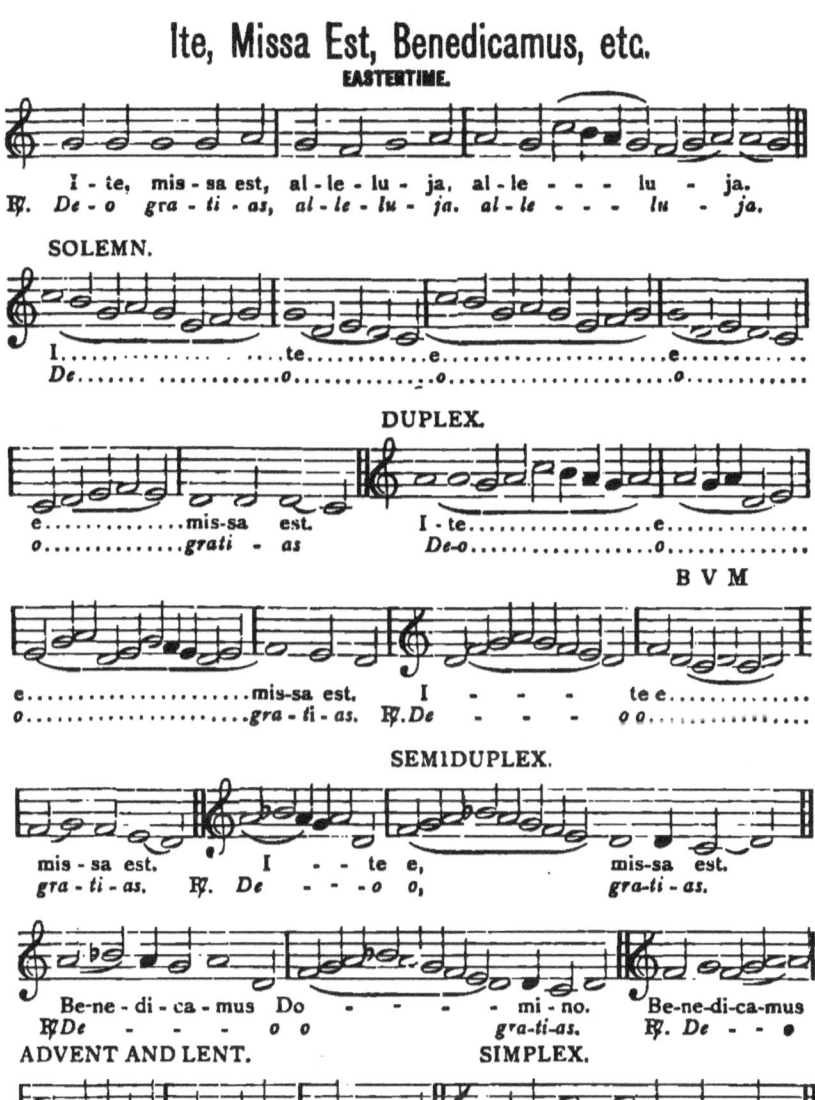

218 — Missa Pro Defunctis.

INTROIT.

MISSA PRO DEFUNCTIS. 371

MISSA PRO DEFUNCTIS.

MISSA PRO DEFUNCTIS.

MISSA PRO DEFUNCTIS. 377
OFFERTORIUM.

f
re - qui - em, do - na e - is Do - mi - ne,
do-na e - is do - na
do - na e - is re - qui - em...... sem-pi - ter - nam.
sem - pi - ter

SANCTUS.

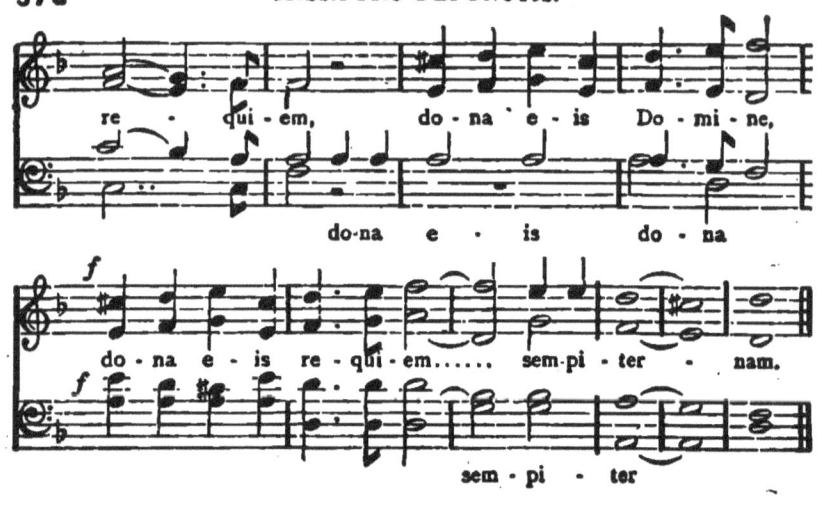

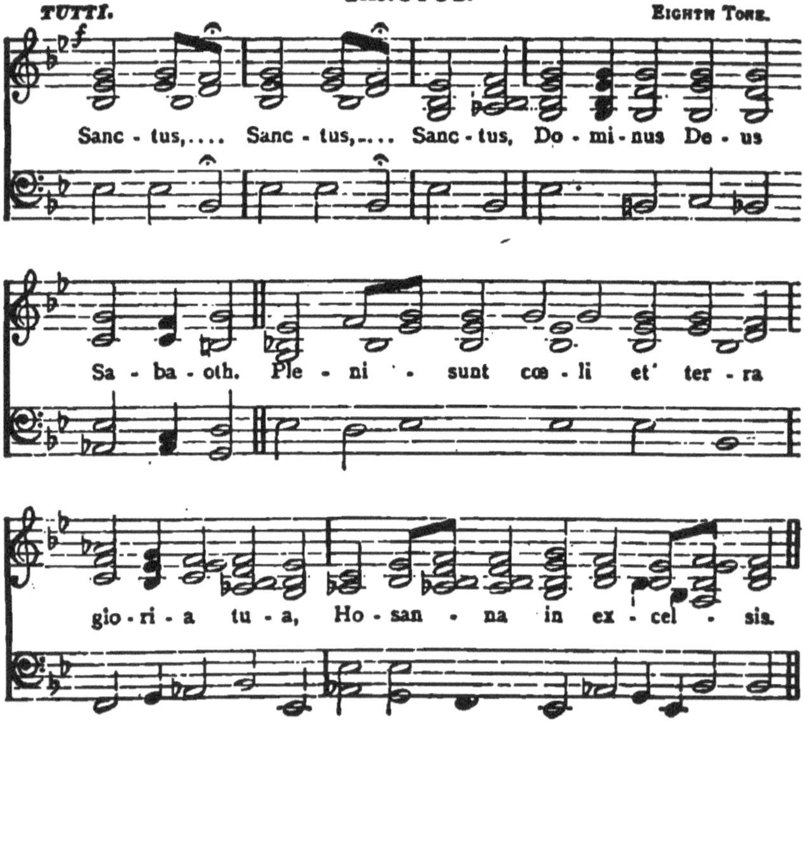
TUTTI.
EIGHTH TONE.
f
Sanc - tus,.... Sanc - tus,.... Sanc - tus, Do - mi - nus De - us
Sa - ba - oth. Ple - ni - sunt cœ - li et ter - ra
glo - ri - a tu - a, Ho - san - na in ex - cel - sis.

MISSA PRO DEFUNCTIS.

219 — LIBERA.

MISSA PRO DEFUNCTIS.

V. Requiem ætérnam dona......... eis, Dómine, et lux perpé...... tua lúceat............ eis.
R. Líbera.

Kýrie eléison Christe eléison Kýrie eléison.

V. Et ne nos indúcas in tentatiónem
R. Sed líbera nos a .... malo
V. A porta .... ínferi
R. Erue, Dómine, ánimam .... ejus
V. Requiéscat in .... pace
R. Amen
V. Dómine exáudi oratiónem .... meam
R. Et clamor meus ad te .... véniat
V. Dóminus vobíscum
R. Et cum spíritu tuo
V. Orémus, etc. —Christum Dóminum nostrum
R. Amen
V. Requiem ætérnam dona ei, ... Dómine
R. Et lux perpétua lúceat .... ei

V. Requiéscat in pace. *R.* Amen.

The Sodality of the Blessed Virgin Mary.

RULES FOR BRANCH SODALITIES.

The object of the Sodality is to promote devotions to the Blessed Virgin Mary.

Branch Sodalities should be affiliated with the Sodality of the Roman College.

The governing body of each branch should consist of a Father Director, a President, Secretary and two Assistants, together with a Council of six or twelve. Other officers may be appointed by this body.

The Sodality should have regular meetings for religious exercises, and should also recite at such meetings, at least, the "Little Office of the Immaculate Conception."

Members should receive Holy Communion once a month, and also upon the principal festivals of the year.

Members who absent themselves from regular meetings should explain their absence to the Prefect.

Members should all contribute towards paying any necessary expenses incurred by the Sodality.

Sodalists should visit at their homes members who are unable to attend the meetings through sickness, and a mass should be offered and special prayers said for the repose of any deceased member's soul.

Candidates for admission should apply to the Father Director or Prefect, and postulants should spend at least one month as a period of probation.

Election of officers should be held annually, and conducted in the manner prescribed by the Father Director, who may, in his discretion. reject any appointment.

NOTE.—The rules for the government of Sodalities and the conduct of officers and members, together with the list of the indulgences within the reach of Sodalists, may be found in detail in the "Manual of the Sodality," (Benziger Bros.), or in the "Manual for the Children of Mary," (John Chisholm, Edinburgh).

Solemn Reception.

The Hymn. "Veni Creator," *is said or sung.*—See page 59.
For translation, see "Come, Holy Ghost, Creator Blest," page 287.

V. Emitte Spiritum Tuum et creabuntur.	V. Send forth Thy Spirit and they shall be created.
R. Et renovabis faciem terræ.	R. And Thou shalt renew the face of the earth.
Oremus.	*Let us Pray.*
DEUS, qui corda fidelium Sancti Spiritus illustratione docuisti, da nobis in eodem Spiritu recta sapere et de ejus semper consolatione gaudere. Per Jesum Christum Dominum nostrum. Amen.	O GOD, who by the light of the Holy Ghost hast instructed the hearts of Thy faithful, grant us, through the same Holy Spirit, to relish what is right, and evermore to rejoice in His consolations through Jesus Christ our Lord. Amen.

BLESSED VIRGIN MARY.

The Blessing of the Medals.

V. Adjutorium nostrum in nomine Domini.
R. Qui fecit cœlum et terram.
V. Domine exaudi orationem meam.
R. Et clamor meus ad te veniat.
V. Dominus vobiscum.
R. Et cum spiritu tuo.

Oremus.

OMNIPOTENS sempiterne Deus, qui sanctorum tuorum imagines (sive effigies) sculpi aut pingi non reprobas, ut quoties illas oculis corporis intuemur, toties eorum actus et sanctitatem ad imitandum memoriæ oculis meditemur has quæsumus, imagines in honorem et memoriam beatissimæ Virginis Mariæ, Matris Domini nostri Jesu Christi adaptatas bene ✠ dicere et sancti✠ficare digneris, et præsta, ut quicumque coram illis beatissimam Virginem suppliciter colere et honorare studuerit, illius meritis et obtentu, a te gratiam in præsenti et æternam gloriam obtineat in futurum. Per Christum Dominum nostrum.
R. Amen.

V. Our help is in the name of the Lord.
R. who made heaven and earth.
V. O Lord hear my prayer.
R. And let my supplication come unto Thee.
V. The Lord be with you.
R. And with thy spirit.

Let us Pray.

ALMIGHTY and eternal God, who hast permitted the images of Thy saints to be sculptured or painted; in order that beholding them every day with our corporal eyes, and meditating upon their actions and sanctity, we may be led to imitate their virtues, deign to bless and sanctify these medals which have been made in honour and commemoration of the most Blessed Virgin Mary, Mother of our Lord Jesus Christ; and grant that whoever humbly invokes the Blessed Virgin before them, may obtain through her merits, grace in this present life and eternal glory in the life to come.
R. Amen.

Here the Medals, are sprinkled with Holy Water.

Each Candidate, holding a lighted candle in the hand, here recites the Act of Consecration in a clear and audible voice.

Act of Consecration.

HOLY Mary, Mother of God, and Virgin, I, *N. N.*, choose thee this day for my Queen, my Patroness, and my Advocate, and I firmly resolve and purpose never to abandon thee, and never to say or do anything against thee nor allow anything to be done against thy honour by those subject to me. I, beseech thee, therefore, receive me as thy servant for ever, assist me in all my actions, and abandon me not at the hour of death. Amen.

When the Act of Consecration has been recited, the Celebrant gives a medal, already blessed, to each Candidate, saying :

Celebrant.—Accipe signum Congregationis B.V.M. ad corporis et animæ defensionem, ut divinæ bonitatis gratia, et ope Beatissimæ Virginis Mariæ Matris tuæ, aeternam beatitudinem consequi merearis; in nomine Patris ✠ et Filii et Spiritus Sancti.

Celebrant.—Receive this medal of the Blessed Virgin Mary as a safeguard and defence for your body and soul, that, by the grace of the Divine goodness, and the assistance of Mary your Mother, you may deserve to obtain eternal happiness; in the Name

Then he adds, turning towards the new Members.

AD majorem Dei gloriam, in laudem beatissimæ Virginis Mariae, in spirituale hujus Congregationis bonum et ex potestate a summo Pontifice mihi delata ego pro tempore hujus Congregationis Praeses vos in numerum Sodalium nostrae Congregationis sub titulo Immaculatae Conceptionis B.V.M., erectae suscipio, et participes reddo et declaro omnium gratiarum et fructuum, privilegiorum et indulgentiarum, quae sancta Romana Ecclesia ipsi primariæ Congregationi Romanæ, cui haec nostra canonice aggregata est, concessit : In nomine Patris ✠ et Filii et Spiritus Sancti. Amen.

SUSCIPIAT vos Christus in numerum confratrum nostrorum et suorum famulorum. Concedat vobis tempus bene vivendi locum bene agendi constantiam, bene perseverandi, et ad aeternae vitae haereditatem feliciter perveniendi ; et sicut nos hodie fraterna caritas spiritualiter jungit in terris ita divina pietas, quae dilectionis est auctrix, et amatrix, nos cum fidelibus conjungere dignetur in cœlis. Per eundem Christum Dominum nostrum. Amen.

V. Confirma hoc Deus, quod operatus es in nobis.
R. A templo sancte tuo, quod est in Jerusalem.
V. Salvos fac famulos tuos, (*or* famulus tuas).
R. Deus meus sperantes in te.
V. Mitte eis Domine auxilium de Sancto.
R. Et de Sion tuere eos, (*or* eas).
V. Domine, exaudi orationem meam.
R. Et clamor meus ad de veniat.
V. Dominus vobiscum.
R. Et cum spiritu tuo.

Oremus.

TO the greater glory of God, and to the honour of the Blessed Virgin Mary, and for the spiritual good of this Congregation, and by the power granted me by our most Holy Father the Pope, I Director for the time being of this Congregation, receive you into the number of the members of our Congregation, erected under the title of the Immaculate Conception, and render you sharers and partakers of all the graces and fruits, privileges, and indulgences which the Holy Roman Church has granted to the Primary Sodality at Rome to which ours has been canonically affiliated : In the name of the Father ✠ and of the Son and of the Holy Ghost. Amen.

MAY Christ receive you into the number of our brethren and His servants. May He give you grace to lead a holy life, opportunity to do good and constancy to persevere therein, that you may arrive happily at the inheritance of life eternal. And as fraternal charity unites us this day spiritually on earth, may the Divine goodness, who is the author and lover of charity, vouchsafe to admit us among the saints in heaven. Through the same Christ our Lord. Amen.

V. Confirm, O Lord, what thou hast wrought in us.
R. Even in thy holy temple which is in Jerusalem.
V. Save thy servants.
R. Who hope in thee, O my God.
V. Send them help from thy holy place.
R. And from Sion protect them.
V. Lord hear my prayer.
R. And let my supplication come unto Thee.
V. The Lord be with you.
R. And with thy spirit.

Let us pray.

BLESSED VIRGIN MARY. 387

The Ceremony concludes with the "Magnificat," *(page* 10,*) or the* "Te Deum," *(page* 325*).*

V. Benedictus es, Domine, Deus patrum nostrorum.
R. Et laudabilis et gloriousus in secula.
V. Benedicamus Patrem, et Filium, cum Sancto Spiritu.
R. Laudemus et superexaltemus Eum in sæcula.
V. Benedictus es, Domine Deus, in firmamento cœli.
R. Et laudabilis, et gloriousus, et superexaltatus in sæcula.
V. Benedic, anima mea, Domino.
R. Et noli oblivisci omnes retributiones Ejus.
V. Domine, exaudi orationem meam.
R. Et clamor meus ad te veniat.
R. Dominus vobiscum.
R. Et cum spiritu tuo.

Oremus.

DEUS, cujus misericordiæ non est numerus, et bonitatis infinitus est thesaurus, piissimæ Majestati tuæ pro collatis donis gratias agimus, tuam semper clementiam, exorantes : ut qui petentibus postulata concedis, eosdem non deserans, ad præmia futura disponas.

Deus, qui corda fidelium Sancti Spiritus illustratione docuisti ; da nobis in eodem Spiritu recta sapere, et de ejus semper consolatione gaudere.

Deus, qui neminem in te sperantem nimium affligi permittis, sed pium precibus præstas auditum : pro postulationibus nostris, votisque susceptis gratias agimus, te piissime deprecantes, ut a cunctis semper muniamur adversis. Per Christum Dominum nostrum.

R. Amen.

V. Blessed are Thou, O Lord, the God of our fathers.
R. And worthy to be praised and glorified forever.
V. Let us bless the Father and the Son, with the Holy Ghost.
R. Let us praise and magnify Him forever.
V. Blessed art Thou, O Lord, in the firmament of heaven.
R. And worthy to be praised glorious, and exalted forever.
V. Bless the Lord, O my soul.
R. And forget not all His benefits.
V. O Lord, hear my prayer.
R. And let my cry come unto Thee.
V. The Lord be with you.
R. And with thy Spirit.

Let us pray.

O GOD, whose mercies are without number, and the treasure of whose goodness is infinite ; we render thanks to Thy most gracious Majesty, for the gifts Thou hast bestowed upon us, ever more beseeching Thy clemency, that as Thou grantest the petitions of those that ask Thee, Thou wilt never forsake them, but wilt prepare them for the rewards to come.

O God, who hast taught the hearts of the faithful by the light of the Holy Spirit : grant us, by the same Spirit, to relish what is right, and evermore to rejoice in His consolation.

O God, who sufferest none that hope in Thee to be afflicted above their strength, but dost afford a gracious ear unto their prayers : we render Thee thanks that Thou hast heard our supplications and vows ; and we most humbly beseech Thee, that we may ever more be protected from all adversities. Through Christ our Lord.
R. Amen.

Act of Consecration.

Most Holy Virgin Mary, Mother of my God, I—though unworthy to be thy servant, moved nevertheless by thy exceeding tenderness, and by the desire of serving thee—choose thee this day, in the presence of my Angel Guardian and of the whole court of Heaven, for my special Mistress, Advocate, and Mother; and I firmly resolve to serve thee always, and to do all in my power to gain others also to thy service. Therefore, I beseech thee, most tender of mothers, by the blood of thy Son shed for me, that thou wouldst receive me into the number of thy devoted clients. Assist me in all my undertakings, and obtain for me the grace so to rule all my thoughts, words, and works, that I may never be displeasing in thy sight, nor in the sight of thy divine Son.

Prayers to be Recited at the Meetings.

(Taken from the "Preci solite a recitarsi nella Congregazione Prima Primaria," Roma, 1823.)

Before the Exhortation.

Come, Holy Ghost, replenish the hearts of Thy faithful, and enkindle in them the fire of Thy love.

V. Send forth Thy Spirit, O Lord, and they shall be created.
R. And Thou shalt renew the face of the earth.

Let us pray.

O GOD, who by the light of the Holy Ghost hast instructed the hearts of Thy faithful, grant us through the same Holy Spirit, to relish what is right, and evermore to rejoice in His consolations, through Jesus Christ our Lord. Amen.

Here part of the Office of the Immaculate Conception is recited (see page vii.) after which an Exhortation is given.

After the Exhortation.

V. Confirm, O Lord, what Thou hast wrought in us.
R. From Thy holy temple which is in Jerusalem.

Let us pray.

Grant us, we beseech Thee, O Lord, the aid of Thy grace, that acknowleding Thee as the author of all good, we may, by Thy assistance, accomplish all that Thou commandest; through Jesus Christ our Lord. Amen.

V. Be mindful of Thy Association
R. Which has been Thine from the beginning.
V. Let us pray for our benefactors.
R. Reward, O Lord, with eternal life, all those who have done us good for Thy Name sake.
V. Let us pray for our deceased brethren.
R. Grant them, O Lord, eternal rest, and let perpetual light shine upon them
V. May they rest in peace.
R. Amen.
V. For our absent brethren.
R. Save Thy servants who trust in Thee, O my God.
V. Send them help, O Lord, from Thy holy place.
R. And from Sion protect them.
V. Lord, hear my prayer.
R. And let my supplication come unto Thee.

Let us pray.

Loosen, O Lord, we pray Thee, in Thy pity, the bonds of our sins, and by the intercession of the Blessed Mary, ever Virgin, Mother of God, the blessed all stain of sin; adorn us with all virtue; grant to us peace and health; drive far off all our enemies, visible and invisible; bridle our appetites; grant us healthful seasons; show forth Thy love towards our freinds and our enemies; guard Thy holy city; preserve our Sovereign Pontiff [N.], and defend all our prelates, princes, and all Thy Christian people from all adversity. Let Thy blessing be ever upon us, and grant to all the faithful departed eternal rest; through Christ our Lord. Amen.

Prayer for a Sick Member.

O ALMIGHTY, everlasting God, the eternal salvation of them that believe, hear us in behalf of Thy servant who is sick, for whom we implore the aid of thy mercy, that, being restored to health, he (or she) may render thanks to thee in Thy Church. Through Christ our Lord. Amen.

For a Deceased Member.

The Psalm, *De Profundis*.

(*For Latin, see page 56.*)

OUT of the depths have I cried unto Thee, O Lord: Lord hear my voice.

2. Let thine ear be attentive to the voice of my supplication.

3. If Thou, O Lord, wilt mark iniquities; Lord, who shall abide it?

4. For with Thee there is merciful forgiveness; and by reason of Thy law I have waited for thee, O Lord.

5. My soul hath relied on His word; my soul hath hoped in the Lord.

6. From the morning watch even until night; let Israel hope in the Lord.

7. Because with the Lord there is mercy; and with Him is plenteous redemption.

8. And he shall redeem Israel from all his iniquities.

9. Eternal rest give to them, O Lord, and let perpetual light shine upon them.

Glory be to the Father, etc.

O GOD, the Creator and Redeemer of all the faithful, grant to the souls of Thy servants departed, the remission of all their sins, that through pious supplications they may obtain that pardon they have always desired; through Christ our Lord. Amen.

May they rest in peace: Amen.

†

Little Office of the Immaculate Conception.

✠

AT MATINS

EJA, mea labia, nunc annuntiate Laudes et præconia Virginis beatæ.
V. Domina, in adjutorium meum intende.
R. Me de manu hostium potenter defende.
V. Gloria Patri, etc. Alleluia.

COME, my lips, and wide proclaim The blessed Virgin's spotless fame.
V. O Lady, make speed to befriend me.
R. From the hands of the enemy mightly defend me.
V. Glory be to the Father, etc. Alleluia.

From Septuagesima to Easter, instead of "Alleluia" is said:

LAUS tibi, Domine, Rex æternæ gloriæ.

PRAISE be to Thee, O Lord, King of everlasting glory.

HYMNUS.

SALVE, mundi Domina,
Cœlorum Regina :
Salve, Virgo virginum,
Stella matutina.

Salve, plena gratia,
Clara luce divina :
Mundi in auxilium,
Domina, festina.

Ab æterno Dominus
Te præordinavit
Matrem Unigeniti
Verbi, quo creavit.

Terram, pontum, æthera ;
Te pulchram ornavit
Sibi Sponsam, quæ in
Adam non peccavit.
Amen.

Hymn.

HAIL, Queen of the heavens !
Hail, Mistress of earth
Hail, Virgin most pure,
Of Immaculate birth !

Clear Star of the Morning,
In beauty enshrined !
O Lady, make speed
To the help of mankind.

Thee, God, in the depth
Of eternity, chose ;
And formed Thee all fair
As His glorious Spouse.

And called Thee His Word's
Own Mother to be,
By whom he created
The earth, sky, and sea.
Amen.

V. Elegit eam Deus, et præelegit eam.
R. In tabernaculo suo habitare fecit eam.
V. Domina, exaudi orationem meam,
R. Et clamor meus ad te veniat.

V. God elected her, and pre-elected her.
R. He made her to dwell in his tabernacle.
V. O Lady, hear my prayer.
R. And let my cry come unto thee.

Oremus.

SANCTA Maria, Regina cœlorum. Mater Domini nostri Jesu

Let us pray.

HOLY Mary, Queen of heaven, Mother of our Lord Jesus Christ,

IMMACULATE CONCEPTION.

menter oculis pietatis, et impetra mihi apud tuum dilectum Filium cunctorum veniam peccatorum ; ut qui nunc tuam sanctam et Immaculatam Conceptionem devoto affectu recolo, æternæ in futurum beatitudinis bravium capiam, ipso, quem Virgo peperisti, donante, Domino nostro Jesu Christo : qui cum Patre et Sancto Spiritu vivit et regnat, in Trinitate perfecta Deus in sæcula sæculorum. Amen.

V. Domina exaudi orationem meam.
R. Et clamor meus ad te veniat.
V. Benedicamus Domino.
R. Deo gratias.
V. Fidelium animæ per misericordiam Dei requiescant in pace.
R. Amen.

Lady, with an eye of pity, and entreat for me, of thy beloved Son, the forgiveness of all my sins that as I now celebrate with devout affection thy holy and Immaculate Conception, so hereafter, I, may recive the prize eternal blessedness, by the grace of Him whom thou, in virginity, didst bring forth, Jesus Christ our Lord : who with the Father and the Holy Ghost, liveth and reigneth in perfect Trinity, God, world without end. Amen.

V. O Lady, hear my prayer.
R. And let my cry come unto thee.
V. Let us bless the Lord.
R. Thanks be to God.
V. May the souls of the faithful departed, through the mercy of God, rest in peace.
R. Amen.

AT PRIME.

V. Domina, in adjutorium meum intende.
R. Me de manu hostinm potenter defende.
V. Gloria Patri, etc. Alleluia.

V. O Lady, make speed to befriend me.
R. From the hands of the enemy mightily defend me.
V. Glory be to the Father, etc. Alleluia.

HYMNUS.

SALVE, Virgo sapiens,
　Domus Deo dicata,
　　Columna septemplici
　Mensaque exornata.

Ab omni contagio
Mundi præservata ;
　Ante sancta in utero
Parentis, quam nata.

Tu, Mater viventium,
Et porta es Sanctorum :
　Nova stella Jacob,
Domina Angelorum.

Zabulo terribilis
Acies castrorum :
　Portus et refugium
Sis Christianorum. Amen.

V. Ipse creavit illam in Spiritu Sancto.
R. Et effudit illam inter omnia opera sua.

HYMN.

HAIL, Virgin most wise !
　Hail, Deity's shrine !
　　With seven fair pillars,
　And table divine !

Preserved from the guilt
Which hath come on us all !
　Exempt, in the womb,
From the taint of the fall !

O new Star of Jacob !!
Of Angels the Queen !
　O gate of the Saints !
O Mother of men !

O terrible as
The embattled array !
　Be thou of the faithful
The refuge and stay. Amen.

V. The Lord Himself created her in the Holy Ghost.
R. And poured her out among all His works.

392 LITTLE OFFICE OF THE
AT TIERCE.

V. Domina, in adjutorium meum intende.
R. Me de manu hostium potenter defende.
V. Gloria Patri, etc. Alleluia.

V. O Lady, make speed to befriend me.
R. From the hands of the enemy mightily defend me.
V. Glory be to the Father, etc. Alleluia.

Hymnus.

SALVE, arca fœderis,
Thronus Salomonis,
Arcus pulcher ætheris,
Rubus visionis :

Virga frondens germinis :
Vellus Gedeonis :
Porta clausa numinis,
Favusque Sampsonis.

Decebat tam nobilem
Natum, præcavere
Ab orignali
Labe Matris Evæ

Almam, quam elegerat,
Genitricem vere,
Nulli prorsus sinens
Culpæ subjacere. Amen.

Hymn.

HAIL, Solomon's throne
Pure ark of the law
Fair rainbow ! and bush,
Which the Patriarch saw

Hail, Gideon's fleece !
Hail, blossoming road !
Sampson's sweet honeycomb !
Portal of God !

Well fitting it was,
That a Son so divine.
Should preserve from all touch
Of original sin ;

Nor suffer by smallest
Defect to be stained,
That Mother, whom He
For Himself had ordained.
Amen.

V. Ego in altissimis habito,
R. Et thronus meus in columna nubis.

V. Domina, exaudi, etc. (*page 390, cum Oratione ut supra.*)

V. I dwell in the highest,
R. And my throne is on the pillar of the clouds.
V. O Lady hear, etc. (*With the Prayer and Versicles, as on page 390*).

AT SEXT.

V. Domina, in adjutorium meum intende.
R. Me de manu hostium potenter defende.

V. Gloria Patri, etc. Alleluia.

V. O Lady, make speed to befriend me.
R. From the hands of the enemy mightily defend me.
V. Glory be to the Father, etc. Alleluia.

Hymnus.

SALVE, Virgo puerpera,
Templum Trinitatis,
Angelorum gaudium,
Cella puritatis :

Solamen mœrentium,
Hortus voluptatis :
*Palma patientiæ,
Cedrus castitatis.*

Hymn.

HAIL, virginal Mother !
Hail, purity's cell !
Fair shrine where the Trinity
Loveth to dwell.

Hail, garden of pleasure !
Celestial balm !
Cedar of chastity

IMMACULATE CONCEPTION

Terra es benedicta
Et sacerdotalis,
Sancta et immunis
Culpæ originalis.

Civitas altissimi,
Porta orientalis:
In te est omnis gratia,
Virgo singularis. Amen.

V. Sicut lilium inter spinas,
R. Sic Amica mea inter filias Adæ.

V. Domina, exaudi, etc., (*page 390, cum Oratione ut supra.*)

Thou land set apart
From uses profane!
And free from the curse
Which in Adam began!

Thou city of God!
Thou gate of the east!
In thee is all grace
O joy of the blest!

V. As the lily among the thorns.
R. So is my beloved among the daughters of Adam.

V. O Lady, hear, etc. (*With the Prayer and Versicles, as on page 390*).

AT NONE.

V. Domina, in adjutorium meum intende.
R. Me de manu hostium potenter defende.
V. Gloria Patri, etc. Alleluia.

V. O Lady, make speed to befriend me.
R. From the hands of the enemy mightily defend me.
V. Glory be to the Father, etc. Alleluia

Hymnus.

SALVE, urbs refugii,
Turrisque munita
David, propugnaculis
Armisque insignita.

In Conceptione
Charitate ignita,
Draconis potestas
Est a te contrita.

O mulier fortis,
Et invicta Judith!
Pulchra Abisag virgo,
Verum fovens David!

Rachel curatorem
Ægypti gestavit:
Salvatorem mundi
Maria portavit. Amen.

V. Tota pulchra es amic mea,
R. Et macula originalis numuqam fuit in te.
V. Domina, exaudi, etc. (*page 390, cum Oratione ut supra.*)

Hymn.

HAIL, city of refuge!
Hail, David's, high tower!
With battlements crowned
And girded with power!

Filled at thy Conception
With love and with light!
The dragon by thee
Was shorn of his might.

O Woman most valiant!
O Judith thrice blessed!
As David was nursed
In fair Abisag's breast.

As the Saviour of Egypt
Upon Rachel's knee:
So the world's great Redeemer
Was cherished by thee. Amen

V. Thou art all fair, my beloved.
R. And the original stain was never in thee.
V. O Lady, hear, etc. (*with the Prayer and Versicles, as on page 390*).

AT VESPERS.

V. Domina, in adjutorium meum intende.
R. Me de manu hostium potenter defende.

V. O Lady, make speed to befriend me.
R. From the hands of the enemy mightily defend me.

IMMACULATE CONCEPTION.

HYMNUS.

SALVE, horologium,
  Quo retrogradiatur
    Sol in decem lineis
Verbum incarnatur.

Homo ut ab inferis
Ad summa attollatur,
Immensus ab Angelis
Paulo minoratur.

Solis hujus radiis
Maria coruscat;
Consurgens aurora
In conceptu micat.

Lilium inter spinas.
Quæ serpentis conterat
Caput: pulchra ut luna
Errantes collustrat.
        Amen.

V. Ego feci in cœlis, ut oriretur lumen indeficiens.
R. Et quasi nebula texi omnem terram.
V. Domina, exaudi, etc. (*page* vii., *cum Oratione ut supra.*)

HYMN.

HAIL, dial of Achaz!
  On thee the true sun
    Told backward the course
Which from old he had run!

And, that man might be raised,
Submitting to shame,
A little more low
Than the Angels became.

Thou, wrapt in the blaze
Of His infinite light,
Dost shine as the morn
On the confines of night.

As the moon on the lost
Through obscurity dawns;
  The serpent's destroyer!
A lily'mid thorns.
        Amen.

V. I made an unfailing light to arise in heaven.
R. And as a mist I overspread the whole earth.
V. O Lady, hear, etc. (*with the Prayer and Versicles, as at page* vii.)

AT COMPLINE.

V. Convertat nos, Domina, tuis precibus placatus Jesus Christus Filius tuus,
R. Et avertat iram suam a nobis.
V. Domina, in adjutorium meum intende.
R. Me de manu hostium potenter defende.
V. Gloria Patri, etc. Alleluia.

HYMNUS.

SALVE, Virgo florens,
  Mater illibata,
    Regina clementiæ,
Stellis coronata.

Super omnes Angelos
Pura immaculata,
Atque ad regis dexteram
Stans veste deaurata.

V. May Jesus Christ thy Son, reconciled by thy prayers, O Lady, convert our hearts.
R. And turn away His anger from us.
V. O Lady, make speed to befriend me.
R. From the hands of the enemy mightily defend me.
V. Glory be to the Father, etc. Alleluia.

HYMN.

HAIL, Mother most pure!
  Hail, Virgin renowned
    Hail, Queen with the stars
As a diadem crowned!

Above all the Angels
  In glory untold,
Standing next to the King

OFFICE OF THE IMMACULATE CONCEPTION. 395

Patens cœli janua,
Salus infirmorum,
Videamus Regem
In aula Sanctorum. Amen.

V. Oleum effusum, Maria, nomen tuum.
R. Servi tui dilexerunt te nimis.

V. Domina, exaudi, etc. (*page* vii., *cum Oratione ut supra.*)

Through thee may we come
To the haven of rest !
And see heaven's King
In the courts of the blest !
Amen.

V. Thy name, O Mary, is as oil poured out.
R. Thy servants have loved thee exceedingly.

V. O Lady, hear, etc. (*With the prayer and versicles, as on page* vii.)

THE COMMENDATION.

SUPPLICES offerimus
Tibi, Virgo pia,
Hæc laudum præconia ;
Fac nos ut in via.

Ducas cursu prospero,
Et in agonia
Tu nobis assiste,
O dulcis Maria.

R. Deo gratias.

THESE praises and prayers
I lay at thy feet,
O Virgin of virgins !
O Mary most sweet !

Be thou my true guide
Through this pilgrimage here,
And stand by my side
When death draweth near.

V. Thanks be to God.

Prayers for Confession.

Before Confession.

O MOST merciful God, I most humbly thank Thee for all Thy mercies unto me; and, particularly at this time, for Thy forbearance and long suffering with me, notwithstanding my many and grievous sins. It is of Thy great mercy that I have not fallen into greater and more grievous sins than those which I have committed, and that I have not been cut off and cast into hell.

O my God, although I have been so ungrateful to Thee in times past, yet now I beseech Thee to accept me, returning to Thee with an earnest desire to repent, and to devote myself to Thee, my Lord and my God, and to praise Thy holy Name for ever.

Grant me, I beseech Thee, perfect contrition for my sins, that I may detest them with the deepest sorrow of heart. Send forth Thy light into my soul, and discover to me all those sins which I ought to confess at this time. Assist me by Thy grace, that I may be able to declare them to the priest, fully, humbly, and with a contrite heart, and so obtain perfect remission of them all through Thine infinite goodness. Amen.

O MOST gracious Virgin Mary, beloved Mother of Jesus Christ my Redeemer, intercede for me with him. Obtain for me the full remission of my sins, and perfect amendment of life, to the salvation of my soul, and the glory of His Name.

Examination of Conscience.

How long is it since your last confession? Did you keep back any sin in your last confession? Did you say your penance? Did you go to Holy Communion without preparing yourself, or after having broken your fast? Have you always said your morning and night prayers? Did you say them badly? Have you used bad words? Did you stay away from Mass on Sundays or Holidays through your own fault? Did you laugh or talk in Church? Have you been disobedient to your parents or superiors? Have you called them names? or grumbled at them? or struck them? Have you been angry or in a passion? or sulky? Have you quarrelled? or fought? or struck anyone? Have you borne malice to anyone? Have you done anything wrong by thought, word, or deed against purity or modesty? Have you got others to do wrong? Have you stolen anything? or done any wilful damage? or kept that to which you had no right? Have you told lies? Have you told lies against anyone? Have you injured your neighbor's characters by speaking ill of him without any reason? Have you eaten meat on Fridays or other days on which it is forbidden? Have you been proud or vain of yourself? or despised others? Have you been discontented? Have you committed sin by eating or drinking too much? Have you wasted your money in drink? or frequented public houses? or gone with bad company? Have you been jealous of others; Have you been idle or slothful? Have you done anything else you ought to confess?

For those who are in the Employment of Others.

Have you been disrespectful to your employers? Have you wasted or wilfuly damaged their goods? or allowed others to do so? Have you stolen from them or given their things away without leave? Have you been idle or careless at your work? or not done what you were told to do? Have you read other people's letters? Have you gossiped about the private affairs of your employers?

PRAYERS FOR CONFESSION.

God is very good. He made you and gave you your soul and body, and everything that you have. He is also very holy and just; and He hates sin. He made heaven for good people, and hell for the wicked. He loves you very much. He was made man for you, and died upon the Cross, with great nails in His Hands and Feet, and a crown of thorns upon His Head, to help you to be good, and to get to Heaven. And when you sin, you offend this good God Who loves you so much.

Try now to be very sorry for your sins, and make up your mind not to sin any more.

ACTS OF CONTRITION.

O LORD Jesus Christ, lover of our souls, who, for the great love wherewith Thou hast loved us, wouldst not the death of a sinner, but rather that he should be converted and live; I grieve from the bottom of my heart that I have offended Thee my most loving Father and Redeemer, unto whom all sin is infinitely displeasing; Who hast so loved me that Thou didst shed Thy Blood for me and endure the bitter torments of a most cruel death. O my God! O infinite Goodness! would that I had never offended Thee. Pardon me, O Lord Jesus, most humbly imploring Thy mercy. Have pity upon a sinner for whom Thy Blood pleads before the face of the Father.

O merciful and forgiving Lord, for the love of Thee I forgive all who have ever offended me. I firmly resolve to forsake and flee from sins, and to avoid the occasions of them; and to confess, in bitterness of spirit, all those sins which I have committed against Thy divine goodness, and to love Thee, O my God, for Thine own sake, above all things and for ever. Grant me grace so to do. O most gracious Lord Jesus,

O my God! I am very sorry that I have offended Thee, because Thou art so good; and I will not sin again.

My Lord and my God, I sincerely acknowledge myself a vile and wretched sinner, unworthy to appear in Thy presence: but do Thou have mercy on me, and save me.

Most loving Father, I have sinned against Heaven and before Thee, and I am unworthy to be called Thy child; make me as one of Thy servants, and may I for the future be ever faithful to Thee. I am now resolved, with the help of Thy grace, to be more watchful over myself, to amend my faults and fulfil Thy law. Look down on me with the eyes of mercy, O God, and blot out my sins.

Say the "Our Father" and the "Hail Mary."

AFTER CONFESSION.

O ALMIGHTY and most merciful God, who according to the multitude of Thy tender mercies, hast been pleased once more to receive me, after so many times going astray from Thee, and to admit me to this sacrament of

Prayers for Holy Communion.

1.—Say these PRAYERS *slowly*, a few words at a time.
2.—It is well to *stop after every few words* that they may sink into the heart.
3.—Each prayer may be said *several times*.

Before Holy Communion.
PRAYER FOR HELP.

O My God, help me to make a good Communion. Mary, my dearest Mother, pray to Jesus for me. My dear Angel Guardian, lead me to the Altar of God.

ACT OF FAITH.

O GOD, because Thou hast said it, I believe that I shall receive the sacred Body of Jesus Christ to eat, and His Precious Blood to drink. My God, I believe this with all my heart.

ACT OF HUMILITY.

MY God, I confess that I am a poor sinner, I am not worthy to receive the Body and Blood of Jesus on account of my sins. Lord, I am not worthy that Thou shouldst enter under my roof; say but the word, and my soul shall be healed.

ACT OF SORROW.

MY God, I detest all the sins of my life. I am sorry for them, because they have offended Thee, my God, Who art so good. I resolve never to sin any more. My good God, pity me, have mercy on me, forgive me. Amen.

ACT OF ADORATION.

O JESUS, great God, present on the Altar, I bow down before Thee, I adore Thee.

ACT OF LOVE AND DESIRE.

SWEET Jesus, I love Thee. I desire with all my heart to receive Thee. Most sweet Jesus, come into my poor soul, and give me Thy Flesh to eat and Thy Blood to drink. Give me *Thy whole Self*, Body, Blood, Soul, and Divinity, that I may live forever with Thee.

In Receiving Holy Communion.

(1) In going to the Altar-rails and returning to your place, keep your *hands* joined, your *eyes* cast down and your *thoughts* on Jesus Christ.

(2) At the Altar-rails, take the Communion cloth and spread it before you under your chin.

(3) Hold your head straight up, keep your eyes closed, your mouth well open and your tongue out, resting on the under lip. Then, with great outward reverence, receive the Sacred Host, saying in your heart, with all the faith of St. Thomas—"My Lord and my God."

After Holy Communion.
ACT OF FAITH.

O JESUS, I believe I have received Thy Flesh to eat and Thy Blood to drink, because Thou hast said it, and Thy word is true.

PRAYERS FOR HOLY COMMUNION. 399

ACT OF ADORATION.

O JESUS, my God, my Creator, I adore Thee, because from Thy Hands I came and with Thee I am to be happy forever.

ACT OF HUMILITY.

O JESUS, I am but dust and ashes, and yet Thou hast come to me, and my poor heart may speak to Thee.

ACT OF LOVE.

SWEET Jesus, I love Thee; I love Thee with all my heart. Thou knowest that I love Thee, and wish to love Thee daily more and more.

ACT OF THANKSGIVING.

MY good Jesus, I thank Thee with all my heart. How good, how kind Thou art to me, sweet Jesus. Blessed be Jesus in the most Holy Sacrament of the Altar.

ACT OF OFFERING.

O JESUS, receive my poor offering. Jesus, Thou hast given Thyself to me, now let me give myself to Thee :
I give Thee my *body*, that it may be chaste and pure.
I give Thee my *soul*, that it may be free from sin.
I give Thee my *heart*, that it may always love Thee.
I give Thee every breath that I shall breathe, and especially my last ; I give Thee *myself* in life and in death, that I may be Thine for ever and ever.
Remember the words of Jesus : "Ask and you shall receive," and

PRAY FOR YOURSELF.

O JESUS, wash away my sins with Thy Precious Blood.
O Jesus, the struggle against temptation is not yet finished. My Jesus, when temptation comes near me, make me strong against it. In the moment of temptation may I always say, "Jesus, mercy ! Mary, help ! "
O Jesus, may I lead a good life ; may I die a happy death. May I receive Thee before I die. May I say when I am dying, " Jesus, Mary, Joseph, I give you my heart and my soul."
Listen now for a moment to Jesus Christ ; perhaps He has something to say to you. There may be some promise you have made and broken, which He wishes you to make again and keep.
Answer Jesus in your heart, and tell him all your troubles. Then.

PRAY FOR OTHERS.

O JESUS, have mercy on Thy Holy Church : take care of it,
O Jesus, have pity on *poor sinners*, and save them from hell.
O Jesus, bless my Father, my mother, my brothers and sisters, and all I ought to pray for, as Thy heart knows how to bless them.
O Jesus, have pity on the *poor souls in purgatory*, and give them eternal rest.
Sweet Jesus, I am going away for a time, but I trust not without Thee. Thou art with me by Thy grace. I will never leave Thee by mortal sin. I do not fear to do so, though I am so weak, because I have *such hope* in Thee. Give

Index.

Daily Prayers.

	Page.
Acts of Adoration, Contrition, Faith, Hope and Charity	vii
Acts of Consecration to the Sacred Heart of Jesus	xi
Angelus, The	43
Divine Praises	ix 33
Indulgence for singing Spiritual Canticles	xxii
Indulgenced Prayers	x
Litany of the Blessed Virgin Mary	ix
Litany of the Sacred Heart	318
Litany of the Most Holy Name of Jesus	viii
Little Office of the Immaculate Conception	390
Memorare	xi
Mass, Prayers at	xi
Mass, manner of assisting at	xx
Prayers for Holy Communion	398
Preparation for Confession and Prayers after	396
Responses at High Mass	367
Sodality of the Blessed Virgin Mary	382
Spiritual Canticles	xxii

Vespers.

First, for Sundays	1
Second, for an Apostle	30
Third, for an Apostle	37
Fourth, for the Blessed Virgin Mary and Virgins	38
Fifth, for Martyrs	52
Sixth, for Martyrs	53
Seventh, for Confessors, etc.	54
Eighth, for Confessors, etc.	55

Special Vespers.

Ascension	58
Christmas	56
Corpus Christi	61
Dedication of Churches	65
Easter Sunday	58
Epiphany	57
Holy Name	57
Holy Family	58
Patronage of St. Joseph	59
Pentecost	59
Precious Blood	63
St. Joseph	62
St. John the Baptist	63
St. Michael	64
Sts. Peter and Paul	65
Trinity Sunday	70

Hymns.

	Page
Ave Maria	41
Ave Verum	129
Angelus	43
Ad regias Agni	9
Audi, benigne Conditor	8
Ave, maris stella	38
Cœlestis urbs Jerusalem	65
Creator alme	7
Crudelis Herodes Deum	57
Decora lux	65
Deus tuorum militum	52
Exultet orbis	30
Festivis resoneut compita vocibus	63
Fortem virili pectore	49
Iste Confessor Domini, colentes	54 55
Jam sol recedit igneus	60
Jesu Corona Virginum	35
Jesu, dulcis memoria	57
Jesu, Redemptor omnium	56
Lucis Creator optime	6
O Maria	48
O Gloriosa Virginum	40
O Lux beata	58
O Quot undis lacrymarum	50
O Salutaris Hostia	20
O Filii et Filiæ	277
Pange lingua, gloriosi	61
Præclara custos Virginum	51
Salutis Humanæ Sator	58
Sanctorum meritis	52
Tantum ergo Sacramentum	26
Te, Joseph, celebrent Agmina Cœlitum	62
Te, splendor et virtus Patris	64
Tristes erant	30
Ut queant laxis resonare fibris	63
Veni, Creator Spiritus	59
Vexilla Regis	8

Anthems.

Alma Redemptoris mater	10–11
Ave, Regina	12
Regina cœli	15 17
Salve, Regina	19

Psalms.

Beati omnes	61
Beatus vir	2
Benedictus	259
Cinfitebor tibi Domine	2
Confitebor—quoniam	64
Credidi, propter	37

INDEX

	Page.
De profundis	56
Dixit Dominus	1
In convertendo	37
In exitu Israel	4
Lauda, Jerusalem	38
Laudate, Dominum	5
Laudate pueri	3
Magnificat	10
Memento, Domine	55
Miserere	258
Nisi Dominus	38
Te Deum, Laudamus	325

Hymns.

No.		Page
	Adoro te devote	34
	Agnus Dei	351
158	A Glorious Voice sounds through the night	256
150	Adeste fideles—with hearts truly grateful	247
66	Ah, her smile makes heav'n rejoice	143
73	Ah, What a Joy, dear Mother	153
173	Alleluia, alleluia, let the holy anthem rise	270
172	All Hail, dear Conquerer! All Hail	269
136	All Praise to St. Patrick	231
28	A Message from the Sacred Heart	97
154	Angels we have heard on high	252
214	Asperges me	331
88	As the dewy shades of even	172
114	As the gentle Spring uncloses	204
30	As the radiant dawn is stealing	99
99	Ave Maria, Guardian Dear	186
122	Ave Maria! Bright and Pure	214
81	Ave Sanctissima	163
162	Benedictus	259
204	Bless me, befriend me	305
16	Behold the Heart Whose love for men	82
107	Bright Mother of our Maker, Hail	196
105	Bring flowers of the rarest	193
104	Children of Mary, high your voices raise	192
175	Christ the Lord is ris'n to-day	272
165	Christians who of Jesus sorrows	262
69	Come and chant the praises	148
96	Come, gather round the altar	182
187	Come Holy Ghost	286
188	Come Holy Ghost, Creator Blest	287
186	Creator—Spirit, all Divine	285
	Credo	341
36	Close veiled in that sweet Sacrament	108
59	Daily, daily sing to Mary	135
80	Daughter of a Mighty Father	162
203	Dear Angel; ever at my side	304
128	Dear Guardian of Mary	220
155	Dear Little One! How sweet Thou art	253

INDEX 403

No.		Page
139	Dear Saint, who on thy natal day	234
181	Dear St. Joseph, Oh, remember	225
	Dies Irae, day of Wrath	372
195	Faith of our Fathers	296
87	Fading, still fading	170
140	Faithful to Thy Spouse and Love	235
132	First Floweret of the Desert Wild	227
29	Form your ranks, Oh! all ye leaguers	98
15	Give me, O Jesus dear, a place to dwell	81
	Gloria	336
65	Glorious Mother! from high heaven	142
1	God of my heart	66
129	Great St. Joseph! throned in glory	221
130	Great St. Joseph, Meek and Lowly	223
177	Haec dies	275
118	Hail! All Hail, Sweet Notre Dame de Lourdes	209
57	Hail! Heavenly Queen	133
98	Hail, Holy Queen, loved Mother to Thee	185
38	Hail, Jesus, Hail! Who for my sake	111
179	Hail the Holy Day of Days	279
102	Hail, Queen of Heaven, the Ocean Star	190
90	Hail, Queen of the Heavens	174
137	Hail, Patron of Erin	232
76	Hail, thou Star of Ocean	157
63	Hail Virgin, dearest Mary	140
119	Hail, Rose of Mystic beauty	210
34	Heart of Jesus Dearest Treasure	104
35	Heart of Jesus we are grateful	106
202	Hark! Hark! The Angels singing	303
208	Hark! Hark! My soul, angelic songs are swelling	310
148	Hark! An awful voice is sounding	245
149	Hark! What mean those holy voices	246
55	Happy we, who thus united	130
189	Have mercy on us, God Most High	289
193	Hear Thy children, Gentle Jesus	294
20	Hear the Heart of Jesus pleading	87
84	Heart of Mary, Heart the purest	167
135	Hibernia's Champion Saint, all hail!	230
3	Holy God, we praise Thy Name	68
126	Holy Joseph, dearest Father	218
101	Holy Mary, Mother mild	189
124	Holy Patron! Thee saluting	216
56	Holy Queen! we bend before thee	131
185	Holy Spirit, come and shine	284
72	How pure, how frail and white	152
32	How shall I ever know the love	102
42	I am my Love's	116
19	I dwell a captive in this heart	86
89	It is the name of Mary	173
4	I love Thee O Thou Lord Most High	69
40	In this Sacrament, sweet Jesus	114
9	Jesus is God, the solid earth	75
167	Jesus! Jesus, behold at length	264

No.		Page
52	Jesus, Jesus, come to me	127
43	Jesus, my Lord, my God, my All	118
10	Jesus, Saviour of my soul	76
8	Jesus, sweet Jesus	74
14	Jesu, the very thought of Thee	80
75	Joy ! Joy, the Mother comes	155
64	Joy of my heart ! O let me pay	141
125	Joseph, pure Spouse	217
206	Know ye that angels silently glide	308
	Kyrie eleison	334
191	Lauda Sion	291
194	Lead, Kindly Light, amid the encircling gloom	294
22	Like a strong and raging fire	89
147	Like the dawning of the morning	244
209	Litany of the Blessed Virgin Mary	312
210	Litany of the Sacred Heart of Jesus	318
211	Litany of the Saints	320
219	Libera	381
171	Lord of Mercy and Compassion	268
97	Look down, O Mother Mary	184
93	Mary, dearest Mother	178
120	Mary ! How sweetly falls that word	211
77	Mary, Mother shield us through life	158
205	Michael, Prince of Highest Heaven	306
161	Miserere mei, Deus	258
215	Missa De Angelis	334
218	Missa Pro Defunctis	370
92	Mother dearest, Mother fairest	177
79	Mother dear, O pray for me	160
83	Mother Mary, at Thine Altar	166
62	Mother of God, we hail thy heart	139
67	Mother of mercy, day by day	145
111	Mother Mary, Queen most sweet	200
47	My God, my Life, my Love	122
51	My Jesus, from His throne above	126
74	My own dear Mother Mary	154
2	Nearer, my God to Thee	67
163	Now are the days of humblest prayer	260
143	O turn to Jesus	240
60	O blest for e'er the Mother	137
168	O come, and mourn with me awhile	265
6	O come, loud anthems let us sing	71
162*	O Cor Jesu	260
145	O dearest Lord, we humbly crave	242
82	O dearest Mother of Mercy	164
68	O Flower of Grace, Divinest Flower	146
166	O Gracious Lord, Creator dear	263
207	O God ! how ought my grateful heart	309
94	O Heart of Mary, pure and fair	179
44	O Jesus Christ remember	119
31	O Jesus Dear, Thy Sacred Heart	101
11	O Jesus, Jesus, dearest Lord	77
12	O Jesus Thou the beauty art	78

INDEX

No.		Page.
49	O Bond of Love	124
134	O Lady high in glory raised	229
50	O Lord, I am not worthy	126
123	O Mary dear mother how fondly I flee	215
70	O Mater Admirabilis	149
103	O Mother I could weep for mirth	191
113	O Mother blest whom God bestows	203
95	O Mother, loved, our sweet delight	180
58	O purest of creatures	134
23	O Sacred Heart	91
27	O Sacred Heart ! O Love Divine	96
18	O Sacred Heart that on the Cross	85
112	O Sanctissima. O Piissima.	202
181	O Thou eternal King Most High	281
151	Oh! Lovely Infant, Dearest Saviour	248
117	Oh, when shall we with Angels bright	208
53	Oh ! What could my Jesus do more	128
115	On this day, O beautiful Mother	206
182	Our Lord is risen	281
200	On bended knee	302
160	Parce Domine	258
25	Peace be still ! our God is dwelling	93
197	Pity, my God, 'tis for our loved land	298
7	Praise ye the Lord	72
144	Pray for the dead	241
217	Responses at High Mass	367
109	Rose of the Cross	198
	Sanctus	348
21	Sacred Heart ! in accents burning	88
45	Saving Host, we fall before Thee	120
153	See, amid the Winter's snow	251
146	See, He comes	243
184	See the Paraclete	283
216	Short Choral Mass	353
190	Sing, my joyful tongue, the mystery	290
152*	Sleep, holy Babe	250
38	Soul of my Saviour	112
170	Stabat Mater, weeping, sore the Mother stood	267
156	Stars of glory, shine more brightly	254
5	Strike, strike the harp	70
100	Sweet Lady of the Sacred Heart	188
192	Sweet Saviour ! bless us ere we go	293
17	Sweet Heart of Jesus, be my love	84
13	Sweet name which makes the dying live	79
10	The Clouds hang thick o'er Israel's Camp	199
174	The dawn was purpling o'er the sky	271
71	The day is o'er	150
157	The Heavens bend	255
85	The Star of the Ocean is risen	167
121	The Sun is shining brightly	212
37	Thou art my hope, dear Sacred Heart	110
164	Thou loving Maker of mankind	261
138	Thou who, hero-like hast striven	233

No.		Page
91	Thro' the world thy children raise	175
180	Thy sacred race, O Lord is run	280
61	'Tis the month of our Mother	138
176	To-day He's risen	273
33	To Jesus' Heart all burning	103
116	To love thee, O Mary	207
26	To thy pure and burning heart	94
133	To kneel at thine altar	228
78	Unfold, Unfold	159
24	Upon the altar night and day	92
	Veni Creator Spiritus	59
142	Veni Sponsa Christi	239
198	Veni Jesu, Amor Mi	299
213	Vidi aquam	329
199	Vivat! Vivat!	301
106	We come, dearest Mother, this beautiful May day	194
141	We come to thee, O happy Saint	237
169	What a sea of tears and sorrows	266
159	What beauteous Sun—surpassing Star	257
39	What happiness can equal mine	113
41	What light is streaming from the skies	115
86	When evening shades are falling	169
46	When our Saviour wished to prove	121
48	When at Thy altar Lord I kneel	123
108	Wilt thou look upon me Mother	197
127	With tender love we come to thee	219
196	Yes, Heaven is the prize	297

www.ingramcontent.com/pod-product-compliance
Lightning Source LLC
Chambersburg PA
CBHW020740020526
44115CB00030B/644